Limited Liability Companies For Dummies®

W9-AUD-021

Preparing to Meet with Your Attorney

When you're getting ready for that first meeting with the attorney who's going to be part of your LLC team, you need to do a couple of things to prepare. Follow this checklist to make sure you have everything set up before the meeting. For more information on preparing to meet with your lawyer and other LLC pros, please see Chapter 3.

- **Create a file for your attorney.** Place copies of all pertinent documents and information in a folder, and attach your contact information to the front.

- **E-mail the attorney to ask if there's anything in particular you should bring to the meeting.** It never hurts to ask.

- **Make copies of all corporate paperwork.** This includes your articles of organization, your operating agreement, and so on. See Chapters 6 and 9 for more information.

- **List immediate projects that the attorney needs to work on.** Gather any important facts or documentation. Make copies for the attorney's file.

- **Jot down the names and contact information of all operating managers and pertinent members.** The attorney will also need information on any other important business contacts.

- **Make copies of all paperwork relevant to the issues that the attorney will be handling.** Include copies of leases, contracts, court notices, correspondence, and filings.

- **Prepare a list of questions that you want answered.** Make a list of the gray areas that the attorney can help you with after you've done your research. Make sure to leave enough space on the page to jot down answers.

Keeping and Maintaining Accurate Records

When it comes to record keeping and LLCs, it's always better to be safe than sorry. Keeping your records in order reduces the amount of risk to your LLC and helps you keep everything running nice and smoothly (see Chapter 11 for more information). Use the following checklist and refer to it often to ensure that your record keeping remains on track:

- Store your records in a special customized company kit.

- Maintain your membership roll.

- Keep your tax and financial records organized.

- Hold regular meetings with the other members and managers of the company.

- Draft resolutions that document major company decisions.

- Document your corporate activities in the meeting minutes.

For Dummies: Bestselling Book Series for Beginners

Limited Liability Companies For Dummies®

State Sales and Use Tax Rates

Whenever you sell products, you must collect sales tax from your clients, and whenever you use products that you haven't paid sales tax on, you must pay a use tax. Both of these taxes are submitted to your state Board of Equalization, or the equivalent tax board in your state.

Each state differs on the percentage of sales and use tax it charges. The tax rates, current as of 2007, are below. These tax rates may change in the future, so it is important to contact your state for updated information or go online to www.myllc.com/dummies where you can find an updated table.

Standard Sales and Use Tax Rates per State

State	State Rate	Range of Local Rates	Local Rates Apply to Use Tax	State	State Rate	Range of Local Rates	Local Rates Apply to Use Tax
Alabama	4%	0% to 8%	Yes/No	Montana	0%	0%	N/A
Alaska	0%	0% to 7%	Yes/No	Nebraska	5.5%	0% to 2%	Yes
Arizona	5.6%	0% to 4.5%	Yes/No	Nevada	6.5%	0% to 1.25%	Yes
Arkansas	6%	0% to 5.5%	Yes	New Hampshire	0%	0%	N/A
California	6.25%	1% to 2.5%	Yes	New Jersey	7%	0%	N/A
Colorado	2.9%	0% to 7%	Yes/No	New Mexico	5%	0.125% to 2.813%	No
Connecticut	6%	0%	N/A	New York	4%	0% to 5%	Yes
Delaware	0%	0%	N/A	North Carolina	4.25%	2% to 3%	Yes
District of Columbia	5.75%	0%	N/A	North Dakota	5%	0% to 2.50%	Yes
Florida	6%	0% to 1.5%	Yes	Ohio	5.5%	0% to 2%	Yes
Georgia	4%	1% to 3%	Yes	Oklahoma	4.5%	0% to 6%	Yes/No
Hawaii	4%	0% to 0.5%	N/A	Oregon	0%	0%	N/A
Idaho	6%	0% to 3%	No	Pennsylvania	6%	0% to 1%	No
Illinois	6.25%	0% to 3%	No	Rhode Island	7%	0%	N/A
Indiana	6%	0%	N/A	South Carolina	5%	0% to 2%	Yes
Iowa	5%	0% to 2%	No	South Dakota	4%	0% to 2%	Yes
Kansas	5.3%	0% to 3%	Yes	Tennessee	7%	1.5% to 2.75%	Yes
Kentucky	6%	0%	N/A	Texas	6.25%	0% to 2%	Yes
Louisiana	4%	0% to 6.75%	Yes	Utah	4.75%	1% to 3.25%	Yes
Maine	5%	0%	N/A	Vermont	6%	0% to 1%	No
Maryland	5%	0%	N/A	Virginia	4%	1%	Yes
Massachusetts	5%	0%	N/A	Washington	6.5%	0.5% to 2.40%	Yes
Michigan	6%	0%	N/A	West Virginia	6%	0%	N/A
Minnesota	6.5%	0% to 1%	Yes	Wisconsin	5%	0% to 1%	Yes/No
Mississippi	7%	0% to 0.25%	No	Wyoming	4%	0% to 2%	Yes
Missouri	4.225%	0.5% to 4.75%	Yes/No				

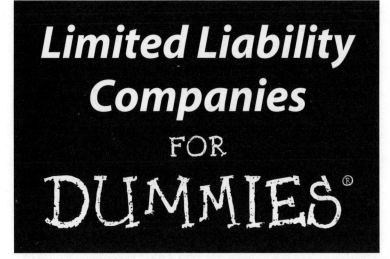

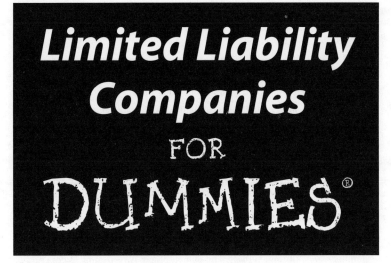

by Jennifer Reuting

Wiley Publishing, Inc.

Limited Liability Companies For Dummies®

Published by
Wiley Publishing, Inc.
111 River St.
Hoboken, NJ 07030-5774
www.wiley.com

WILEY

About the Author

Jennifer Reuting is one of the foremost experts on limited liability companies and corporate structuring. She has been entrusted by thousands of companies over the years to address their individual corporate needs. In 2001, she co-founded Incorp Services Inc., the fourth-largest national registered agent and document filing company with more than 35,000 clients worldwide. InCorp specializes in servicing medium to large businesses, accountancy firms, and law firms.

To service the needs of individuals and small businesses, Jennifer co-founded MyLLC.com, a company that focuses on offering affordable LLC and business entity solutions. Jennifer lends her talents in corporate structuring to the clients at MyLLC.com, providing affordable yet comprehensive LLC solutions.

Jennifer speaks regularly on television and radio shows across the U.S., addressing common business issues, such as the formation and management of limited liability companies. You can also read her articles at www.myllc.com.

Dedication

To my family for their never-ending support; to Martin, who inspires me to no end; to Bobbi for keeping me laughing, even when I'm buried with work; and last but definitely not least, to Doug Ansell, the greatest friend and business partner a girl can have! I am truly blessed.

Author's Acknowledgments

I'd like to thank Michael Lewis for taking a chance on me and Natalie Harris and Vicki Adang for supporting me through this process — their editing has vastly improved my writing, and I have learned a lot in the meantime.

My sincere thanks to my agent, Andy Barzvi, at ICM, whose time and effort have made this opportunity possible. Whoever said agents aren't likeable has obviously never met Andy. Also, I'd like to thank Chris Von Goetz at ICM for being my champion.

A million thanks to Doug Ansell — without him, Incorp and MyLLC.com wouldn't be the amazing companies they are today. I couldn't ask for a better partner, and I can't wait to see what our next adventures are and where our futures take us.

A final acknowledgment goes to attorney David G. LeGrand with the firm Fennemore Craig (`fclaw.com`). His knowledge on LLCs, taxation, and asset protection is unparalleled, and I was incredibly lucky to have him there to check my facts and offer those valuable pieces of advice that help make this book the best on the market. If you're looking for a great attorney, he's your man!

Publisher's Acknowledgments

We're proud of this book; please send us your comments through our Dummies online registration form located at www.dummies.com/register/.

Some of the people who helped bring this book to market include the following:

Acquisitions, Editorial, and Media Development

Project Editor: Natalie Faye Harris

Acquisitions Editor: Michael Lewis

Copy Editor: Victoria M. Adang

Technical Editor: Sarah Spear

Media Development Specialist: Laura Atkinson

Editorial Manager: Christine Meloy Beck

Media Development Manager: Laura VanWinkle

Editorial Assistants: Leeann Harney, David Lutton, Erin Calligan Mooney, Joe Niesen

Cartoons: Rich Tennant (www.the5thwave.com)

Composition Services

Project Coordinator: Patrick Redmond

Layout and Graphics: Jonelle Burns, Carl Byers, Melissa K. Jester, Stephanie D. Jumper, Barbara Moore, Christine Williams

Proofreader: Nancy L. Reinhardt

Indexer: Potomac Indexing, LLC

Special Help: Rueben W. Davis, Christy Pingleton

Publishing and Editorial for Consumer Dummies

Diane Graves Steele, Vice President and Publisher, Consumer Dummies

Joyce Pepple, Acquisitions Director, Consumer Dummies

Kristin A. Cocks, Product Development Director, Consumer Dummies

Michael Spring, Vice President and Publisher, Travel

Kelly Regan, Editorial Director, Travel

Publishing for Technology Dummies

Andy Cummings, Vice President and Publisher, Dummies Technology/General User

Composition Services

Gerry Fahey, Vice President of Production Services

Debbie Stailey, Director of Composition Services

Contents at a Glance

Table of Contents

Introduction

. . . .

*I*ndividuals are now, more than ever, realizing the power of the limited liability company (LLC). If you're like many people, you probably understand
that LLCs are right for you in one way or another; you just don't know the
next steps to take. Maybe you've just purchased a piece of real estate and
know that it should be protected in some way; you just don't know how to
form the LLC and do the transfer. Or, on a whim, you created an LLC for your
current business and can't get any answers on what to do now. How do you
transfer assets? What do you do at tax time? How can you take on a partner?

You now hold in your hands the key to some of the most powerful strategies
of the rich. This book was written to make your life easier and eliminate the
guesswork on forming and owning an LLC. After all, your LLC should work for
you, not the other way around.

After I get into the basics on LLCs in this book, I go into some more-complex
strategies. This info sets this book apart from all the others. The rich have
used a lot of these strategies for decades to operate their businesses, protect
their assets, and pass on their estates. Now, I'm putting the power in your
hands. When you find a strategy that may work for you, sit down with your
team (your attorney, accountant, and/or corporate consultant) and figure out
how to build on it and how to customize it to your specific situation. Use this
book as your starting point. Your possibilities are endless, and your asset
protection and tax strategies should grow along with you.

Now get going on your journey to success and don't look back!

About This Book

Although this book was written in an easy-to-understand, concise manner,
I didn't limit this book to the basics. You'll find that a lot of other books on
LLCs just skim over things, filling their pages with forms (like the ones we
have on the accompanying CD-ROM) and legal statutes that you can easily
access online. They often just cover the basics of filing your articles and creating your operating agreement without delving into the more powerful uses
of LLCs or the strategies that LLCs can be integrated with.

Even though this is a *For Dummies* book, you're no idiot. You don't want to be put to sleep while reading a jargon-laden book on complex strategies that even most attorneys can't understand. You want something that dives deep but keeps it simple, and that's what I strive to give you — well-organized, easy-to-read, and fluff-free information.

Now, even though this book gives you in-depth knowledge on the power of LLCs, it's no substitute for good professional advice. When dealing with this stuff, you'll face some complex legal and tax issues that are unique to your situation. Your attorney, accountant, and corporate consultant should be just a phone call away. Think of this book as a source of knowledge that can lead you to a whole new level of conversations with your team of professionals.

Conventions Used in This Book

I use a few conventions in this book. They're pretty intuitive and easy to understand, but here's the rundown anyway:

- ✔ Any industry terminology that may be new to you will appear in *italics*. Some of these terms are also included in the Glossary.

- ✔ I **boldface** the action parts of numbered steps and keywords or the main points in bulleted items.

- ✔ Sidebars, which are the gray boxes of text, contain fun stories, examples, or other pieces of information that are great to know but not necessary to read if you're in a time crunch.

- ✔ Nine times out of ten I won't spell out "limited liability company" but will instead use the abbreviation "LLC." I can't help it — it's just too easy!

- ✔ When this book was printed, some Web addresses may have needed to break across two lines of text. If that happened, rest assured that I haven't put in any extra characters (such as hyphens) to indicate the break. So, when using one of these Web addresses, just type in exactly what you see in this book, pretending as though the line break doesn't exist.

What You're Not to Read

I know, I know — you're busy! You operate on a need-to-know basis and the rest is just gibberish. Therefore, to speed things up a little, feel free to ignore anything with a Technical Stuff icon next to it. The information in those paragraphs isn't really necessary to understand the topic. Also, the sidebars are fun, but they're sort of a bonus for those who aren't time-impaired. Feel free to skip those too.

Foolish Assumptions

In order for this book to cater to a broad audience, I needed to make some foolish assumptions about you, the reader, and your skill level. After all, it's not *Limited Liability Companies For Attorneys* or *Limited Liability Companies For Real Estate Investors.* It's *Limited Liability Companies For Dummies* (in other words, "everyone"). Let's see if any of these shoes fit:

- ✔ You're a budding (or experienced) entrepreneur, looking for the next leg up.
- ✔ You have a business, and you want to finally get legit and form an entity to protect yourself.
- ✔ You're a real estate investor looking to save some dough and keep your butt out of the courtroom.
- ✔ You're an inventor who wants to protect his patents from a random lawsuit that may be just around the corner.
- ✔ You have intellectual property, and you want to keep it right where it is — in your name.
- ✔ You're old, or young, and are planning your estate.
- ✔ You want to raise money for a project and want a vehicle that can keep things in order and sweeten the pot for your investors.
- ✔ You were born on a day that ends in the letter *y*.

If any of the above assumptions fits your profile, then this book was written especially for you!

How This Book Is Organized

Limited Liability Companies For Dummies, like all *For Dummies* books, is divided into parts and chapters so you can skip around and easily find what you need. I have organized the text into five parts, each with three to five chapters that are commonly related. Here's a breakdown of the parts you'll find.

Part I: LLCs 101

Part I gives you a complete introduction to LLCs. It goes into the basics of LLCs, including how LLCs came into existence, what they are mainly used for, and some of the terminology that you'll see throughout the book. It also looks at the pros and cons of LLCs and compares them to other entities.

In this part, I help you decide whether an LLC is right for your situation. When setting up and running an LLC, you'll most likely want to have professionals on hand, so I show you how to find the right people and create a working team environment.

Part II: First Things First: Forming Your LLC

Part II covers everything you need to know when forming your LLC. In this part, I go over the preliminary decisions that you need to make, including choosing your members, managers, and registered agent. I also include information on choosing your company name and making sure it's available for use. I then talk about choosing the state that you'll form your LLC in and the pros and cons of forming outside of your home state.

At this point, you should have all the preliminary stuff out of the way, so I show you how to create your articles of organization and file them with your state office. In case you're operating as a different entity type, I also cover how to convert your current entity into an LLC. And last but not least, I address state and local licensing issues that your LLC will have to deal with.

Part III: Running Your Brand-New LLC

Part III is for anyone who currently owns an LLC and wants to know what the heck to do with it. In this part, I explain how to create your operating agreement — which, in my opinion, is the most vital chapter in this book. I also cover membership shares: what they are, how to issue them, how to transfer them, and how to sell them to raise capital.

I also go into record keeping. I discuss common precautions and steps you should take to make sure that your contracts are airtight. And you can read about the procedures you need to follow to stay out of court. At the end of Part III, I discuss the dissolution process and what to do when you're ready to call it quits.

Part IV: Making Cents of Taxes and Protecting Your Assets

Part IV contains some of the more advanced strategies. A lot of books don't cover these, but if the wealthy have been using them for generations, why shouldn't you? I start off by going into the basics of LLC taxation. Here, you obtain a good overview of how LLCs are taxed, what IRS filings you need to make, and which forms you need to issue to members.

Then, I dive into asset protection — by far my favorite section of the book. I show you the importance of having an asset protection strategy and how LLCs can be a cheap way for you to gain a pretty powerful defense against creditors and lawsuits. Next up is real estate, the LLC's favorite pastime. Here I show you how LLCs and real estate go hand in hand, and how to properly structure your properties in an LLC (or two or three). Last but not least is estate planning. I go into the current estate tax laws and how LLCs can help save your heirs a fortune when you pass away.

Part V: The Part of Tens

Part V is for all you type-A personalities out there. It gives you the lowdown on important information, with each mini-chapter segmented into ten bite-size sections. First, I go into how to keep your LLC intact so it isn't disregarded by the courts. Next up is the scary chapter. Here I list ten things that you should absolutely avoid while running your LLC. Then I jump back onto a more positive note with "Ten Good Reasons to Form an LLC." The chapter title speaks for itself, and — I have to say — it was one of the easiest chapters to write. After all, I could have written "Twenty good reasons . . ." or even "Thirty good reasons . . .," but my editors wouldn't let me. Grrr.

Part V also includes the Glossary. If you're reading and come across a term that you aren't familiar with, you can turn to the Glossary, instead of flipping through the book for an hour searching for the definition. It should cover all of the legal jargon that goes hand in hand with limited liability companies.

Appendix A is one of the reasons why, if you are flipping through this book at the bookstore, you need to take it to the register immediately. Here I give all of the information that you need to form your entity — for every state! This will cut your research time in half and allow you the extra time to read that fiction book you've been eyeing.

The CD-ROM

Forms, forms, and more forms! That's what you can expect on the CD-ROM that accompanies this book. Forget about drafting stuff by hand — just download the forms from the CD, fill in your info, and submit the papers to the state. Or, for a more finished look, you can copy and paste the text into your own document, add your name and other customized info, hit "Print," and you're done! Your partners won't believe how productive you were!

Icons Used in This Book

In this book, I use little pictures, called *icons,* to highlight important information. When you see these, make sure to pay close attention — otherwise, you may miss some really good info!

This icon flags helpful tips, tidbits, and secrets that may give you an upper hand on your road to success.

If I mention a topic more than once and/or use this icon, then you should make an effort to remember the information. These concepts are often the most important.

Whenever I use this icon, you should watch out! Obtain advice that is specific to your situation from a professional. Otherwise, legal or financial snares can ensue.

I use this icon to flag some technical stuff that may be a little advanced and difficult to understand for the LLC novices out there. When you encounter one of these icons, don't worry — just ignore the information or ask a competent professional for advice.

When you see this icon, know that I've got you covered. Any of the forms or documents that are flagged with this icon are on the CD-ROM that accompanies this book.

Where to Go from Here

One of the many great things about a *For Dummies* book is that you don't have to read it from cover to cover to get to what you need to know. This book was designed to be jumped into, with each chapter standing on its own. Find a topic that interests you and start there! After all, why waste time reading mundane topics that you already know when you can immediately get to the good stuff?

If you're a complete novice and are just dipping your toes into the whole LLC concept, you may want to read Chapters 1 and 2, and then skip to whatever topic interests you most. If you have already formed your LLC and are looking for the next step, you may want to skip to Chapter 9 to find out what you should do next. Only interested in the use of LLCs for estate planning? Skip to Chapter 16. Ready to dissolve your LLC? Feel free to flip to Chapter 12.

Part I
LLCs 101

"Well, apparently our liability wasn't as limited as I thought."

In this part . . .

If you're currently reading this page, it's a good bet that you've heard somewhere that an LLC may be right for you and your business, but you don't know enough to go out and form one. Well, you've come to the right place! In this part, I give you a good overview of what LLCs are, what they're used for, and how they compare to other types of business structures. After reading Chapters 1 and 2, you'll have a basic knowledge of LLCs and will know how to apply them to your situation.

In Chapter 3, I show you how to build your team of professionals, such as your corporate consultant (what I do for a living), your accountant, and your attorney. I give you suggestions on finding them, evaluating them, and working with them after you've decided to take them on.

Chapter 1

What Is an LLC, Really?

*L*imited liability companies have been generating a lot of buzz in the news lately — and for good reason. It's almost as if the corporate gods have smiled upon us and decided to improve upon the corporation and give us the LLC (the acronym for limited liability company). Where the corporation fails, the LLC prevails.

Think of the LLC as a merger of the partnership and the corporation, except it has the best of both worlds — all the good qualities of each and none of the bad. It offers full limited-liability protection to all the owners (like the corporation), yet has a pass-through tax status (like the partnership). In addition, the LLC has a second layer of liability protection that shields the business from any personal lawsuits that may befall you. And it doesn't stop there! The list of benefits goes on and on. In this chapter, I introduce you to those benefits and steer you toward the other chapters in the book where you can gain even more details.

Understanding How LLCs Work

LLCs are a relatively new entity — they are a hybrid between a corporation and a partnership. Therefore, they aren't so easy for some folks to understand at first. Even if you're familiar with corporations — or partnerships, for that matter — you still need to understand some new concepts and a few new terms.

The best and most basic way to understand an LLC is to think of it as a regular partnership, but all of the partners have full *limited-liability protection*. This means that the partners (the *members*) aren't personally responsible for the actions or debts of the company. This is huge! LLCs are more official than regular partnerships in that you have to form them with the state, and you can raise financing by selling off pieces of the company (the membership interests). But when all is said and done, LLCs were made to be easy. They are easy to understand and easy to run. Not to mention, if you make a mistake, the consequences aren't as dire as they would be with a corporation.

LLCs, like most entities, are subject to state oversight. The problem with this is that not all states are on the same page. So in addition to reading this book, you'll need to do a little bit of research so that you can make sure you are complying with the laws of the states you are transacting business in. This won't be too difficult, however, because I have provided each state's information on LLCs in Appendix A to point you in the right direction.

Although in most states, more LLCs are being formed now than corporations, they are still a very new entity. Compared to corporations, which have hundreds of years of case law backing them up, courts still have a lot to decide about LLCs. When operating an LLC, know that some things are based upon assumptions rather than actual legal precedents, and this creates gray areas — and potential problems. After all, you don't want to be the unlucky guy who is stuck in the courtroom when everything you thought you knew about LLCs is overturned. The best way to avoid this is to have a great registered agent or accountant who stays abreast of LLC laws for you. Should any monumental shifts occur in how LLCs are treated, your advisor can fill you in so you can plan accordingly.

Owners: You gotta have 'em

Although LLCs are separate from their owners in a lot of ways, they still need to have them. An LLC without an owner is like a child without parents. It just doesn't happen. In other words, there are no immaculate conceptions when it comes to LLCs.

The owners (see Chapter 10) not only own the entire enterprise and all of its assets, but they generally have the last say. Although they may not manage the business, they choose the managers. They vote on important issues and ultimately control the company's fate.

The owners in the LLC are called *members*. They have units of ownership called *membership interests* that show what percentage of the company they own and how much influence they have when voting on important company matters. Membership interests in an LLC are comparable to stock in a corporation. However, unlike the S corporation (which is often compared to the LLC), LLCs can have unlimited members and any type of members. Members can be citizens of other countries or even entities such as corporations, partnerships, or trusts (see Chapter 10).

The actual term for the members of the LLC and their membership interests varies from one state to another. For instance, in some states, the membership interest is called *ownership interest* or *limited liability company interest.* Just keep in mind that, no matter what they're called, the concepts are still the same.

As you see in Chapter 10, LLCs can have different types of memberships. These are called *classes,* and you can make up whatever rules you want for each class. For instance, one class can have priority on the distributions, while the other class is second in line. Or one class can have a say in managing the company, while the other class must remain silent.

If your LLC has only one member, it's called a *single-member LLC.* Single-member LLCs are treated as sole proprietorships by the IRS for tax purposes. Your state laws, if they even allow single-member LLCs (some don't), may also treat them differently. For the most part, single-member LLCs still offer the liability protection that multiple-member LLCs offer; they just don't have the benefit of partnership taxation and aren't guaranteed the *charging order protections,* which protect the LLC from lawsuits that may be filed against you personally (I discuss this concept in depth in Chapter 11).

Contributions: Where the money comes from

When you buy a share of stock on the stock market, the money you pay is what you are contributing (or *investing*) in return for a percentage of the company's ownership. Well, LLCs are no different. In exchange for their membership interest (see the previous section), members must contribute something to the company. This can be in the form of cash or valuable assets, such as equipment, real estate, services, or even promissory notes (which are allowed in some states). See Chapter 10 for more details on contribution types.

When a member makes a contribution, the other members need to determine the value of that contribution in relation to everyone else's. They then distribute the membership interests proportionally. This is really easy to do when cash is involved. For instance, if Joe, Steve, and Mary each contribute $100,000 in cash, then they each are issued one-third of the company. All of the contributions made by each of the members and their corresponding membership interest are listed in the operating agreement.

Most LLCs issue share certificates that, like stock certificates in a corporation, are evidence of the amount of ownership a member has in the company (see Chapter 10). The share certificate displays the member's name and the number of shares the person owns. To determine the member's percentage of ownership in the company, you divide the number of shares she owns by the total number of shares issued in the company. For instance, if a total of 10,000 shares is issued to all members of the company, and you own 100 shares, then you own 1 percent of the company. If 35,000 shares are issued to all the members, and your share certificate says you have 5,000 shares, then you own around 14 percent of the company. If the company doesn't issue share certificates, then the number of shares you own should be listed in the operating agreement next to your contribution amount. (In Chapter 9, I discuss operating agreements at length and show you how to list your members, their contributions, and membership interests properly.)

Distributions: Getting what you're due

After the company starts turning a profit, the members will no doubt want to benefit. After all, they didn't invest their hard-earned money into the company for nothing — they want to see a return! At certain points in time — usually at the end of the year, but sometimes at the end of each quarter — the company profit is calculated and doled out to each member in proportion to her percentage of ownership. These are called *distributions* and are generally in the form of cash (see Chapters 10 and 13).

LLCs don't have to distribute profits in proportion to the members' percentage of ownership. The members can decide to vary the distributions however they want. The IRS will generally allow this, as long as you pass their tests (mainly to prove that you aren't varying the distributions to avoid taxes). Speak to your accountant if you are interested in doing this.

Distributions also occur if your LLC goes out of business. In this case, the distributions are handled differently. The LLC's assets are liquidated, the creditors are paid back (including any members to whom the business owes money), and then the remaining amount is distributed to the members according to their specific ownership percentages (see Chapter 10). When these final distributions are made, you can't choose how the money is distributed — it must be doled out according to how much of the company each member has. For instance, if you own 50 percent of the company, you can rest assured that you will receive 50 percent of the remaining cash.

The birth of the LLC

The LLC didn't come out of nowhere. Business entities with the same characteristics as LLCs have been around for many years. The origin of LLCs can be traced back to the Germans. In 1892, German law enacted what was called the *Gesellschaft mit beschränkter Haftung* (GmbH) — a modern-day variation of the English private limited company.

After Germany established the GmbH, the concept soon spread throughout Europe and Central and South America. By the 1940s, in France especially, the concept of the limited liability company was becoming more popular than the traditional corporation.

Not that Germany can take all of the credit. In 1874, Pennsylvania authorized the use of a Limited Partnership Association. By 1875, Michigan, New Jersey, Ohio, and Virginia had enacted similar legislation after seeing how the entity type was gaining popularity in Pennsylvania. Unfortunately, the laws of the time required that the company headquarters remain in one of those five states. Because those states weren't huge epicenters of American commerce, the new legislation began to lose popularity.

In 1977, Wyoming decided to spearhead an effort to build upon the antiquated Limited Partnership Association and enacted the first true LLC act. The legislature modeled the act after the German GmbH and the successful Panama version of the LLC. Because of Wyoming, the modern-day LLC protects all partners from the liability of the business and has a double layer of liability protection that protects the business from your personal creditors.

After Wyoming, Florida followed suit in 1982. However, LLCs weren't popular entities. Because they were hybrid entities — between a corporation and a partnership — the IRS had yet to decide how it was going to tax the LLC. After all, would you really want to form an entity without knowing what sort of tax structure would be imposed on you?

Finally, in 1988, the IRS ruling came: LLCs would be taxed as partnerships. The business's profits and losses would flow though to the owners, and the LLC wouldn't be recognized as a separate entity for tax purposes. After this ruling occurred, states began to form their own versions of LLC law.

After a while, the public became more familiar with LLCs and began to form more of them. As they were more commonly used, case law built up, which gave members a more solid idea of what the LLC's legal limitations are.

Popular Uses for LLCs

What are LLCs used for? I think the better question is "what *aren't* LLCs used for?" They are the most flexible business structure around by far. With an LLC, you can choose

✔ How you want to be taxed

✔ How you want to distribute your profits

✔ How you want to manage your LLC

✔ Who you want to manage it

You can even create your own laws, pretty much disregarding those of the state. When you form your LLC, you will create an operating agreement, which I go over in detail in Chapter 9. In this agreement, you dictate exactly how you want to structure your business and how it should be run.

If you are looking to your next business venture, real estate transaction, or are planning your estate, this sort of flexibility probably appeals to you. And when you couple the flexibility with some of the most comprehensive asset protection around, you can see why LLCs are beating out corporations as the entity of choice as the years go on. If you structure your LLC properly, you can also take advantage of the benefits of a corporation, such as corporate taxation and decentralized management.

LLCs are so powerful and are used for so many things that lots of different offshoots are springing up, such as *series LLCs* and *limited liability partnerships* (a version of the professional limited liability company). All have various added benefits that strive to take the LLC even further than it has gone already.

LLCs have many more uses that I don't discuss in this chapter. These range from protecting personal assets to raising capital for a project. As you find out more about LLCs, I hope you begin to understand the power of LLCs and think of the various ways that they can protect you and all that you have worked for.

Running a small business

Tens of millions of Americans operate small businesses. These range from small, home-based businesses on the side to fully operational companies with many employees. For the most part, these individuals are operating without protection. Granted, they may not take what they do too seriously. They may consider themselves independent contractors or consultants, but in today's litigious society, it's a bad move to operate without even a basic level of liability protection.

As *sole proprietors* (the legal term for how these folks are doing business currently — see Chapter 2), they are used to a specific way of being taxed and the informality of not having to keep any records or officially document any of their decisions. Unless they are a full-fledged operation, this is okay. Spending a lot of time and money on this stuff is overkill for the simple, at-home Web page designer, plumber, or dog breeder. I understand.

Professional LLCs protect you from your partner's mistakes

If you are a licensed professional, such as an attorney, accountant, doctor, or engineer, you are probably working with a partner. After all, partnerships can take you much further than you could ever go on your own. Unfortunately, most partnerships are operating with only an agreement and no actual liability protection. If this is the case, you could face some serious trouble.

Partnerships are like chains and are only as strong as their weakest link. An error on your partner's part, whether purposeful or not, could cost you everything. If he does something in the business that causes a lawsuit or results in an angry creditor, then your personal assets are on the block to settle the lawsuit. Even if you have malpractice insurance, the results can be just as catastrophic.

Most states allow you to form a *professional LLC*. This not only keeps both your and your partner's assets safe from any lawsuits or creditors of the business, but it keeps your malpractice claims separate. For instance, if your partner accidentally slips and cuts someone's ear off during surgery (not too likely if you are a dentist, but you get the picture), then that claim will be isolated to his malpractice insurance, and you won't be liable in any way.

For these people (and maybe you), a corporation probably isn't the best choice. Corporations require a lot of paperwork, and the accounting can be tough to keep up with. However, you have another option. You can form a *single-member LLC* (where there is only one owner — see Chapters 4 and 10), which is very similar to the sole proprietorship you're already running. The IRS even considers single-member LLCs (SLLCs) to be sole proprietorships, so you'll see few differences when filing your taxes. Also, formal record keeping isn't required. It's a good idea for you to have a record of any unorthodox business decisions, but other than that, you can just go about your business as if you weren't organized as an LLC in the first place.

Not to mention, forming an LLC is inexpensive. My company forms LLCs for as little as $99, and the state fees are generally pretty low. I wouldn't expect to pay more than $500 total for your single-member LLC, no matter which state you form it in.

Although LLCs and sole proprietorships operate similarly, they have one major difference: asset protection. If you're ever sued by one of your clients or if your business takes on a creditor, you can rest assured that everything you have worked so hard for in life — your house, your car, your bank account, your investments — is safe. In short, for a small-business owner, an LLC is the cheapest, yet most powerful, insurance policy that you can get.

What if you decide that you want to grow by taking on investors? If you're operating as a sole proprietor, what are you going to give the folks in exchange for their investment? Sole proprietorships aren't entities — they have no legal separation from yourself. You can't necessarily distribute pieces of yourself, now, can you? LLCs, on the other hand, have *membership shares* (units of ownership that you give to investors in exchange for the money and other contributions that they give to the business). These ownership units allow them to own a piece of the action — they get rights to vote on important events, receive a percentage of the profits, and even get a chunk of what's left if the business goes under.

Maximizing real estate investments

With all of the characteristics of LLCs, it's almost as if they were made for real estate. Not only does the double layer of limited liability ensure that your assets are protected, but the pass-through taxation that comes with LLCs keeps your tax bill low. You see, if you were to place a piece of rental property into a corporation, you would not only get killed with taxes when you take out the rental income each year, but you would also have some serious tax consequences when you sell the property. Why? Because corporations have what is called *double taxation.* You first pay corporate taxation on the profits, and then the owners are subject to long- or short-term capital gains taxes on those same profits when the money hits their hands. Ouch! It kills me just thinking about it! Even so, I devote a whole chapter (Chapter 15) to the real estate issue.

Real estate investors previously used S corporations (see Chapter 2) to get around the double-taxation issues. S corporations are just like regular corporations but have a pass-through tax status that is similar to the LLC. The problem with S corporations, though, is that the ownership of the entity is severely limited.

LLCs are much more suitable for obtaining your real estate goals. Not only can you transfer the property into the LLC as an initial investment without creating a taxable event, but you can also distribute the profits of the LLC however you want. If you only own 10 percent of the company but want 90 percent of the profits (and the other members are okay with that), then it's doable. This isn't possible for the LLC's corporate brothers. By the way, if you are lucky enough to find partners that are okay with this arrangement, then please send 'em my way!

Not to mention the asset protection. I know, I know, I keep yapping on and on about asset protection, but trust me — it's important. After you realize how much you need to protect your assets, it's already too late. There is something I am going to say that is so important I am going to give it its own line on the page:

There is nothing worse you can do than hold investment property in your own name.

Please read that again and again until it is like a mantra that keeps repeating in your head. Of course, this statement is not 100 percent factual. There are technically *some* worse things you can do, such as: looking down a mortar tube after lighting a firework to see why it didn't go off, professing to the IRS that income taxes are not legal and you don't have to pay them, pointing a gun at the police. . . . Yes, there are a few worse things you can do than hold your property in your own name — but only a few, so please read the above line again. You see, if your tenant slips on the front porch, not only will your property be dust, but also your savings, your other properties, and even your kid's college fund (and possibly even your dog, if he is valuable enough!). If they know you have assets, attorneys and claimants can be vicious beyond belief.

If you are operating as a corporation — regardless of your hideous tax bill — it's a good start, but your protection only goes so far. If you are sued personally, your stock in the corporation is considered a capital asset and can be seized by your personal creditors. So if you run into someone's car while backing out of your driveway, your property can be taken from you. An LLC, on the other hand, has what is called a *charging order protection.* This is a second layer of liability protection that protects your properties from your own personal creditors. Corporations don't have this.

Because the LLC's losses are passed on to the owners, if you own multiple real estate properties, each within its own LLC, and one of the properties encounters a hefty loss, you can deduct that loss at tax time against the income from your other properties. Typically, this sort of loss is only deductible against *passive income,* such as real estate. However, if you work with your accountant or corporate consultant and structure it correctly, you may be able to deduct the loss against *active income* (such as dividends). You can do this by becoming an active real estate investor who spends a certain amount of time each year handling the day-to-day management of the properties.

Planning your estate

Note: If you are immortal, you may skip this section.

LLCs are becoming more and more popular in estate planning (Chapter 16 has the details). Trusts are still king, but now they are generally used in conjunction with LLCs so that your assets are protected while you're still alive. Trusts usually don't provide any asset protection whatsoever, whereas an LLC provides two layers of asset protection (which I discuss at length in Chapter 14).

Within every family looms the perfect LLC

Dan and Denise Sager have two children, Michael, 17, and Mary, 16. One night at the dinner table, Michael has one of his crazy business ideas, but this time it's actually a good one! He suggests they all go into business together with a company that seeks to improve the sales and service of local and national banks. They would sell their program locally and then branch out from there. Their background: Dan is a retired banker with dozens of industry connections; Denise is a retired accountant; Mary could sell ice to Eskimos; and Michael is a jack-of-all-trades with the passion and excitement to keep the project moving.

For this highly motivated, entrepreneurial family, an LLC most certainly works best — but not just any LLC. They know that LLCs are extremely flexible in their organization and operation, so the Sager family discusses each partner's role to decide how to structure their new entity.

The company will be divided into four equal parts, with each family member owning an equal percentage (they're all members) and also handling different aspects of the business. Dan will design the service/sales curriculum that improves each bank's production, while Denise will take care of the accounting. Mary will be a sales associate, and Michael will design and manage the Web site. Because of their children's age, Denise and Dan don't want to empower their kids with a lot of management decisions until they turn 18. So Ma and Pa create a manager-managed LLC in which they are the sole managers and the kids are hired as employees. This way, the kids still get their profit distributions, but they can still be fired (should their grades drop).

With estate taxes as they are, if you have a large estate — more than $1 million — you may want to start gifting your assets to your heirs while you are alive. LLCs are especially useful for this because they allow you to gift small portions of large assets (such as real estate) by gifting the membership shares. They also allow you to maintain control of the assets while you are alive, even if your heir is the majority owner of the LLC. You do this by making yourself a manager of the LLC until your death, at which point your heir will take over.

When you actively plan your estate using trusts and LLCs (and a great estate attorney), you have much more control over what happens to your assets after your passing. An LLC keeps your estate out of probate and avoids the accompanying (astronomical) probate fees. (If you aren't sure what probate is, let me just say that if the Spanish Inquisitors had been just a little bit more vicious, they probably would have just subjected their victims to the bureaucratic nightmare that is probate.) In probate, you leave the major decisions up to a judge, and you never know how things could turn out. With an LLC, you can ensure that your assets go to the right people and don't get dwindled away with legal fees until they turn into dust.

Creating Your Own LLC — How Hard Is It, Really?

It baffles me why so many people go about doing business and owning real estate without the protection of a limited liability company or other entity. They are risking everything! I can only guess that they must be intimidated by the entire process of forming an LLC and think that it's much more complicated than it really is.

It's true that LLCs don't just think themselves into existence. Someone has to create them; but LLCs aren't complicated at all. Some professionals use them in complicated situations, but when it comes to normal, everyday business activities or asset protection strategies, you'll be fine. As you flip through this book, the concepts may seem overwhelming at first, but after getting familiar with a little bit of industry terminology, you should have enough of a basic understanding of LLCs to get started on your own. And, worst-case scenario, if you have a question that isn't answered in this book, feel free to call my office and I will make sure that you get the correct answer.

To create an LLC, you have to draft a short document and file it with your state. This is pretty simple to do and, for the most part, won't require an attorney's help. First, though, you need to do some research so you understand some other elements of LLCs, and then make some decisions on how you want to structure your company.

Educating yourself

First things first, you'll want to gain a little bit of an education about LLCs. I know you're busy, so this doesn't have to be too extensive. You just need to know the basics, and the best way to start is by reading this book. Needless to say, you're on the right track!

You can always use professionals to do the work for you. And that's okay. Hey, I'm all for delegation! Just make sure that you have a good basic knowledge so you can have productive and educated conversations with the people whom you hire. Not to mention, you'll want to have an idea of whether they really know their stuff.

After you understand the basics, call your attorney or accountant and ask about things that pertain to your situation. You may also want to do some research online and set up some free consultations with corporate consulting companies. Also, I have put a lot of in-depth information online at www.myllc.com, where you can read my syndicated articles.

I didn't go in-depth on some advanced topics, like taxes, in this book. For business contracts, I highly recommend *Business Contracts Kit For Dummies* by Richard D. Harroch (Wiley). Also, *Estate Planning For Dummies* (Wiley) by N. Brian Caverly and Jordan S. Simon is really good if you are interested in finding out more about estate planning.

Surveying your assets and making a plan

If you have been working hard all your life, you've probably accumulated some valuable assets. Even if you aren't operating a business, creating an estate plan, or investing in real estate, you likely have some things you want to protect from creditors and lawsuits. Some of these things may include

- Rental real estate
- Vacant land
- Businesses
- Intellectual property
- Expensive equipment (business or personal)
- Vehicles
- Savings accounts, money market funds, and CDs
- Stocks and bonds
- Any appreciating assets

Anything that is of value to you, you should consider protecting in an LLC. Lawsuits and personal creditors abound in today's society, and by leaving anything in your name, you are virtually handing it over to any attorney who wants it.

When using LLCs, consider forming more than one. After all, you never want to put all your eggs in one basket. A good example of this is that if you have multiple rental properties in one LLC and a tenant has an accident on one of your properties, then all the properties will be up for grabs because they are in the same LLC. However, if you were to separate those properties into multiple LLCs (or a series LLC, which I discuss in Chapter 15), then only that one property that was sued can be taken.

If you are a procrastinator, watch out. Wasting too much time to put together your plan and act on it could cost you. Lawsuits come out of nowhere, and Murphy's Law states that you will get sued at the worst possible time. After you are faced with a lawsuit or have a creditor after you, your hands are tied. Any attempt to protect your assets at that point is illegal. Not only will you still lose your assets, but you could also end up with some hefty fines or, even worse, jail time.

Deciding who manages

There are two types of LLCs:

- ✔ Member-managed, where the LLC is managed jointly by all of its members
- ✔ Manager-managed, where the LLC is managed by a separate manager (who can also be a member)

If you are forming a smaller LLC with only a few partners, and each partner will have a say in managing the company, then you may want to choose member-managed. However, if you decide to take on a silent partner and that person will *not* be managing the business, then your LLC will have to be *manager*-managed. The original partners will still be listed as members; however, because not *all* members will be managing, you have to be manager-managed.

In most states, you have to list how the LLC is managed in the organizing document that is filed with the state (called the *articles of organization* — see Chapter 6). If your management structure changes, the organizing document may have to be amended. This will involve fees, so you may want to be as forward-thinking as possible before you do your initial filings and begin operations.

Choosing your registered agent

Before you can file your articles of organization, you need to choose a *registered agent* (sometimes called a "resident agent," "statutory agent," or "RA"). A registered agent is a person or company that is *always* available during business hours, every single day, to accept any formal legal documents for your company in the unfortunate instance that you are sued.

Most registered agents allow you to use their office address for all of your mail and other correspondence. A good registered agent should also stay on top of your state filings for you and make sure that you remain in good standing in the state (or states) that you are registered to transact business in. If you are registered in many states, this can be an onerous task and one that is better left to the professional service companies, or a more expensive option is to use an attorney. See Chapter 5 for more on this.

If your state *does* allow you to serve as your own registered agent, I don't recommend it. Unless you plan on being at your office during business hours every single day, with no exceptions, and you also have a good grasp of all of the state filings that need to be done, I would leave it to the pros. Another consideration is that in the event that you are sued, would you really want a sheriff or process server serving you a lawsuit in front of your customers? Eek! Not me!

Bringing your LLC into existence

Your LLC needs to be registered and receive approval from the state that it is to live in (see Chapter 8). LLCs don't need to reside in the same state as you — they should reside wherever their headquarters is going to be. In the case of companies that don't have headquarters (like Internet-based companies), they should reside wherever the tax laws are most favorable.

Because LLCs are not necessarily perpetual entities (they don't live forever), when creating your LLC, you may have to specify what the dissolution date is to be. Don't worry! You don't actually have to dissolve on this date (as I explain in Chapter 12) — it is mainly just one of those many erroneous procedural things that the state makes you do.

You create your LLC by drawing up a short document called the articles of organization. Your articles contain such basic information as the name of the company, how long the company will exist, the initial members or managers, and the name and address of the company's registered agent. In Chapter 6, I show you how to put together your articles of organization. After you are satisfied with your articles, you file them with your local Secretary of State's office (or comparable state agency).

Operating Your LLC

Now that you've formed your LLC, you're ready to start business operations, right? Well, not exactly. You still have to create your operating agreement and make some very important decisions.

Operating your LLC is meant to be easy. For the most part, if you forget something or fail to document something in writing, the courts will be easy on you. LLCs aren't like corporations where a single misstep can cost you your limited-liability protection. Although this paperwork isn't required, you can save yourself a lot of time, hassle, and potential legal battles by getting it out of the way and making your agreements as tight as a drum.

Creating your operating agreement

Think of your *operating agreement* as a sort of partnership agreement, except with much more power. Your operating agreement is the blueprint for your company. In it, you state your company's policies on important matters including

- ✔ How the company will be managed and by whom
- ✔ How important decisions are to be made
- ✔ How profits are to be distributed among the owners
- ✔ The titles and positions of managers and officers of the company
- ✔ The membership information including who is a member, what that person contributed, and what membership interest they have been assigned

Creating an operating agreement is not easy by any means, but it's vital. With the wealth of information and provisions that I provide you in Chapter 9, it shouldn't take you too long to draft the thing. However, it may take you a while to decide what you and your partners want to put in it. After all, you are creating an infrastructure that needs to serve you for many, many years to come.

After you create your operating agreement, make sure that all of the members and managers of the LLC sign it. Distribute a copy to everyone for their records, and put the original in your company records kit (which brings me to the next point).

Keeping books and records

All companies need to have a records kit. A *company records kit* normally looks like a big, leather binder with the company name emblazoned on the side. The kit can be cheap and low quality — looking like it came from the office supply isle of your local supermarket — or it can be made from the finest leather with real gold plating. No matter how simple or extravagant, every kit serves the same purpose: to house your important company records, such as your filed articles of organization and company charter, your operating agreement, resolutions and minutes from any meetings or voting that took place, your membership roll, and your unissued membership certificates. Of course, if you plan on raising financing or selling your company one day, it may be more impressive to turn over a nice, leather binder! Chapter 11 has more details on records kits.

When you order your records kit, make sure it comes with a company seal. Think of the company seal as your LLC's signature. You will use this to make your company documents and share certificates official.

Paying taxes

The IRS doesn't consider LLCs to be separate from their owners like corporations are. Because of this, LLCs are normally subject to partnership taxation (unless they elect another type of taxation), where the business's profits and losses get passed on to the owners who report their share on their personal tax returns. These portions of profits and losses that get passed on to the members are called *allocations.* This type of taxation is commonly referred to as *pass-through taxation,* which I go over in great detail in Chapter 13.

Because the LLC doesn't actually have to pay taxes itself, the IRS only requires you to file an information statement (IRS Form 1065) that states how the company's profits and losses are allocated among the members. Additionally, the company issues each member an IRS form called a Schedule K-1 that shows the information they need to determine how much tax they must pay on the company's profits.

LLCs aren't required to distribute any cash to the members. However, the members *are* required to pay taxes on these profits. When the company doesn't distribute the profits to the members, but the members still have to pay taxes on the profit out of their own pockets, this is called *phantom income.*

Chapter 2

Determining Whether an LLC Is Right for You

In This Chapter

▶ Assessing the benefits of LLCs

▶ Looking at the drawbacks of LLCs

▶ Comparing LLCs to other business entities

. . . .

*F*or small businesses that want complete limited-liability protection for all of the owners but don't want to pay extra in taxes each year or deal with complex corporate issues, a limited liability company is the perfect entity. But the best part about LLCs is that they don't just shield the owners from lawsuits and creditors; they also offer much more leeway in the business's ownership, management, and tax structure than corporations, limited partnerships, and even sole proprietorships do.

LLCs aren't only an important tool against lawsuits — and in today's lawsuit-crazy society, they are vital to protecting your family's future — but they also offer a variety of tax benefits. Not only that, but they come with the least ownership restrictions, and their maintenance is simple and straightforward. You will find no complex paperwork that will leave you baffled and confused. Whew!

Although LLCs are a powerful tool to lower taxes and protect yourself and your business from lawsuits and creditors, they aren't for everyone. In this chapter, I address the advantages and disadvantages of using an LLC so you can judge for yourself whether an LLC is the right entity for you. I also explain some other types of business structures, such as sole proprietorships, general partnerships, limited partnerships, and corporations. If you are currently in business, this can help you understand the benefits of converting to an LLC.

Reasons to Love LLCs

Everyone seems to be going crazy over LLCs lately, and for good reason. They are one of the most flexible entities — you can choose how to distribute the profits, who manages the business's day-to-day affairs, and how the profits are to be taxed. They also offer a lot in terms of liability protection (hence the name *limited liability* company).

Overall advantages of the LLC include

- ✔ **Personal liability protection:** Any creditors who come knocking or lawsuits filed against your business can't affect you personally. You can rest assured that no matter what happens in the business, your family's assets are safe.

- ✔ **Business liability protection:** An LLC is one of the only entities that prevents personal lawsuits and creditors from liquidating your business.

- ✔ **No separate tax returns:** With a standard LLC, the business's profits and losses are reported on your personal tax returns.

- ✔ **No double taxation:** Unlike some business structures, LLCs can have *pass-through taxation*. This means that the profits won't be taxed at the company level and then taxed as dividends at the individual level.

- ✔ **No ownership restrictions:** You can have as many owners as you need. Even other entities can be owners!

- ✔ **No management restrictions:** Owners can manage and managers can own — you decide.

- ✔ **Flexible tax status:** You can choose from a multitude of ways to be taxed, depending on what works best for your situation.

- ✔ **Flexible profit distribution:** *You* decide what percentage of the profits to give to whom — no matter how much of the company the person actually owns.

In the following sections, I provide you with a more detailed overview of each of these advantages that LLCs offer.

Personal liability protection: Keeping your personal assets safe

An LLC protects you from the liabilities that you inevitably come across during the normal, everyday course of business. Should your business get sued or go bankrupt, your *personal assets* (home, car, investments, and so on) and other businesses (if they are in different LLCs) *cannot* be taken away. Only the assets included in the LLC that got sued are at risk. Because LLCs protect your personal assets, I think everyone who is in business or real estate should use one.

Too many victims of frivolous lawsuits have shown up at my office wondering what they can do to get out of them — asking how they can save their home and bank accounts that are about to be taken away. Unfortunately, at this point, it's always too late. If only they had spent some time planning, working with advisors like me, they could have saved everything.

Business liability protection: Keeping your business safe if you face legal headaches

Normally, when you have shares in a corporation or other entity, those shares are considered personal assets and can be taken away from you if you face a *personal lawsuit* (one not related to your business) or if a creditor turns up seeking payment. However, LLCs are unique because they offer double protection against lawsuits. LLCs offer *business liability protection* — protection for the business from your personal lawsuits or creditors — not just personal liability protection (as described in the previous section). So if *you* are sued, your business or asset(s) in the LLC can't be taken away from you. (Chapter 14 has more details about asset protection.) This extra level of protection is also called *dual protection*.

When formed and maintained properly, LLCs will always hold up in court. When a creditor sees that you have shielded your assets with an LLC, he very rarely goes through the hassle of taking you to court. And everyone knows that avoiding a lawsuit is always better than winning one.

Because the LLC offers a double layer of protection that corporations don't, I often advise my clients to form a *holding LLC* for their personal use. That holding LLC contains any stock the client may have in other corporations and other personal assets. That way, in the event she is sued, her assets are protected.

No more double taxation: Putting a stop to Uncle Sam's double-dipping

One of the key differences between an LLC and a corporation is the way that the entities are taxed. Corporations pay taxes separate from their owners, while with LLCs, the business's profits and losses can go directly on the owners' individual tax returns. This is called *pass-through taxation* — the income and expenses pass through to the tax returns of the owners.

Although LLCs can elect corporate tax status, the typical LLC chooses pass-through tax status. Using this tax status avoids one of the biggest downfalls that corporations are faced with: double taxation. *Double taxation* occurs when the corporation *and* the individual both pay taxes on the same profits as they are distributed. This additional layer of taxation can make a world of difference to a small business. LLCs are great because they avoid double taxation completely. (Chapter 13 covers LLCs and taxes in depth.)

Pass-through taxation makes LLCs perfect for holding real estate and other appreciating assets. Can you imagine paying the capital gains tax twice? Also, don't forget — filing taxes as an LLC is simple. You don't have to file separate tax returns. You just include the Schedule K information in your personal tax return and you're done!

LLCs that opt for a pass-through tax status are still required to pay self-employment tax. The self-employment tax rate for 2007 is 15.3 percent of the first $97,500 of income and 2.9 percent for all income greater than $97,500.

Avoiding ownership restrictions: Divvying up the pie however you want

Some business structures, such as S corporations (as described later in this chapter), have severe ownership limitations. Often, you're limited in the number and types of owners, be it other companies or non-U.S. citizens. LLCs have no such problem. You can issue as many shares as you want to any individual (no, your pets don't count!) or any company, no matter what entity type it is. In Chapter 10, I show you how to issue, transfer, and cancel membership shares.

This freedom of ownerships has made LLCs the entity of choice for raising money for your business from angel investors or private equity firms. Often, you will want to develop a new product or grow into a new market. With LLCs, you have the flexibility (remember — no ownership restrictions) to issue membership shares in exchange for investment.

No management restrictions: Choosing who gets a say in the operations

When it comes to the management of the business, an LLC can be managed by

✔ **Its members:** When you select member management for your LLC, all of the business's members have an equal say in the day-to-day operations. For the most part, they all have the right to sign contracts and enter into debts on behalf of the business. If you don't want one of your members to have this sort of power, then member-management is definitely not for you.

✔ **Separate managers:** These folks may or may not hold a stake in the company. Most companies that are larger than two or three operating partners will choose manager management. When you elect manager management, you can have as many of your members be managers as you want; however, not all of them have to be if you don't want them to. For instance, if you have a silent investor who is only in it for the return and doesn't want to be hassled with business affairs, you may elect all the members but him to be managers.

Say that you are raising money for your new enterprise, and you want your investors to profit from the business's success, but you don't want them to have a say in the day-to-day operations. In this case, I would advise you to form a manager-managed LLC, in which you would place yourself as the manager, and the investors would solely remain members.

The fact that you can specify separate managers is a trademark quality of LLCs that helps separate them from sole proprietorships and general partnerships. In general partnerships, all members are owners and all are equally (and personally!) liable for the business. In limited partnerships, you can have members who also manage the business; however, they don't have any sort of limited-liability protection. I get into the specifics of these business types later in the chapter.

Normally when setting up the LLC — in the articles of organization, as a matter of fact — you designate your new company as being either *member-managed* or *manager-managed.* I go into further detail on these two types of setups in Chapter 6.

The management aspect is one reason why LLCs work well in estate planning. You can place your assets in an LLC with the kids as the full owners ("members") and yourself as the manager. This way, you still control the company, while your kids can receive profit distributions. Upon your death, the assets will still be in their name, and a new manager will be elected.

Flexible tax status: Minimizing how much you send to the IRS

As the owner of an LLC, you have the unique ability to choose how you want to pay taxes on your business. LLCs can be taxed as partnerships (with pass-through taxation) or as sole proprietorships (if the LLC has only one member); or they can even choose to be taxed as S corporations (which I explain in further detail later in the chapter). Although you can't necessarily flip back and forth from one type of taxation to another very easily, this sort of flexibility is unique to LLCs. For instance, corporations can't choose to be taxed like partnerships. Sole proprietorships can only be taxed like sole proprietorships. LLCs have a choice, and in the business world, flexibility and choices can determine success or failure.

Corporate taxation works for growing companies that want to reinvest their profits to help build the company. This is because the corporate tax rate is lower than the personal income tax rate that the members have to pay when pass-through taxation is elected. As long as you don't intend on paying yourself the profits (in which case you will be faced with *double taxation*), then a corporate tax status is probably your best bet. If you *do* need to take out some extra money for yourself one year, you can always opt to raise your salary slightly or have your LLC loan you the money. Chapter 13 has more information on partnership and corporate tax structures.

For example, say you have just started your business, and you don't foresee taking any profits from the business for the next five or so years. You can be taxed like a corporation during that time and then switch to an LLC tax status when you start earning more profits. That way, after you are making more profits, you can take them for yourself without having to worry about double taxation.

To change your LLC's tax status to corporate, you must file IRS Form 8832, Entity Classification Election. You can refer to Chapter 13 for more information on how to file this form.

After you elect corporate taxation, you can't change back to pass-through taxation for five years. This makes sense if you want to retain all of the profit for building your business, but you should still be cautious.

Flexible profit distribution: Deciding who gets how much moolah

With most entities, if a shareholder owns 10 percent of the company, he can only receive 10 percent of the profits that are distributed, no more and no less. With an LLC, you have freedom to choose! You don't have to split the profits in accordance with the percentage of ownership. If all the members agree, you can give 40 percent of the profits to someone who owns 20 percent of the business, or give 10 percent to someone who owns 50 percent.

Say you and John decide to partner together to create a Web design company. You have chosen to partner fifty-fifty, and you are putting in the initial $20,000 needed to get the venture started. You'll both be sharing the workload. But, is it fair to split the profits fifty-fifty when you put in the initial investment? You think not!

Being the smart cookie that you are, you decide to form an LLC. You distribute 50 percent of the company to John and 50 percent to yourself. In your operating agreement, you state that you'll take 10 percent interest on your initial investment ($2,000), and then split the profits fifty-fifty.

Drawbacks to LLCs

Unfortunately, all roses have thorns, and this holds true with LLCs. Although they're great for many things, LLCs aren't the perfect fit for everyone. For one, LLCs are relatively new entities with very few precedents, so people often are uncomfortable using them. LLCs are also still restricted by a lot of partnership laws, such as transferring ownership and a limit to the life span of the business.

The main disadvantages I cover here are

- ✔ **The new kid on the block:** LLCs are new entities and not very well understood, and there aren't a lot of precedents in LLC law to validate them.

- ✔ **Limits on transferring ownership:** You can't just transfer your ownership to another person when you want out of the business. Certain formalities must be followed.

- ✔ **Limited life span:** By law, LLCs can't live forever. You have to choose a dissolution date.

✔ **Partners are preferred:** I know, I know — I said earlier in the chapter that LLC don't have any ownership restrictions. Well, in a few states, this isn't exactly the case — you may actually have to have a minimum of two members because single-member LLCs are not allowed. In Appendix A, I tell you whether your state allows single-member LLCs.

✔ **Extra costs:** When compared to doing business as a sole proprietor or general partnership, any cost is an additional cost because very few fees are associated with those two business structures. However, while LLCs are imposed with some extra filing fees (and in some states, taxes), just think of it as the best insurance policy you can find for the money. Chapter 8 covers some of the fees LLCs face.

✔ **Self-employment taxes:** Unless specific criteria are met, all members of the LLC must pay self-employment taxes at the current rate of 15.3 percent. This rate is imposed on all of the business's profits and can sometimes even be higher than the double taxation that corporations face, depending on the amount of profit the LLC has. (Chapter 13 goes into taxes and how you can minimize them.)

In the following sections, I delve into some of the disadvantages of using an LLC in more detail. This way, you can easily determine whether an LLC is the right entity for you.

Still working out the kinks

The LLC is a very recent development, and the laws that support it are changing constantly. When something such as an entity type exists for a long time in the United States, it develops a large amount of case law that supports its existence and upholds it structure. *Case law* is the history of decisions made by judges in regard to the entity. For instance, if a judge disregards your LLC because certain formalities haven't been followed, then judges in future lawsuits can do the same thing, based on the previous judge's decision.

In the case of the LLC, very little history and case law exists to substantiate its existence. Therefore, you run the risk that, should you go to court, some of your assumptions about LLCs may be overturned by the judge. Without any case law for guidance, a lot of elements of the LLC are left for speculation.

This isn't all. Because LLCs are newer entities and not entirely understood by everyone, some more conservative investors may be turned off by the idea of investing in an LLC and may decide to invest in a more traditional business structure, such as a corporation.

Difficulty in transferring ownership

It is common for LLCs to restrict the transfer of ownership. Although this used to be a requirement of LLCs, it is now more customary than anything else. Basically, if a member wants to sell or transfer his shares, he can only assign the membership interest, not actually transfer the ownership. So the person purchasing the membership only has rights to the profits that are distributed; he has no voting rights and no control over the business operations.

However, don't fret too much — this can be more of a positive than anything else! An *assignee* (the person or company purchasing the membership) can become a full member upon the approval of the majority of the other members. All it takes is a quick vote. But keep in mind that to fully transfer your membership shares, you must be sure that the other members will approve the transfer; otherwise, the assignee may end up as a silent partner with no voting rights or control! (See Chapter 10 for more on transferring ownership.)

If you intend on taking your company public, bear in mind that you probably won't be able to do it with an LLC. Ownership is not freely transferable in an LLC, and this prohibits the free exchange of ownership. This may also prevent your business from being acquired by a public company in exchange for its stock because it creates a taxable event. This isn't really a dire problem though. You can always change from an LLC to a corporation.

Limited life spans: Setting an end date before you get started

The IRS doesn't allow LLCs to live forever — they must have limited life spans. Normally when you form an LLC, you must state the *date of dissolution* — the date that the partners will wrap up the business's affairs and close it down. Don't worry! This isn't as ominous as it sounds.

During the dissolution, the partners can always vote to continue the business instead of dissolving it. If the entire idea of forced dissolution sounds pointless to you, you're in good company. The only reason why the IRS has enforced this law is to legally separate LLCs from corporations, which live forever. Otherwise, nothing would really differentiate them. Because the members can always just decide to continue the business operations, the dissolution date required when forming the LLC is just used to please the IRS. You can find more on dissolutions in Chapter 12.

Check your state's laws regarding the maximum allowed life span (also called *duration*) of the LLC. It is common for LLCs to be limited to a life span of 30 years (which the members can vote to prolong at the end of the term). Some states allow you to choose a *perpetual duration,* which means you never have to dissolve. If you choose a perpetual duration, then you may be able to avoid the dissolution problem entirely!

Understanding Other Business Structures

Not all business structures are created alike. In fact, the differences can be vast, and the choice you make can spell life or death for your business. LLCs aren't right for every situation, so in this section, I explain the other major entity types so that you have a good understanding of the options that are out there and can consider whether one of these entity types might work best for your situation.

Because every situation is unique, you should only use this chapter as a starting point. Contact an attorney or corporate consulting firm for advice on what entity is right for your business now and for your future goals.

Going it alone: Sole proprietorships

Your kid's school bake sale, your stall at the local flea market, the consulting job you did where you weren't on the payroll — all perfect examples of sole proprietorships. A *sole proprietorship* (or "SP" for short) automatically exists whenever you are engaging in business by and for yourself, without the protection of an LLC, corporation, or limited partnership. Although it sounds fancy and complicated, forming an SP is *easy.* In some states, you only need a business license to get up and running.

Even though the sole proprietorship is simple to set up, it has many disadvantages. When you are operating as an SP, your personal assets are completely at risk from being seized by a lawsuit gone bad or an angry creditor. There is an old saying, "You aren't in business until you've been sued," and as an SP, you are handing over all of your hard-earned assets (your home, your car, everything) on a silver platter. So, if you're out selling cookies and somebody chokes on the oatmeal specials, you may be cashing out your kids' college fund sooner than you think.

Unlike LLCs, which have membership interests, sole proprietorships don't have interests or any other form of ownership in the company. Your business is *you.* You can't sell little pieces of yourself, now, can you?

Adding a partner: General partnerships

When a sole proprietorship brings on its first partner, a *general partnership* is formed. Occasionally, partners will create a general partnership agreement, but often no other paperwork is completed and no filings need to be made.

When it comes to lawsuits and creditors, a general partnership ("GP" for short) is even more dangerous than a sole proprietorship. When operating as a GP, each partner is equally responsible for all of the business's judgments, taxes, and debts. This means that not only are you personally responsible for the business's debts and obligations, but you are also personally responsible for your partner's wrongdoing or debts! So if your partner at your bakery is delivering cookies and hits someone, that person can sue your partnership and take away your house, car, and other assets, as well as your partner's.

Unlike LLCs, which have membership interests, general partnerships don't have interests or any other form of ownership in the company. Remember, in a GP, your business is you and your partner. So, unless you can cut yourself up into little pieces and place them for sale, an LLC is definitely the way to go.

Throwing in a little legal protection: Limited partnerships

Think of a *limited partnership* ("LP" for short) as a general partnership with a little bit of protection against lawsuits thrown in. Whereas a general partnership doesn't protect any of the owners against the business's lawsuits and creditors, an LP protects the investors, or silent partners (also called the *limited partners*). Limited partners can receive profit from the company, but they don't manage the business's day-to-day operations. If the business goes south, the limited partners only risk losing the money they have invested in the company, while the managers (called *general partners*) still put all of their personal assets at risk.

I'm often asked why anyone bothers to use a limited partnership, especially considering that they're somewhat complicated to set up and they lack basic liability protection for the general partners. These reasons alone make the limited partnership a bad choice for business owners; however, because of their limitations on the decision-making power of the limited partners, LPs are still great for use in estate planning (for example, the kids can receive money from, but not manage, the assets of the limited partnership).

Separating yourself from your business: Corporations

Unlike LLCs, *corporations* are completely separate from the owners (think of them as a separate person or entity). Because of this, corporations pay taxes at a special corporate tax rate. Corporations only pay taxes on the profit that is left in the company at the end of the year. For this reason, corporations can be useful for a newer business that wants to reinvest its profits in the business.

The downside to corporations is that the profits are subject to *double taxation,* meaning the profits that get distributed to the shareholders (the owners) are taxed twice — first as corporate taxes, then again as income to the shareholder. To avoid this, many upstarts are now operating as LLCs.

A corporation also protects its owners from lawsuits and creditors; however, unlike an LLC, it doesn't protect the business from the liabilities of the owners. So if the owner of a corporation is sued for personal reasons, her ownership of the corporation is considered to be a personal asset of hers, and the creditor can take her business away. This *dual protection* an LLC provides is a key reason to operate as an LLC.

Because of their complete flexibility of ownership and management structures and their lengthy history of case law, corporations are an ideal choice for business owners intent on taking their company public.

Easing the tax burden: S corporations

An *S corporation* is structured exactly the same as a regular corporation (you even form it as a regular corporation!); however, it's taxed like an LLC, with pass-through tax status, instead of like a corporation. This avoids the double taxation that corporations are disliked for. Designating a corporation as an S corporation is easy. You just have to file Form 2553, Election by a Small Business Corporation, within three months of formation.

S corporations and LLCs have two major differences, one good and one bad:

✔ **Fewer self-employment taxes:** Unlike LLCs, S corporations can hire their owners as employees, which means the owners are paying average, everyday payroll taxes that any employee would pay. With LLCs, the managing members aren't considered employees and are therefore required to pay a pretty hefty self-employment tax.

> ✔ **No free contributions:** When you transfer an asset into an LLC in exchange for membership interests, no taxable event occurs. Not so with S corporations. Contributions (and distributions of assets) aren't tax free!

S corporations have severe ownership limitations. Non-U.S. citizens and other entities can't own shares in an S corporation, and the number of shareholders is limited to 100. Also, all shares are equal, meaning that the officers of the company can't create special *classes* of shares (which allow some members to vote while others don't, or some members to get priority on profits while others take the back seat, and so on) like they can in an LLC.

Newly emerging entity types

After LLCs became popular, a lot of states lobbied for other types of similar entities to be created under the U.S. Corporation Law. This resulted in the limited liability partnership (LLP), the limited liability limited partnership (LLLP), and the Series LLC. It is impossible to cover all of the intricacies of each one, and not all of these company types are available in every state; therefore, I just give you a brief overview of each one.

To find out if these entity types are available in your state, call your Secretary of State's office (flip to Appendix A for contact info). Just be careful — these entities are pretty new and aren't well understood by the courts.

Limited liability partnership (LLP)

The *limited liability partnership* (LLP) is a cross between a limited partnership and a corporation. In a way, it offers the best of both worlds. The LLP is exactly like a limited partnership (see the earlier section) in that it has both general partners and limited partners and *pass-through tax status* (the owners pay the company's taxes on their personal tax returns).

The LLP differs from a limited partnership in that, like a corporation, it offers *all* business partners protection from lawsuits filed against the company and creditors seeking payment from the company, not just the limited partners. However, in exchange for this added protection, the limited partners have full management rights in the company. They are no longer resigned to their role as silent partners.

Limited liability limited partnership (LLLP)

The *limited liability limited partnership* (LLLP) is another modification of the limited partnership. The LLLP has general partners who operate the business and limited partners who own the business but aren't allowed to deal in day-to-day management activities, just like a limited partnership does.

The difference is that an LLLP can only be created when there is more than one general partner and more than one limited partner. But an LLLP is a great entity — it protects *all* partners in the business from lawsuits and creditors, not just the limited partners. So far, only Colorado, Delaware, Florida, Georgia, Kentucky, Maryland, Nevada, and Texas allow LLLPs. Currently, they are normally created by forming a standard limited partnership, and then applying for LLLP status with the state.

Series LLC

I'm a big believer in forming a different entity for each of your assets (real estate, intellectual property, and so on) so you can separate each asset from the lawsuits and creditors that your business may face during its normal operations. This is a very good business practice, and it has become so popular over the last couple of years that states have started enacting series LLCs, which streamline the entire process of protecting several assets.

Instead of having multiple LLCs to file, manage, and pay taxes on, a business owner or real estate investor can form a *series LLC* — one entity that has multiple cells. Think of a *cell* as a protective barrier around the asset — nothing can touch it. It's as if the asset is within its own LLC. Additionally, you only file one tax return and are only required to deal with the upkeep of one entity, not multiple ones. This definitely helps solve a lot of the paperwork headaches associated with managing multiple entities!

Say you are a real estate investor and own three houses that you rent out. You can form a series LLC and place each house into one cell of that series LLC. After your assets are placed in the series LLC, if a renter sues you, only the one property that is involved in the lawsuit can be seized, not the other two. And because all the houses are under a series LLC, you reduce the amount of paperwork you have to handle.

As of the publishing of this book, series LLCs are currently available in the following states: Delaware, Illinois, Iowa, Nevada, Oklahoma, Oregon, Nevada, Tennessee, and Utah.

Chapter 3

Getting the Help You Need for Your LLC

In This Chapter
▶ Knowing which professionals you need
▶ Adding the right experts to your team
▶ Minimizing how much you pay in fees

*B*uilding a business is a journey, and the best time to prepare for the future is now, when you're just beginning. Over the next couple of years, situations will arise where you need immediate help — be it taxes, lawsuits, human resources, or administrative stuff — and you need a team of professionals ready and waiting to jump in at a moment's notice.

No matter what, you need professionals to handle certain matters as you run your business. For example, you need an accountant to handle tax issues; a bookkeeper to maintain your accounts; a good small-business attorney to handle legal issues; a corporate strategist, a financial planner, a real estate broker, a banker . . . the list goes on and on.

You can figure out how to do all of this yourself, but the question is, do you really want to? Although you should have a good, basic knowledge of all aspects of your business, you should spend your time working on the parts of your business that you do best and entrust tedious, time-consuming tasks outside your area of expertise to the professionals. And when it comes to tax issues, you don't want to make mistakes that could (very literally) cost you!

This chapter gives you tips on finding the professionals you need and how to let them know exactly what you want from them. Do you really need to hire an attorney, accountant, or professional incorporating company to form your LLC? Not necessarily. I personally believe that you only need to consult an expert when you are dealing with multiple companies, a lot of money or assets, or anything else out of the ordinary. For example, you may only need to talk to an attorney when you're dealing with multiple LLCs or have a large amount of assets that need to be transferred. Even then, in the interest of saving money, you should have the attorney review your structure and only write out the more complex agreements that you can't do yourself or can't find in this book. With that in mind, this chapter also tells you what you can do to save money while working with these often pricey pros.

Picking Out the Right Professionals

Every great leader knows that the people who surround him make all the difference in success or failure. These people can make or break your business, so you need to choose them well and choose them *now*. After all, the last thing you want to do when faced with a catastrophe is to hastily try to find an attorney, accountant, or banker who will back you up.

Sometimes it's difficult to find someone whom you can trust with some of the most important elements of your business. Where do you even begin to look? Well, put the Yellow Pages away because that's a headache waiting to happen. The following sections give you tips for finding the best of the three types of professionals you really need for your business:

- ✔ Attorneys
- ✔ Accountants or CPAs
- ✔ Incorporating companies

I can't stress enough the importance of building your team early and fostering these relationships. Facing a lawsuit or a tax audit isn't the best time to start interviewing professionals. Under these circumstances, you'll most likely make hasty decisions and choose someone with a reputation that is unknown to you. You may end up paying too much or find yourself in a worse situation than you started in because of their lack of expertise. Build your team now — although it may cost you a little bit of time and maybe some money, it will serve you well in the coming years. I promise.

You need to find professionals who not only have great reputations, but also share your principles and ideals. Are you risk-averse? Or do you prefer more aggressive strategies? These are the sort of perspectives that you and the professionals you work with must agree on from the get-go. Also, don't underestimate the rapport you should develop with your advisors. You want to have long, trusting relationships with these people — that's hard to do when you don't really like them.

Hiring a good attorney

Most of you won't need an attorney to form your LLC, but you'll need one waiting in the wings when the occasional legal issue crops up. What's that old adage? "You aren't in business until you've been sued." Lawsuits abound, and after the public smells your first sign of success, there will be people looking for any reason possible to sue you. Trust me — after you've been served, you'll be so glad that you took the time to find the perfect attorney to lead the way.

Sometimes you must consult with an attorney, especially if you're forming a nonstandard LLC, creating multiple LLCs that are to work together, or converting your existing business to an LLC and it has assets that need to be transferred. (See more about these types of LLCs in Chapter 2.) You should also consult a securities attorney if you will be selling a large quantity of ownership shares of your LLC to raise capital.

Forget about hiring a fancy-pants corporate attorney who charges an arm and a leg. It doesn't matter whether your lawyer's office has Italian marble flooring or shag carpeting, as long as he knows what he's talking about. If his clients are Fortune 500 companies, chances are you can't afford him. Plus, he wouldn't be dealing with small-business issues on a day-to-day basis anyway — you want someone with the *right* experience.

Getting referrals

Finding a great attorney isn't always an easy task! Often people suggest contacting your local bar association for a referral. This is normally pointless because the person you speak with hasn't had any personal experience with the attorney, and she does little to assist you. Usually, she just provides the names of attorneys who have paid the bar association to do so. Some bar associations even charge you for the referral!

The best way, by far, to find the perfect lawyer is to ask around. Talk to everyone you know who has a small business — especially those who have formed LLCs — and ask them about their lawyer. Get them to speak candidly with you — find out what they *truly* think of the person's legal expertise and work.

Don't have a lot of entrepreneur friends? Join the SBA (U.S. Small Business Administration, www.sba.gov) and go to their meetings or small-business networking events. You may also be able to get some good referrals from your other business contacts, such as your banker, real estate broker, accountant, investment advisor, and incorporating company. After exhausting these various sources, you should be able to come up with at least three good attorneys to contact.

Researching attorneys

Before you call the attorneys to set up an appointment for a consultation, do your homework and find out a little bit about them. Sites that offer good attorney background information include:

- **LawyerDex.com,** www.lawyerdex.com: My personal favorite, this site not only offers detailed information about attorneys, such as schools and biographies, but also allows users to comment on their experiences with attorneys, so you can gain firsthand knowledge of clients' experiences.

- **FindLaw.com,** www.findlaw.com: This site supplies lengthy firm profiles and extensive background information on each attorney.

- **Martindale.com,** www.martindale.com: At this site, you get a firm profile and some background information on each attorney.

When you are looking at individual lawyers' profiles, I would recommend that you focus on attorneys whose area of expertise is limited to small-business issues. If an attorney practices in a wide range of areas, such as business formation and personal injury, I would count her out. You want an attorney who is dealing with issues similar to yours on a day-to-day basis, not someone who is scouring the hospitals looking for her next client. Also, read as much information as you can about the attorney's history and background; does it sound like someone who has focused her career on working with businesses such as yours?

Choosing an attorney

When calling prospective attorneys, let them know right off the bat what you're looking for: a good small-business attorney who can help you help yourself. You are looking for a long-term business relationship. If it's obvious that the attorney isn't for you, disqualify them now — not during a face-to-face meeting where you may not only be wasting your time, but you may also be paying them for the pleasure.

When screening attorneys, evaluate them on two aspects:

- **A personal basis:** Do you like this person? What do your instincts tell you? Can you trust her? How would you feel working with her for a decade or longer?

  These are tough questions, but also the most pertinent. You're looking to establish rapport and a long-term relationship with this person — it's a waste of time even trying to do that if you don't even like her.

- **Her level of aggressiveness:** It should match yours. If she is extremely conservative and risk-averse in her strategies, and you are the adventurous type and like to live on the edge of the law, then the relationship should probably end after the phone call. If, however, you're in agreement about how aggressive one should be when using entities to lower taxes and avoid lawsuits, then you should set the appointment.

After you have found one or two lawyers whom you like, set up an appointment for a one-hour consultation. (See the "Bringing the Pros On Board" section for advice on your initial meeting.) You may be charged for this time, but if you come in prepared and full of questions, it will be well worth the money.

Getting a great CPA or accountant

Do you need a tax professional to assist you in creating your LLC? Not usually. When using multiple entities, you definitely want a tax specialist to review your strategy to ensure that no tax traps are looming. But unless that's the case, you don't need a fancy tax advisor or CPA (Certified Public Accountant) to help you create the LLC. Down the road, however, you *will* need a more experienced eye for the difficult stuff that comes about *after* you form the LLC: choosing your accounting year, setting up your books, creating a bookkeeping system, creating financial reports, setting up payroll and withholding, calculating IRS payments, and filing end-of-the-year tax returns. So it's a really good idea to find a tax specialist now.

Already have a tax advisor whom you want to use? Believe it or not, that person may not be qualified! LLCs are a newer entity and not well understood by most people. Therefore, your personal tax advisor — or the tax advisor for another business you own — may *not* be the most suitable person to advise you on issues regarding your LLC. You need someone who has been around the block a couple of times — someone who is knowledgeable about federal and state LLC tax laws.

Doing a little homework

Before seeking out a tax professional, I encourage you to understand as much as you can about LLC tax law — on a federal *and* state level. When you have a basic understanding of tax law, you can not only have an intelligent conversation with the advisor you choose, but you also can accurately evaluate his level of expertise. (Reading this book is a good step in that direction!)

If you don't know where to look for information on LLC tax laws, flip to Appendix A, where I list Web sites that have information about state statutes regarding LLCs. This gives you a starting point. After you're familiar with the information there, you can find more information at www.corpfiling.com. You can do the research anytime you want from the comfort of your own home.

When you're ready to start shopping around for a tax specialist to add to your team, ask other small-business owners, particularly those who have LLCs, who they use and whether they recommend them. If you don't know anyone who can give you a referral, try going to networking events and SBA meetings. You can also ask your banker or real estate broker for suggestions.

Choosing a tax specialist

There are many types of tax specialists, so which do you use?

- ✔ An **accountant,** who may or may not have a degree in accounting, is someone who captures the financial information of a company and monitors those results. She creates and distributes financial statements to the company's managers for them to use in their planning.

- ✔ A **CPA,** which stands for "Certified Public Accountant," is a regular accountant. However, they are certified by the state as experienced and educated in the field. In states where accountants aren't regulated, hiring someone with this designation can help you make sure that the person who is working for you actually knows what he's talking about.

- ✔ A **bookkeeper** is commonly someone without any advanced degrees in accounting who sets up accounting systems for companies and handles their books (such as accounts payable, accounts receivable, and payroll).

Plan on having a reputable accountant or CPA on hand for the more complicated issues that may arise. Eventually, you'll need his expertise. If you have any tax questions regarding the formation of your LLC, you can consult this person.

CPAs can get expensive! That's why I don't recommend using them for the everyday accounting needed to run your business, such as bookkeeping, profit and loss statements, accounts payable and receivable, and financial reports. However, you should still delegate these duties to someone who is experienced in this area, such as an everyday accountant or bookkeeper.

Normally, unless you are scouting out a pricey CPA, accountants won't charge you for a consultation. Still, go to the meeting prepared (see "Bringing the Pros On Board" later in this chapter). You can use the consultation to absorb all the knowledge that this person has to offer. Go to the meeting loaded with questions!

You and your tax advisor need to agree on how aggressive you plan to be when it comes to tax matters because tax issues and laws are mostly based on interpretation. Some people see tax benefits that can be passed on to their clients where others don't. For example, does your CPA shy away from risk when you would rather pay less tax now and risk the chance of penalties later? Consider how your advisor's approach will fit with yours. (See the chapters in Part IV for more on taxes.)

I don't recommend entrusting the tax elements of your LLC to your attorney, unless he is specifically a tax attorney. When using multiple LLCs, or even corporations, in a tax strategy, I always advise running your plan by an experienced accountant first to make sure that all the pieces fit.

Considering incorporating companies

Don't know what an incorporating company is exactly? Sure you do! Remember those ads offering to form your LLC for $300 or $400? Normally, those ads are placed by *incorporating companies* — companies whose sole business is forming corporations and LLCs.

When I started in this business in 2002, there was very little competition. Now, it seems, companies are popping up everywhere, ready to take your money for doing relatively little work. The truth is that a lot of newer incorporating companies are doing exactly what this book tells you to do — they even use the state forms as opposed to their own customized articles of organization (see Chapter 6)!

Using an incorporating company to form your LLC makes sense when you

✔ **Want to save time:** For the most part, incorporating companies normally don't do anything more for you than you can do for yourself, but they have the process down pat and can handle the paperwork for you. Their much lower fees sometimes makes it worth it! They can save you days of tedious research and bureaucratic hassles.

✔ **Want to customize your company's articles and operating agreements:** You may want these documents to reflect specifically what you're trying to achieve. If you want to make changes to the standard operating agreement included on the CD that came with this book, but don't know how, an incorporating company can help you.

✔ **Are forming multiple LLCs and want an expert to look over your structure:** Some brick-and-mortar incorporating companies (the ones that operate outside of the online realm) have consultants who can review your strategy with a skilled eye and set you up in the proper business structure.

✔ **Are forming an LLC in a different state than you live:** Different states come with different laws, and a good incorporating company in all 50 states will be well aware of how the various governments operate. It can also serve as your registered agent, hand deliver your filings, and make sure you stay in compliance while you're living hundreds of miles away.

Good incorporating companies also normally assign you a knowledgeable consultant who will get to know the ins and outs of your business. The company will also have small-business attorneys and accountants on staff who can work with you and your consultant on a continual basis. These folks can delve into complex, multi-entity, and estate-planning strategies. They can also look at the asset protection and tax aspects of your business so you don't wind up with different, sometimes conflicting, opinions from different experts. For instance, the tax-reduction plan that your accountant sets out for you may conflict with the lawsuit-proof plan that your attorney has constructed. Good incorporating companies avoid this by having all experts work together.

Online incorporating companies have their place — they save precious time by preparing the documentation for you. However, you must do your research to make sure the company you're using is reputable. Most just fill out the same forms, or some version thereof, that are included on the CD that accompanies this book. See! By using this book, you've already saved yourself hundreds of dollars in needless fees.

If you decide to use an incorporating company, use these questions to find a quality firm:

✔ Do you have an attorney and accountant on staff to advise me on legal and tax issues?

✔ Will you assign a consultant to work with me on an ongoing basis?

✔ Are you located in all 50 states? If not, are you able to help me form an LLC in my state?

✔ Will you customize the company to my needs?

✔ Will you customize the articles of organization or just use state forms?

Bringing the Pros On Board

Whether before or after you have formed your entity, you need to meet with the professionals you want to add to your business team. These professionals need to know the ins and outs of your business — especially if they are working on a particular case or project.

It's your job as the head honcho to make sure that you choose people you can work with for the long term and that the lines of communication are constantly open. You're the leader, and it's your responsibility to make sure that your team members always act in line with your vision — and your ethics.

Gathering information for the meeting

I'm going to specify what to do before meeting with your attorney, but these steps are applicable to *every* member of your team. Before your big meeting, make sure to do the following:

- ✔ **Create a file for your attorney.** You'll place copies of all pertinent documents and information in a folder that you can take to your meeting. Staple your business card or write your contact information on the front.

- ✔ **Send an e-mail to the attorney and ask if there is anything in particular she wants you to bring to the meeting.** Most of the items included in this list will be sufficient, but you never want to make assumptions, so always ask.

- ✔ **Make copies of all your corporate paperwork.** This includes your articles of organization, your operating agreement, your minutes, and so on. If you don't have all of these things, don't fret. Just make copies of what you do have and put them in the file.

- ✔ **Think about any immediate projects that you need her to work on.** Write down or gather any important facts or documentation. Make copies and put them in the file.

- ✔ **Write down the names, phone numbers, and addresses of all operating officers, directors, and/or pertinent shareholders.** Also, if the attorney will be corresponding with any key employees or if she will need to be in touch with any important business contacts, be sure to include their information as well. Make a copy and place it in the file.

- ✔ **Make copies of all paperwork relevant to those issues that your attorney will be handling.** You may need to include leases, contracts, court notices, correspondence, filings, and so on. Place the copies in your attorney's file.

- ✔ **Prepare a list of questions that you want answered.** After doing your research and educating yourself, you'll definitely have gray areas that need more explanation (the next section can help you get started). Write these questions down and put them in your own file so you don't forget to ask them. Make sure to leave enough space on the page to jot down the answers!

I can't overstate the importance of being knowledgeable before meeting with your professionals. Not only will you have a much more fulfilling conversation, but you'll also be a lot more productive. You'll also save money! After all, the more prepared you are and the more information you provide, the fewer billable hours the attorney or accountant has to spend digging up details!

The Glossary contains some common terms relating to LLCs, corporations, and real estate that you should know. Refer to the Glossary as often as necessary to get comfortable with the lingo, especially when you need to talk shop with pros!

When it comes to working with your team of professionals, communication is key. Without open lines of communication, everyone won't be on the same page, and your team can hurt your business more than help it. Plus, you often pay a lot of money to work with these folks. Why not make the most of your cash by being prepared and speaking directly?

Preparing questions to ask the pros

Below are some questions that you can ask when you interview a professional who you may want to add to your business team. Use his answers to decide whether he is qualified to entrust with your business.

- ✔ **What size of businesses do you normally work with?** Unless you're starting out as a billion-dollar enterprise (very unlikely), you need someone who deals with businesses like yours on a regular basis.

- ✔ **Do you handle litigation?** If you are sued and go to court, you need someone who has experience speaking in front of a judge and jury.

- ✔ **What is your fee structure?** You need to make sure that the fees are in your budget range. See more on this in the next section.

- ✔ **What work will you handle personally?** Often, attorneys and accountants hand work off to junior staff, including paralegals and less-experienced accountants. What work will that be? If the work that the professional plans to hand off isn't pertinent in your opinion, then find out whether the rate will be discounted.

- ✔ **Do you work with LLCs often? Do you recommend them to your clients?** This is a new field, and you want someone who has experience in it. If the person never recommends LLCs to any of her clients, chances are she is unfamiliar with the entity and shouldn't be your front-runner if you're intent on using an LLC.

Conducting the meeting

You've screened the attorney or accountant through an initial phone call, and you've prepared all of your paperwork and questions. Now you're ready to meet face to face with the person whom you're considering hiring.

At the beginning of the meeting, give a quick background of yourself and your company. Hand the professional the folder containing your records (make sure they are all copies!), and then let him know what you're looking for and the budget that you have to work with. Be open and honest. If you don't have a lot of money, say so. Perhaps he can help you find a solution.

The meeting should be professional and relaxed. If you've done some research, you should be knowledgeable enough to have an intelligent conversation with the person and be able to evaluate whether he is qualified. Use the questions from the previous section to steer the conversation and to get a sense of whether this person is a good match for your needs.

Friendliness is important when fostering relationships, but overfriendliness can cost you — literally! Whenever you chitchat about the weather, the clock keeps ticking, and the money runs out the door. So keep small talk to a minimum and immediately get to the business at hand.

Just as you'll be evaluating the attorney or accountant, he'll be evaluating you. Put your best foot forward. Let him know that you value open communication and are looking for a great, long-term working relationship. Tell him that you pay fairly and on time — and make sure that you stick to your word!

Establishing a working relationship

After you've decided on a professional, let him know. If the person is an attorney and insists on a retainer, and you are okay with it, pay him the money (but first see the upcoming "How to Keep Professional Fees Low" section).

Most companies will never make you sign a contract, so be wary of one that requests you do. This is a new relationship and deserves a trial period. If, at any time, you feel that you don't mesh with the person, or you decide that he is unqualified for the type of work that you want him to do, then don't hesitate to terminate the relationship and go with your second choice. The sooner, the better.

However, if the relationship seems to be going smoothly, make sure to keep in contact with the person on a regular basis. When nothing is going on, you don't have to hassle him, but if your attorney or accountant doesn't know who you are when you call, you should probably make it a point to keep in touch more often.

How to Keep Professional Fees Low

When you're trying to build your business — and watching every penny that you have — being inundated with legal and professional fees can be overwhelming. Part of being a prudent entrepreneur or real estate investor is watching your money. After all, as Benjamin Franklin said, "A penny saved is a penny earned."

You can do a couple of things to keep a lid on the ever-growing pile of bills. I cover these topics in the following sections:

✔ Do a lot of the research yourself.

✔ Don't choose lawyers and CPAs who mostly deal with Fortune 500 companies (unless you are one).

✔ Negotiate all fees and fee structures upfront.

✔ Stay away from retainers.

✔ Use services that are experts at document preparation for routine paperwork.

With any sort of tax professional, your rule of thumb should always be that they save you more money in taxes than the amount you pay them.

Do your own research

Although most law is open to interpretation, a lot of the practical stuff that you need to know to form and manage your LLC properly is just bland, factual stuff. The only difficult part is trying to stay awake long enough to absorb the information.

Now, thanks to the Internet, you have access to the same information that your attorney has. For the most part, attorneys don't do a lot of research anyway — their paralegals do it. And if they can do it, you can do it. After all, it's *your* business. Being knowledgeable about certain LLC laws can only benefit you.

You will want to research information including:

✔ **Federal laws (U.S. corporation code and partnership law):** Most LLC law is governed by the state. However, the federal government has laid out a lot of guidelines that are important to know. These are sort of "default laws" that will come into effect if your state is silent on a particular issue.

Where to find LLC laws and regulations

If you have decided to go it alone and don't have a professional on hand with ready knowledge about basic laws, then you'll definitely need to spend some time in the library or on the Internet. Knowledge is important, and you won't be able to move forward with confidence unless you know your legal limitations and requirements, such as tax laws and your state's formation laws. When researching laws, you only have to look at a few sites to find the information you need:

✔ **Secretary of State:** In Appendix A, I provide you with the Web site address of your state's Secretary of State's office. In most states, you file your articles of organization with the Secretary of State, thereby creating your new LLC. This is the first stop in your journey.

✔ **The Internal Revenue Service,** www.IRS. gov: Here you can find all federal tax information for LLCs. Start by doing a search for

Publication 3402, "Limited Liability Companies Overview," and Publication 334, "Tax Guide for Small Businesses."

✔ **The U.S. Department of Labor,** www.DOL. gov: After you begin to hire employees, this site will be invaluable to you. It offers information about wages, benefits and healthcare, unemployment insurance, and other human resources issues.

✔ **The Securities and Exchange Commission,** www.SEC.gov: Thinking about taking your company public in the future? Looking to raise money by selling membership shares? The SEC regulates all *securities* (the sale of stock and membership shares) in the United States. In addition to visiting this site, you may want to research your state's securities regulations, because both will be applicable.

✔ **IRS regulations:** These are federal tax laws and incredibly important for you to know.

✔ **State statutes:** LLCs have different rules and regulations from state to state, especially when it comes to paperwork and reporting requirements. You must know your state's LLC laws before forming and running your LLC.

✔ **Civil codes:** This is the area of private law (as opposed to criminal law). If someone were to sue you, they would do so under the civil codes.

✔ **Securities laws:** These are federal and state laws that govern the sale of *securities* (stock, investments, and so on) to protect investors from fraudulent investments.

✔ **Labor law:** Labor law encapsulates all laws relating to employees, including topics such as hours, pay, safety, and discrimination.

In Appendix A, I list where each state's statutes can be found. The LLC information that you can't find in this book you can find on the Internet. You have no excuse!

When doing your own research, be careful not to get ahead of yourself and jump into things, such as complex asset protection strategies, that are beyond your knowledge. This can be dangerous. If you're not sure about something, a ten-minute phone call to your attorney should clear everything up. You may have to pay for the attorney's time while he's on the phone with you, but you'll still be saving money in the long run by doing most of the legwork.

Use the "legal coach" approach

With all of the lawsuits nowadays and pages and pages of laws, codes, and case law to interpret, attorneys are a necessary evil. Unfortunately, most people can't afford an expensive attorney who handles *all* of their legal issues. The bills would bury you. So, what's the solution?

After you have found an attorney who you are interested in working with, see how she feels about being more of a *mentor,* or a "legal coach," so to speak. Instead of handling *all* of your company's issues and legal filings, she would assist you and check your work. She will work *with* you, not just *for* you. In essence, she helps you help yourself. It's hard to tell upfront which attorney will go for this type of arrangement, so the best thing you can do is just ask.

This is a newer approach that's gaining popularity because of the skyrocketing legal fees that small businesses face, but as you can guess, a lot of attorneys don't like it. It means less money for them. An attorney may also decline to be your mentor by saying the relationship would create a malpractice risk — although this isn't the most valid excuse. Let her know that you will pay fairly and *on time.* If she isn't up for it, thank her for her time and move on. Don't begin the attorney-client relationship and assume that you can develop a mentor relationship. Announce your intentions in advance. Being straightforward will save you a lot of time and headaches later.

When it comes to larger lawsuits and litigation, I always recommend letting your attorney handle everything 100 percent. When your business is at stake, you don't want to argue your case by yourself. Keep a small sum in reserve that can cover your legal fees should a lawsuit or criminal case arise.

Negotiate upfront

Many clients don't realize that they can negotiate attorney fees, especially flat fees. If you don't feel comfortable bargaining, then you should only evaluate firms that have lower fees, such as small firms. At larger firms, don't be lured by the rookies who charge lower hourly rates — they may take four times as long to do the work. You don't want to be charged for the associate's on-the-job training.

Attorneys can bill you in several ways, so it's important to find out upfront what your attorney's policy is. Some popular fee structures are:

- ✔ **Flat fee:** For common issues that normally take a set amount of time to complete, such as forming your LLC, attorneys normally charge a flat fee. However, if a surprise arises and extra work needs to be done, you'll be billed for it.

- ✔ **Hourly rate:** This is the most common form of legal fees. Generally, this fee ranges in the hundreds ($100 to $600 per hour). Often, attorneys request that you put down a deposit (called a *retainer*) that they can deduct fees from. Retainers can range from $500 to $50,000 (although the amount is closer to $1,000 to $5,000 for most small-business attorneys), depending on the work that is required.

- ✔ **Contingency:** When you sue someone, this payment is normally a percentage of whatever amount you win in the case. If the attorney loses the case, you don't have to pay him; however, you'll still have to put up money to cover his expenses.

Before you can negotiate a lower fee with your attorney, you need to know exactly how and how much you will be billed. How much will a particular job cost? If your attorney bills hourly, get an estimate. Also, find out how he bills phone calls. Does he bill in 20-minute increments or round it up to the next hour? Knowing as many specifics as possible helps save you moolah.

Negotiating can be tough for some people to swallow. But don't worry; this isn't a flea market where you have to haggle until you're blue in the face. You just have to let the attorney know that his price is a little out of your budget. Ask him whether he would be willing to work at a slightly reduced rate until your business is off the ground and you have more money to pay. If he says no, then you need to consider whether you can actually afford him. If you can't, walk away and find someone who you *can* afford.

In most states, you aren't legally required to have your fee arrangements (such as the hourly rate, the retainer, if any, or the flat fee) in writing if the amount is under $1,000. However, regardless of the amount, you should always request that your arrangement be put in writing. This helps curb any surprises that may come your way later.

With specific projects, try to negotiate flat fees instead of hourly fees. Flat fees, although they sound like a lot in the beginning, are normally much less in the long run.

Stay away from retainers

Some attorneys demand *retainers* (a fee you pay ahead of time that keeps the attorney on your team for when you eventually need him). Try to negotiate your way out of paying a retainer. Let him know that you will pay on time. If you don't, *then* he can impose a retainer. If he still insists that you put money down, find someone else. Otherwise, you may write a check for $10,000 (or more!) — money that you can use to build your business. In the meantime, the attorney will most likely be charging your account with reckless abandon, and before you know it, you'll need to refresh your account and write another $10,000 check.

Not only are retainers expensive, but if you don't like the attorney's work, you'll have a hard time getting your money back. Thousands of dollars is a lot to lose when testing out an attorney.

Use other types of professionals

Most legal and tax work is pretty mundane. Small-business attorneys often deal less with complex legal theory and more with administrative paperwork and filings. Their experience can speed up the process and make sure that it gets done right, but they're not the only ones who can help you.

Often, you can hire paralegal services or incorporating companies to handle a lot of the mundane tasks, such as minute meetings, corporate compliance, and so on. They don't provide you with detailed information or legal advice, but they're great at document preparation. It beats paying an attorney four to ten times the amount for doing the same thing. Just keep in mind that you should still have an attorney review your business structure if it's somewhat complex.

Part II
First Things First: Forming Your LLC

The 5th Wave   By Rich Tennant

"Dave used his time well while waiting for the state to approve the Articles of Organization."

In this part . . .

In this part, you'll find out about the preliminary stuff
you need to know to form your LLC, such as what state
is best for your LLC and what decisions you and your
partners need to make before creating your articles of
organization.

Then, in Chapter 6, I show you how to create your articles
of organization so they're unique to your company. After
all, each company is different, so why shouldn't its LLC
be also? And of course, after your articles are created,
you have to file them, and I show you how to do that in
Chapter 8.

If you aren't forming a new company — meaning your
company is already operating with the public — I show
you in Chapter 7 how to transfer your assets and business
operations over to your newly formed LLC.

Chapter 4

Making the Big Decisions: Choosing Members, Managers, and a Name

▶ Figuring out who to bring on board

▶ Choosing who will run the day-to-day operations

▶ Capturing your business's essence with the perfect name

As Benjamin Franklin once said, "Those who fail to prepare, prepare to fail." In this case, setting up your plan of action is not only practical, it's necessary. You need to decide all sorts of things before preparing and filing your articles of organization (see Chapters 6 and 8) and making your LLC official. Don't overlook this chapter! Taking a wrong step today could end up landing you in a world of filing fees — or even lawsuits! — tomorrow.

In this chapter, I cover some of the basic things that you need to know or do before you prepare and file your articles of organization — such as choosing your members, setting up the management of your company, and determining whether the name you want for your LLC is available for use.

Choosing Your Members

LLCs are like children — they need parents! No matter what, your LLC must have at least one owner, preferably two or more. The owners of the LLC are called the *members*. One of the best characteristics of LLCs is that anyone or anything can be a member. In other words, any person or entity— an individual, other LLCs, corporations, trusts, limited partnerships, and so on — can be a member. Also, assuming you haven't elected to be taxed like an S corporation (which I cover in further detail in Chapter 13), you aren't restricted in how many members you can have — you can have 1,000 members if you like! Or more! This is one of the main reasons why LLCs are becoming so popular for raising capital.

The amount of the business you own is called your *membership interest*. Normally, your membership interest is represented on a piece of paper called a *share certificate* or *membership certificate*. The percentage of your membership interest in relation to all of the membership interests that the company has issued is called your *membership percentage* or *ownership percentage*.

If you want more information on the ins and outs of membership shares, I recommend that you read Chapter 10 before preparing and filing your articles of organization.

Selecting your partners

Who you select as your partner (or partners!) in the company will probably be the number-one determining factor of whether your business venture succeeds. Although partnerships can increase productivity tenfold and give you an edge over your competitors, they can also be quickly torn apart, taking everything that you have worked for down with them. I'm not saying you shouldn't take the plunge and tie yourself up with a long-term business partner, but I will tell you this: You *must* make sure that everyone is on the same page from the get-go and that there are procedures in place for when disagreements occur.

Generally, most partnerships have what is called a *partnership agreement*. With LLCs, you normally create this in your operating agreement. Although this doesn't need to be completed until after your articles of organization have been filed, you should still sit down with your partners and negotiate the majority of it. Why? Because the process of doing so is a great way to see how well you fit with a potential partner and whether your visions of the company are in line. This discovery process is an important step to take before jumping in.

In the next section, I go over how to determine ownership percentages (how much of the company each member gets). Although this is important, it's not the only thing that you should address before filing your articles of organization. You need to go over a few other points, such as

- ✔ How will you make decisions? Can any one partner unilaterally make a decision on her own? What happens in the event of a disagreement? A common practice with fifty-fifty partners is to include a trusted associate and give her 1 percent of the partnership so her decision can settle a disagreement.

- ✔ If a member wants out, and the other members want to buy her shares, how is the value of those shares determined? You can seek a third party to appraise the value of the shares, such as a qualified accountant, or you can create a formula. Additionally, must the money be paid upfront, or will a payment plan suffice?

- ✔ If a partner leaves the LLC, is a noncompete agreement in place to prevent that person from competing with the business? Does anything prevent him from taking the business's clients or trade secrets?

- ✔ When are you and your partner planning to retire? If this is relatively imminent, then you should put a clause in your agreement that allows — or forces — a partner to retire at a certain age and sell his membership shares to the other members. Will you allow partial retirement?

You may want to have your small-business attorney work with you and your partner(s) to draft the agreement. They can offer valuable suggestions, assist in the negotiations, and keep everyone from getting deadlocked on certain issues.

Divvying up the pie

Now, before you officially form your LLC, is the best time to get together with your partners and/or investors and decide what and how much each person is going to contribute. Contributions can come in many varieties — money, equipment, real estate, services, promises for the future (we've all heard that before!), or any combination of these things. In return for contributing to the business, everyone gets a percentage of the business. Because the value of the contributions isn't set in stone, the actual percentage that each partner receives is entirely up for argument. (I recommend reading *Stress Management For Dummies* by Allen Elkin [Wiley] when dealing with the aftermath.) For instance, if you're responsible for 30 percent of the total initial investment in the company (from all the members), you will most likely receive 30 percent of the company.

The percentage that you or your partners own of the company *matters* — it matters more than titles or other positions. Your membership interest allows you to vote on important matters such as who manages the company and how your partners can transfer their shares. It also determines what percentage of the profit you receive when your company is sold or dissolved.

Double liability protection doesn't fly for single-member LLCs

For many years, professionals and consultants argued about whether single-member LLCs were allowed the same double liability protection (as discussed in Chapter 2) as multiple-member LLCs. Finally, in 2003, a case came up (In re: Albright, No. 01-11367, Colorado Bankruptcy Court, April 4, 2003), and the court decided that this double protection (also called *charging order protection* [see Chapter 11]) doesn't apply to single-member LLCs because there are no innocent partners to protect (the reason why the charging order exists in the first place).

Up until this time, many attorneys and financial planners were setting their clients up in single-member LLCs under the assumption that the business liability protections would apply. Needless to say, they're lucky they weren't the debtor in the case in Colorado!

LLCs normally don't allow shares to be transferred freely like corporations do. This means that after you are invested in the company, you may have a hard time selling your interest or even transferring it to a family member. This is one of the reasons why you should choose your partners carefully — you could be stuck with them longer than you think!

Getting the skinny on single-member LLCs

LLCs that have only one member are called *single-member LLCs,* or "SLLCs" for short. If you're planning on operating as an SLLC, you may have a hard road ahead of you. Sorry, but it's true.

First and foremost, it is common for LLCs with only one member to not be treated as LLCs at all. Under federal law, an LLC with a single owner is considered a *proprietorship* or *disregarded entity.* The IRS doesn't consider the single-member LLC to be separate from its owners, as are corporations and other LLCs. This causes problems because, legally, nothing separates the single-member LLC from a sole proprietorship (the default form of business that I discuss in Chapter 2).

Why is this so bad? Sole proprietorships don't offer any personal protection from the company's lawsuits and creditors. Therefore, if you are legally considered a proprietorship, you might as well not form any entity in the first place. After all, isn't safeguarding your assets and minimizing personal risk the name of the game?

If you are set on pursuing your entrepreneurial endeavors on your own, don't fret. There are solutions! In Chapter 10, I go into ways that you can avoid some of the headaches inherent in operating as a single-member LLC.

The Power Source: Deciding Who Manages the LLC

Businesses don't operate themselves — someone needs to manage them! Often, you don't have to immediately decide exactly who will manage and what their specific roles will be, but most states require that you give a basic idea of how your company will be managed in the articles of organization. If your state doesn't require this, then you will most likely have to state it in your operating agreement. So why delay in figuring out how you want to structure your LLC's management? Start now!

An LLC can be managed two ways:

- ✔ **Member-managed:** This is where the LLC's members (the owners) also deal in the business's day-to-day operations. If this is selected, *all* members are also managers — you can't prevent one member from getting involved while allowing the rest. But if you have confidence in your partners' business plans, then by all means, why not include everyone in the decision-making process?

- ✔ **Manager-managed:** This is where a separate manager (or two or three . . .) handles the business's day-to-day operations. This is a good choice if only one member wants to manage and/or an outside person would be a good manager. Some benefits of manager management include alleviating confusion and breaking up the workload.

Just as there's no limit to the number of members an LLC can have, there's no limit to the number of managers that an LLC can have, but I would choose wisely if I were you. Managers have absolute authority to obligate the business to contracts, loans, debts, and so on. It only takes one manager to do this — even if it is without the knowledge of the others. Therefore, all of the members must absolutely trust whoever is chosen as a manager.

When the members manage

Member management is the most common choice for smaller businesses. When an LLC is managed by the owners (also called the *members*), all owners are equally responsible for the LLC's management. However, you shouldn't worry that one of your partners will mismanage the company and land you in the poorhouse, because all managers of the LLC are exempt from being legally responsible for the debts of the LLC. For instance, if the LLC is sued, the managers can't be held personally liable for the business's actions. They can rest comfortably — anything that they didn't invest in the LLC (like a car, house, or wedding ring) is untouchable by outside sources.

A lot of small businesses choose this method of operation because they normally don't have any outside investors, and the business owners also want to have a full say in how the business operates.

If you are a larger company with a lot of members, then you may want to think twice about choosing member management. Think about it — if each member has a say in the day-to-day operations of the business and you have 25 members — it will be a total mess! That's like having 25 CEOs! Not only is it unrealistic, but it will also lack credibility if you are ever taken to court.

If you choose member management, you can lose your double-liability protection — the biggest benefit to operating as an LLC in the first place. You see, if a creditor gets a charging order against your membership interests and those interests come with management rights, he can use his management powers to distribute a good portion of the profits to himself to pay off the claim. See Chapter 11 for more information on charging order protections.

In Minnesota and North Dakota, the managers are called *governors*.

When separate managers manage

When you select manager management, you must choose at least one manager — even if he or she is also a member. Also, the manager doesn't even have to be a he or a she! You can select an entity (an LLC, corporation, limited partnership, and so on) to manage the LLC. Of course, whoever manages that entity will be the true manager of the LLC!

Why would you have separate managers manage? Maybe one of the members wants to remain a silent partner. He's willing to risk his money but doesn't want to be bothered with the everyday business decisions that the managers are confronted with. Or, say that none of the members has time to actually manage the business, so they want to hire an outside CEO who can do a better job than they ever could. There are a million reasons why you may want separate managers!

Managing her LLC means she can have her cake and eat it too

Jill's family and friends have been pressuring her to start a bakery for years now, and Jill finally relents. She is looking forward to the challenge and has even taken business classes to learn how to run the company. She puts together a business plan so she can look for financing. Her credit isn't great, so that leaves her with the option of going to an investor.

Jill's cousin is a very successful lawyer and offers to loan her the money. He trusts Jill's

expertise and is willing to be a silent partner. He lives on the other coast, so he can't be active in the business's day-to-day operations anyway. Considering this, Jill sets up an LLC. She issues 50 percent of the membership interests to herself and 50 percent to her cousin in exchange for the startup capital. Jill then designates the LLC as being manager-managed with herself as the only manager.

All managers in the LLC have an equal right (also called *legal authority*) to bind the entity to the terms of a contract or to the sale or purchase of goods. The government can intervene at times when a foolish manager goes out and does something that obviously is not in the company's best interest, but is in *his* best interest. But, ultimately, it's hard to prove. The best word of advice I can give someone going into their first partnership is to choose your partners carefully. If you think your future partner is capable of fanatically indebting your entire business — make sure to run away as fast as you can!

Manager-managed LLCs are commonly used in estate planning. You can give membership shares in the LLC to your children every year, while still being the only manager of the LLC. While you're alive, your children can't make management decisions regarding the money but can receive profits from it (Finally, a true gift that keeps on giving!). Then, when you pass away, they are elected as the new managers and have full rights and use over the LLC's assets. (For more on LLCs and estate planning, see Chapter 16.)

When you have a manager-managed LLC, the Securities Exchange Commission or your state securities division may determine that you are involved in the sale of securities if your members are investing in an LLC that they have no say in managing. This isn't necessarily a bad thing. Just be sure to speak with someone qualified before disallowing any of your investors decision-making power in the company's operations.

Establishing the Best Name for Your LLC

Naming your company can be one of the most agonizing and time-consuming parts of starting your business. Not only do you want to be creative, but you also want to be original — in fact, so original that no one else is currently using a similar name. This isn't something that can be put off, either. The name of your LLC must be on your articles of organization. So before your company is even formed, you and your partners must decide on the name.

Playing — and winning — the name game

Your name is your calling card. It's what you want to imprint into the minds and hearts of your customers. A good name will make potential customers want to get to know you. A bad name will be forgotten in the blink of an eye.

Sit down and think long and hard about your product or service and what you're trying to achieve. Look at your competition and see what names they're using. Try to find a way to separate yourself from the competition. Look at your market and determine the best way to present your company to your potential customers.

So many factors come into play when selecting a name that your head will spin! You need to keep in mind a few things.

- ✔ **Don't restrain yourself!** Don't be afraid to release those genius marketing skills you've been hiding all these years.

- ✔ **Be careful about using a specific location, product, or service in your business name.** The world is changing at a spectacular pace, and businesses are constantly evolving. You don't want your name to hold you back or become antiquated as your business moves forward.

- ✔ **Make sure your name is easy to pronounce.** You don't want people to avoid saying your name because they're afraid of mispronouncing it. Remember — if a first-grader can't read it, ditch it.

- ✔ **If you're looking to expand internationally, make sure that the name you choose doesn't have any negative connotations in the countries you are hoping to operate in.** Otherwise, you could end up with a very funny, yet very expensive, story to tell.

Nowadays, most words seem to be already in use or trademarked. If this is the case for you, then try to create new words. Coin a word or a group of words that emits a feeling and is catchy and memorable. Yahoo! and Google weren't words found in the dictionary, yet that hasn't stopped their immense success.

Let the ideas fly!

After you have all of this in your mind, it's time to hold a brainstorming session, better referred to as a "namestorming session"! Lock yourself away in a quiet room with a pad of paper and write down every name you can think of. Try to come up with 50 names! 100! Don't leave your namestorming session until you're completely depleted and can't come up with another single name.

After you've finished your namestorming session, cross out the names that you don't like and rewrite the list of the names you do like. Put them in order of importance, with the ones you absolutely *love* at the top of the list. Now you're ready to see what's available for use.

Checking out your potential domain

Start with the *domain name,* which is usually the dominant part of the address for your Web site. For example, in `www.yourllcname.com`, "yourllcname" is the domain. The Internet is the core of business nowadays and is only getting bigger. It should be a huge priority on your part to make sure that your name is marketable in the online realm as well. Consider the following:

✔ Does the name you want translate easily into a domain name?

✔ If the name is long, can you register its acronym?

✔ Is the name you want memorable?

✔ Is the name easy to spell and pronounce?

Go down your list of names until you find one that translates into a domain name. To check whether a domain is available, go to `www.godaddy.com` and do a domain search. Cross out the ones that don't have exact or similar domain names available — that way, you won't have to deal with the problem later on when you grow and decide to build a Web site.

After you have a list of names that you want to proceed with, you need to check whether that name is available in your state and whether it has already been trademarked by someone. If the name has been *trademarked,* that person or company has the exclusive right to use that name, and you'd better choose an alternative. Trademark infringement is not a road you want to travel.

Determining whether the name is trademarked

When a company wants to protect its name from being used by other companies in similar industries, it obtains a state or federal trademark. A *state trademark* gives the trademark holder exclusive rights to use the name in that particular state. A *federal trademark,* filed at the U.S. Patent and Trademark Office, gives exclusive rights to use the name throughout the entire nation. This means that, for the most part, the company with that name or set of words trademarked is the only one that has the right to use those words in the business sectors in which it is trademarked.

Because the federal trademark is usually easy and inexpensive to do, I recommend that you skip the state trademark and focus on the federal one.

Before ever entering into business and committing to a business name, it's imperative that you do a comprehensive trademark search for the name that you want to use. Either you or an experienced law firm or trademarking company can do this. If the name you're interested in is available, I recommend registering it as a trademark immediately, so you have the exclusive right to use the name. Better safe than sorry.

If you fail to find out when you're just starting your LLC whether the name you've selected has been trademarked by another individual, then you may have to change to another name down the road. This could seriously hurt your business — especially if sums of money have already been dumped into marketing. Worse than this, you can be sued for trademark infringement, and you may be forced to pay damages on any losses the other company may have incurred because you used its name. These damages are, more often than not, ill-founded but can still amount to a *huge* amount of money.

Conducting a name search in your state

If the name you've chosen conflicts with a name already in use in your state, your articles of organization will be rejected when you file them with the Secretary of State's office. What constitutes "conflicting"? It depends on the judgment of the person at the Secretary of State's office who reviews your articles. But you can still get a relatively good idea of the names trademarked in your state by conducting a name search in your state.

Searching national trademarks

You can conduct a trademark search online at the U.S. Patent and Trademark Office's Web site by searching its TESS (Trademark Electronic Search System) database. Go to www.uspto.gov and do a search for Trademarks.

Some results should be displayed. If you find some words that are similar to yours, you may still be okay. Check the International Classification (IC) code by clicking on the result that's similar to what you want to use. The IC is located next to the Goods and Services and looks like this: IC 032.

If you'll be doing business in that particular industry, then there is a conflicting trademark and you should consider using another name. To see the list of IC codes and industries, go to www.myllc.com/dummies.

For more information on conducting trademark searches, read *Patents, Copyrights & Trademarks For Dummies* by Henri Charmasson (Wiley). You should also consider speaking with an attorney or service company that specializes in trademarking.

You can perform a name search by going to your Secretary of State's Web site (see Appendix A for a list of state Web sites). Normally, you can search the state's listing of entities (LLCs, corporations, limited partnerships, and so on) that are filed in that state. Enter the name you want to use — leaving off all identifiers, such as "LLC" or "limited company" — and click search. If there are names that are very similar to yours, you may have to choose a new name.

If your state doesn't allow the online search of records, you can call the Secretary of State's office at the phone number provided in Appendix A.

If you see a conflicting name, but the company is in a revoked status (meaning the company is officially "dead" in the eyes of the state), you should be able to use the name.

If you are still unsure about the availability of the name you want to use, contact an incorporating company for assistance. You can go to www.myllc.com for a free name search. All you have to do is enter the name into the search box. Then you'll be asked to select the states you want to do the name search in (yes, you can search more than one at once!). Your results will be e-mailed to you within a few hours.

When selecting the states that you want to conduct your name search in, remember to include states that you will be transacting business in. Otherwise, you could be stuck trying to register in those states but not able to use your own name!

If your name is available in your state to form your LLC, that doesn't necessarily mean it's free to use. Make sure that there are no state or national trademarks for the same name in your classification of goods and services.

Reserving your name

Imagine . . . you go through the painstaking process of selecting a name, checking to see if it's available, and filing a trademark. Then, after you prepare your articles and submit them, you realize that the name you want isn't available. Someone took it in those few weeks between checking the name and submitting your filing. Now, you've wasted precious time and money and have to start the process all over again.

If you want to avoid this, you should reserve your name as soon as you know it's available and decide that you want to use it. Each state has its own laws as to what needs to be in your company name. Before reserving your name, you should double-check to make sure that you are in compliance with all of your state's laws. Otherwise, your articles of organization or name reservation may be rejected, and that could be costly.

Before reserving your name, your name should meet the following criteria (and any others that are particular to your state):

- **Make sure your name designates that the company is an LLC.** You can typically use such designators as "Limited Liability Company," "LLC," "L.L.C.," "Limited Company," and so on. Check your state's requirements for a more specific list of identifiers that can be used in your state. This designator should be placed at the end of your company name, not anywhere else.

- **Make sure your name doesn't include any restricted words**. Each state has its own set of words, such as "bank," "securities," "financial," "insurance," and so on, that are restricted from general use. To include one of these words in your name, you usually must get approval from a particular state department, such as the department of securities.

- **Make sure your name doesn't conflict with other names on file in your state.** See the "Conducting a name search in your state" section for more on this.

✔ **Make sure there are no other trademarked names that are similar to yours.** See the "Determining whether the name is trademarked" section for more specifics.

✔ **Make sure you have determined who will be filing your articles of organization for you.** The person or organization filing the articles must be the same person who is on the name reservation; otherwise, you could have a problem getting the Secretary of State to release the name. For instance, if the name reservation is in your name, but your incorporating company is filing the articles, the articles probably will be rejected until you sign off on the use of the name.

When you're ready to reserve the name, you can normally do so by going to your Secretary of State's Web site (see Appendix A for contact info) and downloading the form. Fill in the form and mail it to the Secretary of State. (If you don't want to do this yourself, ask your registered agent to do it for you.) Some states allow you to do the name reservation online but may charge more for the convenience. You can usually reserve your name for 60 days (or more in some states). The process and fees for name reservations vary from state to state.

Unless you have a very popular name or you'll be waiting for some time before filing your articles, you may not need a name reservation. If you'll be filing your articles within a week of the name reservation and you have an obscure name, you should consider whether it's worth the hassle.

Want to do business under more than one name? First, figure out what name you want to call your LLC, then, after your LLC is formed, you can file a *fictitious firm name application* (also called a "DBA") at your local clerk's office.

Chapter 5

Choosing the Best State for Your LLC

*L*et's say that you've lived in California, maybe even the same city, your entire life, and now you'd like to create an LLC all the way across the country in Florida. Why Florida? Well, this is where you believe your retirement community real estate project will have its greatest chance to flourish. Too bad you don't live in Miami where your LLC should be established! Not to fret . . . .

It's a common myth that you need to form your LLC in the state that you live in. LLCs are completely separate from their owners — they're like their own individual person that you have full control over. They can live wherever they want to live, wherever is best for them. When your LLC does business in a particular state, it must be registered with that state, but where your LLC is actually *formed* is entirely up to you. The state where your LLC is formed is called its *domicile*.

In this chapter, I give you an overview of some of your options when it comes to deciding where to form your LLC. I help clear up some of the confusion that comes with the term "tax haven," and also point all of you multistate moguls in the right direction when it comes to registering to transact business in multiple states.

Your State or Not Your State, That Is the Question

When choosing a state to live in, your LLC cares little about the weather and even less about the school districts. Your LLC is pretty easy to please . . . give it favorable laws and low taxes and you'll have one happy camper! You can choose any state (or even country!) that you want for your LLC — the world is your oyster! But this leads us to the main problem that you're facing — all states are not created equal. Some states are better than others. So, how do you choose?

Before you can answer the question of which state to form your LLC in, you must first answer this question: What business do you want to do? You must have a clear picture of what sort of business you'll be transacting and where. You need to know what your future plans are — do you want to go public or stay small? Is your business ingrained in your community or does it exist in the Internet realm and have no real territory? What are your priorities? Would you rather save taxes or avoid extra paperwork?

LLCs bring with them fantastically flexible options that make them suitable for any industry, for any location, for any dream. If you've read this far, you probably already know that an LLC is right for you. But which LLC? Each state makes its own laws regarding LLCs and because of this, LLCs tend to look, feel, and act differently depending on where they are formed.

The laws surrounding LLCs vary from state to state — not a lot, but enough to warrant this little warning. To assist most states in coming up with some standard LLC statutes, the federal government enacted the Revised Uniform Limited Liability Company Act (RULLCA) — a set of laws regarding the LLC that the various states could pick and choose from as they saw fit. Although most states just copied the entire act directly, some states decided they wanted to be rebels and strayed from the format the federal government laid out. Some of these states were well intentioned and offer *more* protection and flexibility, while others decided to offer less. I try to give advice that can be used for forming LLCs anywhere in the U.S., but because of these rogue operators, it's always a good idea to look at the specific laws for the state that you choose to form your LLC in.

Forming an LLC in your home state

If you're opening up a bricks-and-mortar business that is only operating in one state — for example, a local shop that deals heavily in the community — you should just make it easy on yourself and form your LLC in that state.

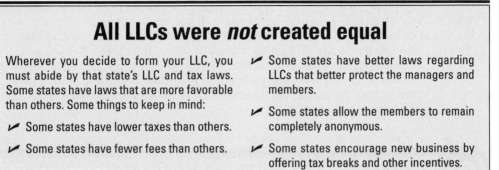

All LLCs were *not* created equal

Wherever you decide to form your LLC, you must abide by that state's LLC and tax laws. Some states have laws that are more favorable than others. Some things to keep in mind:

✔ Some states have lower taxes than others.

✔ Some states have fewer fees than others.

✔ Some states have better laws regarding LLCs that better protect the managers and members.

✔ Some states allow the members to remain completely anonymous.

✔ Some states encourage new business by offering tax breaks and other incentives.

Sometimes a business is only a good business because of its close proximity to interested customers, resources, and land. Running this type of company means that you'll have to register to transact business in that particular state and will also be subject to its laws, so you might as well save on filing fees and paperwork hassles by keeping everything in your home state.

And of course, if you're lucky enough to live in a state that has a really low tax structure, then why form out-of-state at all? In Appendix A, I list the business taxes imposed on LLCs in all 50 states. There, you can compare your state's tax structure with the tax structures of other states. Just keep in mind that I only list the taxes imposed on LLCs with partnership taxation (the most common type), so if you have elected to be taxed as a corporation, then you should definitely speak with your accountant and/or a multistate registered agent who should be familiar with the tax structures of all 50 states.

If you have a bricks-and-mortar operation in more than just your home state, then you will be required to register to transact business in those other states. This is called *foreign filing.* When you have foreign filed, you are now required to comply with all of the laws and the paperwork of that state.

Looking for LLCs out-of-state

If you don't have a bricks-and-mortar business — maybe you're running an Internet company or a consulting or service business that isn't restricted to a particular state — and you live in a high tax state, then I urge you to consider forming your LLC in another state. After all, some states have worked very hard to structure their tax and LLC laws to make it desirable to domicile companies there. Would you really want to let them down? I know, I know . . . the entire idea of forming your LLC in a faraway place can be somewhat daunting at first, but don't let the idea overwhelm you.

Right now, go to Appendix A and compare the tax structure of the state that you live in to those of the other states. If it looks like you can do much better (for instance, you live in California!), then you should definitely consider domiciling your LLC in another state. But which state? Well, Nevada and Delaware stand out among the rest. They are actively trying to lure businesses by keeping their taxes low (or having none at all!) and making sure they provide the proper legal support for small businesses (such as Delaware's Chancery Court).

For very little money, you can go to a multi-state registered agent or corporate consulting company that specializes in working in all 50 states and have them tell you what needs to be filed and even file the documents for you! These companies specialize in taking the headache out of operating out of different states. They can save you from spending your valuable time doing research, preparing paperwork, and standing in line at the government offices.

Nevada: The small business tax haven

Nevada is notorious for being the ultimate state for small businesses. When Nevada wrote its LLC laws, it decided to allow one person to be all positions, which means that even though the LLC is considered a partnership, by law there needn't be two members. I don't condone single-member LLCs (see Chapter 4 for more details), but this is just one representation of the flexibility that Nevada offers.

But, wait! That's not all! That number-one reason every entrepreneur and real estate mogul out there goes on and on about the benefit of Nevada is that there are no taxes. Yes, you read correctly. No taxes. Zero. Zilch. Nada. And I mean *nada* . . . no franchise taxes, no corporate taxes, no personal income taxes . . . I guess all of that gambling has paid off! So the next time your best friend loses $200 at the craps table, make sure to thank him.

So no taxes is pretty cool. Okay, *very* cool. But there's more! In Nevada, the members are not on the public records. This means that you can own an LLC and no one will even know about it. The managers are listed, so this only works if you are manager-managed (see Chapter 4), but this is pretty powerful, nonetheless. Why? Well, if a lawyer doesn't know you own anything, she'll most likely not want to sue you!

Some benefits of forming in Nevada are

- ✔ One person can be all positions
- ✔ Single-member LLCs are allowed
- ✔ No personal income taxes
- ✔ No corporate taxes
- ✔ No franchise fees
- ✔ Members are not public record

✔ Nominee managers are legal (see Chapter 14 for more information)

✔ Non-U.S. citizens can be managers and/or members

✔ Low filing fees

Wyoming is also a great state to form your LLC in and even beats Nevada in some ways. Wyoming is a notoriously pro-business state, and it's where LLCs were first pioneered in the United States! It offers a lot of the same benefits as Nevada, but it's a lot more under the radar — it doesn't have that "tax haven" stigma that Nevada has. Also, the fees are about 75 percent less. However, Wyoming has its drawbacks, such as not allowing single-member LLCs.

Delaware: The heavy hitter with the Chancery Court

Great expectations? Designing an LLC that needs room to grow? Then Delaware is the state for you! Delaware is perfect if you intend to grow really large and do business in several different states.

Most public companies want to be in Delaware because of its Chancery Court and its long history of case law. The state is so great, in fact, that the majority of public companies listed on the stock exchange are domiciled in Delaware. That's a pretty big reputation for such a little state!

Considering it's so great, I should probably be a little bit more specific about what the Chancery Court actually is. Although it sounds like something out of the game of *Monopoly*, the *Chancery Court* is a special court the makes decisions on business matters. Delaware is the only state with such a court. Most states' courts are very backlogged, and it can take years for a judge to hear and decide on your lawsuit. Delaware can get things resolved in weeks instead of years.

That alone should be good enough, but the Chancery Court goes a step further. When you go to court in other states, you never know how much your judge *actually* knows about business. ("You mean to tell me that his honor was just promoted from traffic court?" You get the picture.) In Delaware, though, all judges in the Chancery Court are experts in matters of business and are renowned for their fair and educated decision making. After all, don't you want to feel comfortable that the person deciding the fate of your company will be more fluent in the laws of LLCs than petty larceny?

Some of Delaware's benefits include:

✔ The ever-famous Chancery Court

✔ 300 years of business case law to lead the way

✔ Delaware allows series LLCs (see Chapter 2)

✔ Fees are relatively low

✔ No state tax on LLCs that are formed in Delaware but don't operate there

Working with a State-Required Agent for Your LLC

"Where should we send your lawsuit?" If this question were posed to most business owners, they'd probably give the wrong address, if any at all. For this reason, states now require a business to have what is called a *registered agent* (which is interchangeable with the term *resident agent*). In the state in which you form your LLC and in every state that you're doing business, you must have a registered agent.

A registered agent's primary duty is to be open during business hours in the event that your company is sued and paperwork needs to be served. Fun job, huh? This person also accepts government documents, such as correspondence from the Secretary of State's office, the clerk's office, and the state tax bureaus, on behalf of your company and then forwards them on to you. The agent's office can also serve as your corporate headquarters in the state your LLC was formed in if you don't have an office there.

Why you need a registered agent

In some states, you can serve as your own registered agent (provided you have an office address in the state). However, there are multitudes of reasons why this isn't a good idea:

- ✔ Someone must be at the registered agent's office address during all business hours and must agree to sign for government papers. If the court service comes to drop off legal documents and you're not around, you could lose the lawsuit by default!

- ✔ If lawsuits are filed at your business address, imagine what your customers and employees will think.

- ✔ You lose some of your privacy. By using your registered agent's address on all of your state filings, you have an additional level of privacy.

What your agent should do for you

Due to the sad truth that a registered agent's primary function is to sit and wait for a lawsuit to arrive, most registered agents now provide extra services. After all, you're a well-behaved citizen and are most likely not getting sued very often, so what's a registered agent to do all day?

They try to busy themselves and warrant their fees by taking on such important tasks as keeping your LLC in compliance with all of the state-required filings, forwarding your mail, and protecting your identity. Because of these extra tasks, registered agents have gone from being a legal irritant to becoming one of the most important members of your team. Their responsibilities include

- ✔ Having a separate business location and being open during normal business hours to accept lawsuits and filing documents, which they forward immediately to you

- ✔ Protecting your address by allowing you to use their address as your corporate headquarters

- ✔ Forwarding your mail and government notices each business day

- ✔ Reminding you of any filings that are due in the state and making sure you stay in compliance

- ✔ Filing your documents (if necessary) with the requisite state and local bureaus

- ✔ Assisting you in finding state-specific tax and legal professionals

Finding and working with an agent

Finding a registered agent shouldn't be too difficult. The best way to find an agent is by calling up your Secretary of State's office and asking if they can recommend anyone. Some state offices will do this; others try to remain impartial. You can also find an agent by doing a Google search or by going to www.registered-agent-information.com. This Web site doesn't list agents for every state, but if you e-mail them, they can point you in the right direction. This Web site includes information on all of the registered agents in a particular state, their pricing, and customer reviews.

First and foremost, when interviewing a potential agent, get a feel for her policies on dealing with lawsuits. You and your registered agent must agree that any legal paperwork she receives on your behalf will be brought to your attention immediately. Perhaps you decide that she will call you and summarize a document's contents and then have it delivered to you overnight. Or maybe she'll e-mail you a copy of the documents and then send the originals to you. Just be sure both of you are clear on what procedure will be followed. The same method should be used for state documents and various tax notices as well.

Whatever the delivery method you and your agent agree on, make sure you can track your package.

One characteristic to look for when choosing a registered agent is how long that person or company has been working with the Secretary of State's office. If your registered agent has close relationships with the administrators at the Secretary of State's office, then there's a good chance your filings will be completed much faster and issues can be resolved easily. Also, it's a good sign of

Summons served. Or was it?

You formed an LLC for your restaurant and even found ways to keep customers coming back for more. The company is thriving, and your bank account is growing faster than you can plate the next meal. Life is good. Then one day you find out that last spring a customer got food poisoning from your shellfish, you were sued, the case went to trial, and worst of all . . . you lost! By "default judgment!"

Whoa, whoa, whoa! How does something like this happen? As your kitchen equipment is hauled away for auction, you curse at your cousin Bob. Why? Because he was on file as your registered agent, and he never notified you of the summons to appear in court! You weren't

even there to defend the restaurant against claims that you suspect weren't even true. Maybe it wasn't the shellfish (after all, you tried it yourself!), but something else the customer ate earlier that day.

Of course, this is a nightmare scenario, but it does demonstrate the importance of selecting a reliable registered agent. This also can happen if the summons is misplaced at your busy establishment or simply ignored by an ignorant employee. So how do you defend yourself from such a nightmare? Choose a qualified registered agent and keep communication lines open. It may save your business from going under one day.

legitimacy. If the administrators at the Secretary of State's office have never heard of your registered agent, then there's a good chance that person or company isn't doing a lot of work there.

If you'll be doing business in multiple states, your registered agent should also be located in those states. That way, your filings, your invoices, and your records can be consolidated, and you have one firm that knows the ins and outs of your business and can handle you in multiple jurisdictions. You should also make sure that the agent can collect, complete, and file your state and local business licenses and permits for you. (See Chapter 8 for more on business licenses and permit filings.)

Although registered agents don't come free, their services are minimal in price, usually only costing a few hundred dollars per year (a pretty fair price for everything they do!). Most fees are billed annually and at the time your LLC was initially created. If your agent requests that you sign a contract with her for a number of years, I would think twice. There are a lot of really legitimate agents out there who don't require contracts — why lock yourself in if you don't have to?

Make sure your agent always has your current contact information. If your agent can't find you, she'll have trouble forwarding Uncle Sam's letters to you. I have had numerous clients who used my company as their agent to maintain their privacy, and they were *so* private that they wouldn't even share their correct contact information with *me!* Needless to say, tracking them down to forward their legal paperwork wasn't always the easiest task!

I would suggest choosing an individual within your LLC to maintain regular contact with your registered agent. This helps avoid any unnecessary confusion about who the agent is supposed to contact in the face of a lawsuit. With that said, all members should feel comfortable contacting the agent at any time.

Attorneys will try to place themselves as your registered agent. Although they are qualified to be your agent, be aware that they tend to be much more expensive than commercial registered agents. Not only that, but if they aren't the most qualified attorney to handle a particular legal battle, you have to go through the fun of explaining to them that you don't want to use their services on a lawsuit that was served to them.

Registering Your LLC in Multiple States

Say you have a restaurant in Florida, your home state, but want to expand to Georgia and North Carolina. After you open your locations in those states, you are *doing business* there. By law, if you're doing business in other states, you must register in those states (this is called *foreign filing*). The foreign-filing process is similar to the actual formation process, but it's always in addition to the initial formation. Your *domicile* (the state where your LLC is formed) won't change; you'll just be allowed to transact business in the other states you've registered in.

Not foreign filed anywhere? Doing business only in the state where your LLC is formed? Then you're simply called a *domestic LLC.*

What "doing business" really means

The term *doing business* is important in LLC law because it creates the guidelines under which you may or may not be required to foreign file. Of course, you'll want to foreign file in as few states as necessary. With each additional state come additional laws to learn and red tape to follow, as well as some pretty hefty fees. Unfortunately, as you find out in the next section, foreign filing is sometimes necessary.

It's hard to determine whether you're actually "doing business" in another state. What if you shipped your product across the country to a single customer, yet most of your business is accomplished in your LLC's home state? Which state's laws must you follow? Remember, each state's laws are different. Here are a few questions to point you in the right direction:

 ✔ Does your LLC operate out of a physical office or retail store in the state?

 ✔ Are you physically there, meeting with customers (instead of just speaking with them over the phone or by e-mail)?

✔ Does a large portion of your LLC's revenue come from that state?

✔ Do any of your employees physically work in the state? Do you pay state payroll taxes?

If you answered yes to any of these questions, then there's a good chance that you are doing business in the state and are required to foreign file your LLC there.

Even though you may be making money from customers in a particular state, it doesn't necessarily mean that you're transacting business there, as far as the law is concerned.

Doing business in multiple states? You must foreign file!

Yes, it's a necessary evil, but with the help of your registered agent and perhaps a good advisor, foreign filing can be a breeze. Just be aware that if you're planning on doing business in numerous states, the filing fees can get pretty hefty, especially considering that a lot of states charge more for filing foreign LLCs than they do for domestic ones. Unfortunately, you can't get out of the fees, but at least you can try to incorporate this cost into your budget.

Tsk, tsk, tsk . . . Haven't foreign filed?

So, you've been doing business in a state and haven't registered there . . . what do you do? First, call your attorney. Second, drive immediately to the police station and turn yourself in. Don't worry — just kidding!

The reality is that nothing major will happen to you. If your LLC is sued, you can still defend it in the local courts. However, if you decide that you want to sue someone in that state, you definitely need to register there first.

As for penalties, some states are harder than others. You may have to pay the fees that should have been paid, plus possible fines and interest. However, most states are just happy to have the business and will waive the fines and fees just to get you in compliance. In other words, it's not such a big deal. Just make sure you register ASAP!

Knowing you are *not* doing business in a state

The Revised Model Business Corporation Act (RMBCA) gives criteria for when an entity is *not* transacting business in a state. Although it was written for corporations, the act also applies to LLCs.

Not sure if you are technically "doing business" in a particular state? If you are doing any of the things listed below, then you should double-check with a corporate consultant in that state because you will likely have to foreign file.

✔ Maintaining, defending, or settling any proceeding (that is, being involved in a lawsuit)

✔ Holding meetings of the board of directors or shareholders or carrying on other activities concerning internal corporate affairs

✔ Maintaining bank accounts

✔ Maintaining offices or agencies for the transfer, exchange, and registration of the corporation's own securities or maintaining trustees or depositaries with respect to those securities

✔ Selling through independent contractors

✔ Soliciting or obtaining orders, whether by mail or through employees or agents or otherwise, if the orders require acceptance outside this state before they become contracts

✔ Creating or acquiring debts, mortgages, and security interests in real or personal property

✔ Securing or collecting debts or enforcing mortgages and security interests in property securing the debts

✔ Owning real or personal property

✔ Conducting an isolated transaction that is completed within 30 days and that is not one in the course of repeated transactions of a like nature

✔ Transacting business in interstate commerce

If you're doing one or two of the above things, then chances are, you aren't required to foreign file in that state. If you're doing a lot of the above things, then you may want to contact your attorney for his advice on the issue.

Preparing and filing the paperwork

Registering (also called *qualifying*) your business in another state is remarkably similar to the formation process. This stuff should almost be second nature after creating your original LLC (I cover those steps in Chapter 6). Registering is relatively easy, and generally, foreign entities have less paperwork to deal with in terms of certain licenses and permits after the registration is completed. Whew . . . something to look forward to!

When you register, you submit an application for a certificate of authority. You can normally download the basic form off the Web site for the Secretary of State in the state you are attempting to register in, or you can have your incorporating company create the application for you.

When filling out the application, you'll most likely have to provide the following:

- ✔ **The name of your foreign LLC:** List the name as it appears on the articles of organization in your home state.

- ✔ **The name of your foreign LLC in the state you are registering in:** If your name isn't available in the state you're registering your LLC in, you may have to select an alternate name to do business under.

- ✔ **Entity domicile:** This means the date and state that the LLC was formed in.

- ✔ **Resident agent name and address:** Give the name and address of your LLC's resident agent in the state you are registering to do business in.

- ✔ **Your principle office address:** It's common to put your resident agent's address here as your principle office in the state. However, you can also list your corporate office address, if you have one.

- ✔ **Name and address of each manager and/or member:** The information that is required here varies from state to state. Contact your incorporating company if you have any questions.

- ✔ **Signature of a manager or member:** One manager or member's signature is required to file the registration.

- ✔ **Signature of resident agent:** Your resident agent is required to sign the application stating that he has agreed to be your resident agent.

Before your application can be approved by your Secretary of State, it must be signed by your resident agent in that state. If you're registering to transact business in multiple states, you may have a hard time keeping everything in order and staying on top of your filing dates. Trust me, running a company is hard enough without all the tedious paperwork involved in maintaining your LLC's compliance in a zillion jurisdictions.

For a nominal fee, you can have a multi-state resident agent company serve as your resident agent in all of the states in which you're doing business. The company can assist you with the filings, stay on top of your paperwork, and even let you know when your filings are due!

In some states, before you can file your application, you must show a proof of good standing in the state your LLC was formed in. This is often called a *certificate of good standing* or *certificate of existence.* The certificate shows the state that you are foreign filing with that your LLC is in good standing in the state that it was formed in. To make it even *more* difficult, some states require that you provide a certified copy of your articles of organization. You can contact the Secretary of State's office in your home state to obtain these documents, or you can have your incorporating company do it for you. After you have obtained your certificate of good standing (and your certified copy of your articles, if required), you should send it in with your application.

Maintaining your multi-state LLC

Although it may sound sexy to say you're a nationwide company, every state you register in to transact business brings a pile of paperwork and loads of fees. Some of your annual or biannual filings may include

- Annual report of members and managers
- Annual publication in a local newspaper
- Franchise tax reports
- Income tax reports
- Business licenses

This is just a short list — there could be many others. It really depends on the state. Because of the multitude of filings that are required for every state you are transacting business in, you may want to consider hiring an incorporating company to handle everything for you. That way, you maintain compliance and can spend your time running your business rather than struggling with strange filings for states you aren't familiar with. Many companies offer services tailored to each state. For instance, IncorpServices.com is one of the four multi-state registered agent companies in the United States and offers a Company Compliance & Resident Agent Service that tracks your filings, filing dates, mail forwarding, and so on. It also has an online system where you can view all of your filing dates, your filings, your corporate documents, and so on.

Want to change your home state?

When Bart opened Bart's Bikes, he was a different man. He lived on Venice Beach and was a California boy at heart. But as the company grew, so did he. Soon, he was doing business in Oregon too, and little did he know that Oregon was a bike lover's paradise. Within months, Bart's Bikes took off. Bart, getting older and wanting to trade in his surf board for some hiking boots, decided that a move to Oregon was in order.

Within a year, all of Bart's business was in Oregon, and he decided to close up shop in Venice Beach, leaving that life behind for good. Now Bart faced a predicament. Bart's Bikes, LLC was formed in California and foreign filed in Oregon. Bart wanted to change his company's domicile to Oregon. After all, why should anyone put up with California's high taxes and exorbitant fees if he doesn't have to?

Bart heard about a process called *domestication*, where he could file some forms with the new state's Secretary of State's office and make that state the LLC's new domicile. Unfortunately, Bart discovered that Oregon is one of the states that does not provide for domestication. In this case, he had his attorney assist him in withdrawing and dissolving his California-based LLC and transferring the assets to a new, Oregon-based LLC.

This organization system is a huge help because your filing dates vary from state to state, and it helps you avoid paying hefty late fees for missed filings. The other multi-state registered agent companies are CSC, CT, and NRAI.

Withdrawing from a state

What happens when you're no longer doing business in a particular state and don't want to keep up with the paperwork of being registered there? It's very simple to withdraw (or *cancel*) your LLC — you just file a *certificate of cancellation* with the Secretary of State's office in the state you want to withdraw from.

The certificate of cancellation is a pretty standard form and contains some basic information, such as

- ✔ The name of the LLC as stated on its articles of organization

- ✔ The name of the LLC as it is doing business in that state, if different

- ✔ The effective date of the cancellation, if different from the filing date

- ✔ Any other information that the manager or member filing the certificate of cancellation feels is relevant

You can normally just download this form off the Secretary of State's Web site and mail it in with the filing fee. You don't really need an attorney to file the certificate of cancellation. However, you should seek legal advice if the entity you are withdrawing has assets or physical locations in that state.

Chapter 6

Creating Your Articles of Organization

*T*he articles of organization is your LLC's most important document. Why? Because you can't even be an LLC until you create and file your articles of organization with your Secretary of State's office. After this is done, your LLC is formed.

With so many uses for LLCs and all of their flexibility, why on earth would you want your LLC to look and act the same way as someone else's? If you are raising money for a multimillion-dollar real-estate venture and your Uncle Joe is running a paper route, do you really want both companies operating under carbon-copy LLCs? Heck no! You need something that is customized to your specific needs.

Because LLC law is so vague, you easily can customize your LLC by choosing the right rules and operational guidelines to include in your articles of organization (which this chapter covers) and your operating agreement (see Chapter 9). Think of writing your articles of organization for your LLC as drawing up plans for your dream house — why own prefab when you can have custom built?

You need to be careful when filing your articles of organization. Although most of the designing and customizing of your entity is done in your operating agreement, some states may require you to include certain *provisions* (a fancy name for the sections of your articles of organization) in your articles. It can be sort of tricky — all states differ slightly in their requirements, so if you are creating and filing your articles yourself, you definitely need to look up your state's rules. I provide Web addresses in Appendix A where you can find the LLC laws for each state you are filing in.

What You Need to Know Before You Begin

Before creating your articles of organization, you need to establish some pretty important things:

- **What is the name of your LLC? Is the name available for use?** (See Chapter 4.) Any particular name may be available for your LLC, but is it available for use in your state? Has it already been trademarked by another company? Trademark infringement can be a time-consuming and costly experience. Even if you have no evil marketing intentions of making money off someone else's name, the courts won't be lenient. Just as with a speeding ticket, ignorance is not a defense (and we've all tried that one before!).

- **What is the purpose of your LLC?** This is an easy one. Before going into business, you need to know what sort of business you are in! This can be as specific or broad as you like. However, I recommend that you keep your company's purpose broad so you aren't limited by what you put in your articles of organization. (See "The Purpose & Powers of the LLC" later in this chapter.)

- **Is your LLC going to be member-managed or manager-managed?** (See Chapter 4.) Are all investors going to have a say in the day-to-day business decisions, or will a select few handle everything? Do you want to manage your own LLC, or would you rather step back and let someone else handle it?

- **Who will be the initial members?** (See Chapter 9.) In some states, you're required to list your initial members on your articles of organization — especially if you are member-managed. Therefore, you should have an idea of who the initial members of the company will be before forming. You can always change this later; however, it can be time consuming, depending on the process that you lay out in your operating agreement.

- **In which state(s) are you going to form your LLC?** (See Chapter 5.) LLC and tax laws vary from state to state — some states have no taxes, others have less paperwork, and others less disclosure — and you should take this into consideration when determining where to form your LLC. Also, Chapter 5 helps you figure out whether you are doing enough business in a particular state to be required to register there.

- **Who is going to act as your registered agent?** (See Chapter 5 again.) Every LLC needs to have a registered agent acting on its behalf in *every* state in which it is doing business. Have you chosen your registered agent for each state you are registering in? Bear in mind that you must rely on this business if your LLC is ever served with a lawsuit.

Preparing for What the States Require

As LLCs started to become popular, the federal government worried that there were too many differences between states' laws. Some differences are okay, but you can imagine the confusion if every state had its own idea of what an LLC was and how it was supposed to operate. It would be mayhem! To avoid this problem, the federal government came up with a nifty set of guidelines called the Uniform Limited Liability Company Act (ULLCA, for short). This act laid out what the government believed were ideal laws for the creation and management of LLCs in each state.

The ULLCA offers plenty of guidelines on how states should recognize and regulate LLCs, including

- Limitations in the name of the LLC — there must be a designator, such as LLC
- Provisions that allow for name reservations
- Requirements on designating a registered agent (Please refer to Chapter 5 for more information on working with a registered agent.)
- The nature of business that the LLC can state in its articles of organization
- The designation of an LLC as a separate legal entity
- The process of filing the articles of organization with the state
- The process of amending the articles of organization
- The process of filing an annual report
- Provisions limiting the liability of the managers and members
- Laws regarding membership shares
- Dissolutions of LLCs
- Foreign registrations and withdrawals of LLCs

I recommend reading over the ULLCA. You can view the entire act at www.myllc.com/dummies. However, keep in mind that each state can pick and choose what it wants to take out of the act. Many states have come up with their own sets of laws that vary slightly from other states' guidelines. In Appendix A, I provide you with a list of the Web address and phone number for the Secretary of State's office (where you will file your documents) in each state, as well as the LLC statutes in each state's laws.

All states have basic layouts of articles of organization, based on the state's LLC laws, that you can adopt. Even if you aren't setting up a complex business structure or doing anything too fancy with your LLC, you should add some provisions specific to your LLC to the state-provided articles of organization.

If your state allows it (most states do), you should retype the articles into your own document so it looks more professional. A lot of important people likely will be looking at these articles — bankers determining your eligibility for a business loan, investors looking to buy in, and so on. You want to demonstrate that you take pride in your company documents. I show you how a formal articles of organization should look at the end of this chapter.

In the end, your LLC's documents should fit your business like a freshly tailored suit. The articles of organization and the operating agreement (discussed in Chapter 9) together should outline all the voting rules and restrictions, as well as the management structure.

Throughout the book, I give examples of provisions you can include, and I even supply you with a CD full of the state articles of organization forms. But wait! If I don't recommend going with generic formation documents, why am I only supplying you with generic forms?

First, it would be impossible to include *all* of the possible variations of the articles of organization for every state in this book. Instead, I give you the barebones articles that each state requires (although you should still check your state's tax laws) and then give you extra provisions that you can add to customize the LLC to your needs.

When it comes to customizing your LLC, you get into a lot more specifics in the operating agreement (see Chapter 9) than you do in the articles of organization. If you don't see an important provision here, it's probably because I felt it best to include it in the operating agreement instead. I like putting most of the provisions in the operating agreement because the operating agreement isn't on public record like the articles of organization is. Privacy is important, especially when it comes to protecting yourself against lawsuits. And if you change the articles, you have to refile them with the state, and that costs money. You don't have to pay a dime to change your operating agreement.

Choosing Provisions for Your Articles of Organization

The articles of organization are made up of *provisions,* which are just parts. Some provisions are legally required to be in your articles, but you can pick and choose other ones to customize your LLC to your specific needs. Choosing the best provisions for your articles of organization can mean the difference between just getting by in your business and being more successful than you ever thought possible!

The articles of organization are public record, which means that anyone can view them. If there is anything you don't want the world to know, you should instead put it in your operating agreement, which is normally kept in the private company files.

All states have their own forms that you can use for your articles of organization. You can fill out basic information and file them with the Secretary of State's office. This is definitely the easiest way to go; however, you must be aware that what the state provides is just the bare bones and isn't tailored to your specific needs and/or line of business.

Provisions that the articles must (must!) have

Most states' articles of organization are pretty similar. Here is a list of provisions that are normally required in each state, along with an example so you can get an idea of the provision's content and wording. You can find the actual language of the provision on your state's generic articles of organization, which I have provided on the accompanying CD.

The LLC Name

Your company name must separate your LLC from other companies so you avoid trademark infringement. The name also should be easy to pronounce; it's also a good idea to confirm that the name translates well in other languages in case you eventually do business overseas. Refer to Chapter 4 for more specifics on naming your LLC.

An example provision:

> *Article I. Name.*
>
> *The name of the Limited Liability Company is _____ (hereinafter referred to as the "Company").*

Company Address

Some states require that you put your company address in the articles of organization. I always recommend using your registered agent's address. Just make sure your agent has okayed this in advance and can forward your mail every day. Also be aware that, often, the state won't let you use a P.O. Box.

An example provision:

> *Article II. Principle Place of Business*
>
> *The address of the Company's principal place of business in this state is:*
>
> _____.

The Purpose & Powers of the LLC

Here you designate what sort of business you'll be engaging in. Although some states require you to be more detailed, most states allow you to be really broad and say that the LLC isn't limited in its purpose and has the power to engage in any activity it wants. I always feel that the broader you make this statement, the less you are limited in the future should you decide to venture into other business areas. Sometimes envisioning where your business will be at its ten-year mark can be an impossible feat, so to be safe, always stick with the idea that "broader is better!"

An example of a broadly stated provision:

> *Article III. Purpose & Powers*
>
> *The purpose for which this Company is organized is to transact any or all lawful business for which Limited Liability Companies may be organized for, including, but not limited to:*
>
> > *a. Carrying on any business or any other legal or lawful activity allowed by law.*
> >
> > *b. Acquiring, owning, using, conveying, and otherwise disposing of any interest of real and/or personal property.*
> >
> > *c. Manufacturing, buying, selling, and distributing goods, wares, and merchandise of every class and description, both real and personal and tangible.*
> >
> > *d. Engaging in any services — with the exception of services deemed "professional" by the laws of the state — which include but are not limited to: consulting, brokering, and dealing.*
> >
> > *e. To have and exercise all rights and powers that are legally available to a Limited Liability Company, now and in the future.*
>
> *The foregoing purposes and powers thereof shall not be held to limit or restrict in any manner.*

Duration of the Company

One tricky thing about LLCs — by law, they can't live forever (also called a *perpetual duration*). This is one of the things that legally separates LLCs from corporations.

Even though some states allow you to state "perpetual duration" on your articles of organization, this may open you up to avoidable liability in the future. To be safe, I would put 30 years, which is a fairly standard duration. This doesn't mean that in 30 years you'll be required to dissolve — you can always renew your LLC when the time comes.

A sample provision:

> *Article IV. Duration*
>
> *In accordance with all state statutes, the duration of the company shall be thirty (30) years. However, the Company may still have the option of dissolving during this term.*
>
> *The Company may, in its Operating Agreement and amendments thereof, confer additional powers upon its managers and members, so as they are not in conflict with the law.*

Registered Agent

Your registered agent can be your greatest asset — especially if you are organized in a state other than the one you live in (see Chapter 5). First of all, it's the law to have a registered agent, and secondly, a registered agent can handle much of the paperwork involved in maintaining compliance in your state(s).

A sample provision:

> *Article V. Name & Address of Registered Agent*
>
> *The Name of the Company's initial Registered Agent is:*
>
> _____
>
> *The Address of the Company's initial Registered Agent is:*
>
> _____
>
> _____

In the event of a lawsuit, your registered agent is of the greatest importance; therefore, you *must* have someone who is experienced in this area take on this role. This address is where all legal papers will be sent, along with state or federal notices and other tax-related documents. It's better to have everything forwarded to you from your registered agent than to worry about losing something critical at your place of business. This address provides a sanctuary for vital legal and government papers to reside and can work to protect *you*.

Member-Managed or Manager-Managed

Whether your LLC will be managed by its members or separate managers is something that you need to decide before creating your articles of organization. In Chapter 4, I discuss the benefits and drawbacks of both types of management structures.

A sample provision:

> *Article VI. Management*
>
> *The Company shall be managed by (choose one: <u>its members</u> / <u>separate managers</u>).*

Names and Addresses of Managers and/or Members

Most states require that you state the names and addresses of the managers and/or members in the articles. Because the articles of organization are public record, try to state as little as is legally allowed. If you are manager-managed and have the option of stating either your managers or your members, always opt to disclose your managers.

Other states only require the names to be stated on the Initial List of Managers and Members (the exact name of this filing varies from state to state), which is a completely separate filing. Again, if you want to keep your privacy, see if the registered agent will allow you to use his address as each member's address.

A sample provision (when stating managers):

> *Article VII. Managers*
>
> *The names and addresses of the persons who will be serving as managers: (Recognize that this list may be tailored during the Company's first and subsequent annual meetings if new members are voted upon by managing partners.)*
>
> _____   _____
>
> _____   _____
>
> _____   _____

If you are in a state where the members must be disclosed in the articles of organization, yet you still want privacy in order to protect your assets, you should talk to an attorney about getting a revocable living trust to serve as a member. This protects your identity (the name of the trust will be on record), but as a beneficiary of the trust, you will still own the membership shares.

Some states require that you state the amount of each member's initial contribution (money, services, equipment, whatever) and the percentage of profits that each member gets. If you don't yet know this information, you can do one of two things:

- ✔ State what you *do* know, and then amend the articles later (which can be a hassle — not to mention costly!).

- ✔ Domicile your LLC in another state that doesn't require this disclosure, and then foreign file in the state that you're operating in.

Organizer

In most states, an _organizer_ must sign the articles of organization (for more details, see the "Choosing who signs" section later in this chapter). This provision states who the organizer is and her place of business. The purpose is to verify that the information contained in the articles is factual. However, the organizer has no true legal responsibility or further obligation to the LLC. This provision should always come last in the articles of organization.

An example provision:

> _Article VIII. Organizer_
>
> _The name and address of the Organizer of the Company is:_
>
> _____
>
> _____
>
> _____

Additional provisions you can include

If the provisions provided in the generic state forms were adequate for everyone, there wouldn't be too many customized LLCs. Quite a few provisions can be included that most LLC novices (and some professionals!) don't know about and states aren't legally required to provide you with. I give you the most common ones here. Because you can customize your LLC in so many different ways, your attorney can assist you in drafting other provisions that will meet your specific needs, if necessary.

Indemnification of Managers and Members under State Law

When you are _indemnified,_ you can't be held personally responsible for the acts of the company or even for your acts on behalf of the company. This is normally provided in state law, but it's always good to publicly state in your articles of organization that each member is permitted the maximum indemnification available to them.

A sample provision:

> _Article IX: Indemnification of Managers and Members_
>
> A. _Under the current law, including any amendments hereafter, each manager shall be entitled to the fullest indemnification available to them._
>
> B. _Each manager shall be liable to the Company for the following actions:_
>
>> 1. _The breach of the manager's or member's loyalty to the Company, or its members._

    2. *To be liable hereunder the manager in question must have acted in a malicious or grossly negligent manner, as defined by law.*

    3. *A transaction in which the manager benefits to the detriment of the Company or its members.*

    4. *An action for which there is no indemnification provided by law.*

C. *This indemnification shall not deter or cancel out other rights to which the manager or member is entitled.*

Voting Rights

Voting rights are usually dispersed among members in one of two ways:

- **All members get one vote.** A member who owns 2 percent of the company has the same voting power as a member who owns 98 percent of the company.

- **Each percentage of membership interest gets one vote.** A member with a 2 percent share of the company gets two votes, while the member with the 98 percent share gets 98 votes.

The voting rights in one state vary from those in another. However, this is one of the rare cases where you don't have to follow the law! You can create your own rules — all you have to do is state your preference in your articles of organization. If you want each member to have a percentage of votes equal to her percentage of ownership, then be sure to include this provision in your articles of organization.

A sample provision:

Article X. Voting Rights

In regards to the voting rights, each member will be entitled a single vote for each percentage of membership the member has in the company.

Provisions for professional LLCs

In most states, if you are a licensed professional you must have a special provision in your articles of organization designating you as a *professional LLC* (or PLLC, for short). A PLLC is very similar to a standard LLC; however, professionals can't be exempt from malpractice, so they have less liability protection. The PLLC's formation is the same, but the articles are slightly different, and the filing fee may be slightly higher, depending on the state.

Not sure whether you're considered a professional? If you are in a profession requiring a license, then you most likely need to form a PLLC. These professions are typically

- ✔ Doctors
- ✔ Chiropractors
- ✔ Dentists
- ✔ Architects
- ✔ Engineers
- ✔ Accountants
- ✔ Lawyers

If you are still unsure about whether you are required to form a PLLC, contact your local Secretary of State's office or an incorporating company.

California currently doesn't allow professionals to operate under LLCs. If you are a professional operating in this state, you should consider forming a professional corporation instead.

When creating your articles of organization for a professional limited liability company, keep in mind the following points:

- ✔ Typically, there are name restrictions. You must add the word "Professional" or the letter "P" to the designator. In some states, the name of the LLC must contain the professional's name. For instance, if you are a doctor and your name is Jane Goodman, then your professional limited liability company can be called "Jane Goodman, MD, P.L.L.C."

- ✔ You can't state a broad purpose; it must be specific to the service you are providing. Replace the Purpose provision that I provide earlier in the chapter with this one:

  Article III: Purpose & Powers

  The Company is a Professional Limited Liability Company.

  The purpose for which the Company is organized is to engage in the professional service of: _____.

- ✔ Most states restrict PLLC members to those professionals who are operating in the business. This can be a problem if you want to have silent investors who own membership shares. Check your state statutes to find out the specific regulations for your state.

- ✔ In some states, you may need to have your licensing board approve your articles of organization and sign them before the Secretary of State will accept them for filing. Contact the Secretary of State's office to see if this is required. If it is, you may need a good dose of patience — these things can take time!

✔ The fees may be slightly higher when forming a professional LLC. Also, if you are using the generic, state-provided articles of organization, you must check to see if you need to use a different one for PLLCs.

It's a Wrap! Putting It All Together

After you figure out what provisions you're going to include in your articles of organization, you need to wrap everything up into a professional-looking document. One option is to just amend the state's generic form with your extra provisions, but do you really want to walk into a bank, ask for a million-dollar business loan, and then hand them articles that look like a patchwork quilt of legalese? Not likely.

Different states require different formats, and you should probably contact your Secretary of State's office to make sure that it doesn't have any special requirements as to how the articles of organization are laid out. However, most states have the basics in common, and with that in mind, here are a few tips:

✔ Always print your articles of organization on regular 81/2-x-11-inch white paper. Use black ink and only print on one side of the paper (no double-sided copies). Make sure that the articles are clean and legible.

✔ Spell your company name exactly as you want it to look on your checks, letterhead, and other official documents.

✔ Structure the document into articles, sections, and subsections. This makes referencing different provisions a breeze. For example, Article A, Section 4, or Article II, Section B, Subsection 4. To better understand what I mean by structure, see the sample articles of organization in the "Examining your completed articles" section later in this chapter.

Articles of organization are pretty simple, and for the most part, you can draft them yourself. If you don't feel like researching laws and typing out provisions, consider going to an incorporating company. They are generally well versed on creating articles of organization (after all, they do it every day!) and will charge a heck of a lot less than an attorney will.

Choosing who signs

So you've put all this work into forming your articles of organization and now you need to sign it, right? Not exactly. Believe it or not, in most states, a manager or member doesn't even need to sign the articles before filing them!

Most states assume that when an LLC is organized, it hasn't had its first member meeting. At that meeting, managers are traditionally elected. If the LLC doesn't have any managers, they can't exactly sign the articles, now, can they? Most states also assume that you are forming your LLC through an attorney or incorporating service, and to make it easy for everyone, states allow someone at the law firm or incorporating company to sign the articles instead of the client. That is why most states allow an *organizer* to sign and file the articles of organization.

The organizer doesn't have to be associated with your company, and she isn't a manager or member (unless you want her to be). She is simply the person who creates the LLC. After the LLC is formed and the managers and members are assigned, the organizer fades away — she has no future position of power in the company.

Although most states allow an organizer to sign the articles of organization, some states require a manager and/or member to sign. Some states even require the articles to be notarized! A quick way to determine who must sign the articles of organization in your state is to look at the filing form for your state (which is included on the CD).

While this all sounds simple, there's a catch. In most states, the LLC's registered agent is required to sign the articles of organization before it can be filed. The agent normally signs an Acceptance of Appointment document that is appended to the articles. This can be a little bit of a headache for most people, especially if you live in a different state than the one you're filing in. In that case, I recommend that you make sure that the company filing your articles and the registered agent for your entity are one and the same.

Examining your completed articles

Voilà! Finis! You've created your articles of organization. If you are creating an LLC for a standard business, the finished product should look something like this:

Articles of Organization of

Your Company Name, L.L.C.

I, the undersigned, am eighteen years of age or older and am acting as the Organizer of this Limited Liability Company. I hereby adopt the following Articles of Organization:

Article I. Name

The name of the Limited Liability Company is **Your Company Name, L.L.C.** (hereinafter referred to as the "Company").

Article II. Principle Place of Business

The address of the Company's principal place of business in this state is: **10 Main Street, Suite 1, Anywhere, CA 90068.**

Article III. Purpose & Powers

The purpose for which this Company is organized is to transact any or all lawful business for which Limited Liability Companies may be organized for, including, but not limited to:

A. Carrying on any business or any other legal or lawful activity allowed by law.

B. Acquiring, owning, using, conveying, and otherwise disposing of any interest of real and/or personal property.

C. Manufacturing, buying, selling, and distributing goods, wares, and merchandise of every class and description, both real and personal and tangible.

D. Engaging in any services — with the exception of services deemed "professional" by the laws of the state — which include but are not limited to: consulting, brokering, and dealing.

E. To have and exercise all rights and powers that are legally available to a limited liability company, now and in the future.

The foregoing purpose and powers thereof shall not be held to limit or restrict in any manner.

The Company may, in its Operating Agreement and amendments thereof, confer additional powers upon its managers and members, so long as they are not in conflict with the law.

Article IV. Duration

In accordance with all state statutes, the duration of the company shall be thirty (30) years. However, the Company may still have the option of dissolving during this term.

Article V. Name & Address of Registered Agent

The Name of the Company's initial Registered Agent is: **MyLLC, Inc.**

The Address of the Company's initial Registered Agent is:

1817 Morena Blvd., Suite A

San Diego, CA 92110

Article VI. Management

The Company shall be managed by separate managers. The company shall be considered "manager-managed."

Article VII. Managers

The names and addresses of the persons who will be serving as managers:

Jane Doe

1817 Morena Blvd., Suite A

San Diego, CA 92110

Article VIII: Indemnification of Managers and Members

Section A

Under the current law, including any amendments hereafter, each manager shall be entitled to the fullest indemnification available to them.

Section B

Each manager shall be liable to the Company for the following actions:

1. The breach of the manager's or member's loyalty to the Company, or its members.
2. To be liable hereunder, the manager in question must have acted in a malicious or grossly negligent manner, as defined by law.
3. A transaction in which the manager benefits to the detriment of the Company or its members.
4. An action for which there is no indemnification provided by law.

Section C

This indemnification shall not deter or cancel out other rights to which the manager or member is entitled.

Article IX. Voting Rights

In regards to the voting rights, each member will be entitled a single vote for each percentage of membership the member has in the company.

Article X. Organizer

The name and address of the Organizer of the Company is:

John Smith

1817 Morena Blvd., Suite A

San Diego, CA 92110

IN WITNESS WHEREOF, the undersigned have signed these Articles of Organization on this _____ day of _____, 20_____.

_____

John Smith, Organizer

Certificate of acceptance of appointment of Registered Agent:

I, **Jennifer Reuting on behalf of MyLLC, Inc.**, hereby accept appointment as Registered Agent for the above named Limited Liability Company on this _____ day of _____, 20_____.

_____

Jennifer Reuting, on behalf of MyLLC, Inc.

Chapter 7

Converting Your Current Business into an LLC

. . . .

In This Chapter

▶ Determining whether a conversion is for you

▶ Understanding the tax implications

▶ Completing the conversion

. . . .

Chances are, if you're considering forming an LLC, you're starting from somewhere. LLCs are relatively new entities, and if you've been in business for a long time, you're probably operating your business or maintaining your assets as a sole proprietor, partnership, or corporation. You likely know the benefits of operating under an LLC, but how do you convert your existing business into one? Forming the LLC is the first step, which I cover in Chapters 4 and 6, but then you need to get your assets into the new entity and begin operations. This isn't always easy.

When you're in the throes of a bustling business, the last thing you want to do is cause any more chaos by changing your infrastructure and switching to a completely different entity type. In most cases, you have to navigate a tax minefield and spend a lot of time changing contracts, business loans, and even marketing materials over to your new name. Although it can be hairy, the conversion to an LLC is normally well worth it in the long run — I promise!

Throughout this chapter, I show you how to convert your current business structure into an LLC, no matter the entity type that you are currently using. I also show you how to avoid most of the fees and taxes that pop up and how to avoid unknowingly falling into a tax trap that you can't get out of. Although this process may seem complicated on the surface, the situation isn't as dire as it first appears. With proper planning and some of my tax-saving tips, you can be operating under your new LLC in no time!

When to Consider Converting to an LLC

Life is good. Your business is flourishing, and you have just decided to take it to the next level. As you operate more and more with the public, your chances of being sued increase tenfold. You know that you need the liability protection and the reassurance that an LLC brings. And if you're operating as a sole proprietorship or general partnership, you are probably thinking that you may want to acquire loans and investors as you grow. For all of these things, you need a powerful and flexible entity, and as you're aware, the LLC is your best bet.

In Chapter 2, I compare LLCs to all of the major forms of doing business — sole proprietorships, partnerships, corporations. If you haven't read that chapter yet, I suggest that you stop here and backtrack to discover the benefits and drawbacks of an LLC in comparison with the entity structure you are currently operating under. After you understand the pros and cons of your entity versus an LLC, call your attorney or corporate consultant to discuss what is right for your specific situation. If you don't have anyone who knows the different entity types and can advise you, call 888-88-MYLLC (888-886-9552) and speak with a consultant there. Get the information any way you can, because at the end of the day, the details of your business determine whether an LLC is right for you. The glove doesn't fit everybody.

When I use the term *conversion,* I'm not only talking about converting a corporation, limited partnership, or other *incorporated entity* (an entity that needs to be filed with the state to exist); I'm including any form of business that you are operating — sole proprietorships and general partnerships are included too. After all, converting a business from your own name to an LLC can be a complicated transaction.

Here are a few reasons why you may want to convert to an LLC:

- ✔ You're operating as a sole proprietorship or general partnership and are afraid of being sued by a customer or employee.

- ✔ Your company — which is currently a corporation — is becoming more and more profitable, and your corporate tax is up to almost 35 percent. You realize that your tax burden would be less if you were to operate as an LLC instead.

- ✔ You just purchased real estate in your own name, and you want to protect the property from lawsuits, but you also want an entity that you can transfer assets in and out of without causing a taxable event.

- ✔ You are currently operating as a sole proprietorship or general partnership and have decided that you want to raise financing to get the business off the ground.

Now, these aren't all the reasons you might want to convert your business to an LLC; I couldn't possibly list them all here. However, this list gives you a taste of why converting your entity into an LLC could be an incredibly powerful step on your path to success.

The Drawbacks of Conversion

Unfortunately, converting to an LLC is easier said than done. If you have an operational business, you can't just tack the words "LLC" or "Limited Liability Company" at the end of your name and be done with it. You have to go through the painstaking process of transferring your assets, one by one, from the old entity to the new. You also have to change your contracts over, which can be a huge financial burden if there are fees or if you have to renegotiate them. You can also trigger taxes, fees, and penalties, which can cost you up the wazoo!

A few pitfalls that you should be aware of include:

- ✔ You may have to find a partner if you are operating on your own and your state doesn't allow single-member LLCs.

- ✔ If you have a partner, you may not be able to change ownership percentages without being subject to some pretty hefty taxes.

- ✔ If you have a corporation, you may be subject to being taxed *twice* on everything that you own before you can contribute it to your new LLC. That can be a *huge* tax burden.

- ✔ If you are transferring real estate, you may have to pay a transfer tax and/or other taxes. You may also have to negotiate with your mortgage company to allow you to transfer the title without having to first pay off your mortgage.

- ✔ You may have to transfer some contracts over to the new entity. If the contract doesn't allow a transfer, you may have to renegotiate it and/or buy it out.

You *can* take some steps to lessen the burden; however, before you jump into a conversion, it's a good idea to sit down and come up with a plan. Not to mention, you'll need to add up these costs and make sure you can afford it!

Navigating the tax minefield

When deciding to convert your business into an LLC, first and foremost you need to look at what sort of tax burdens the conversion will entail. During the conversion, you need to transfer each and every asset from the old entity to the owners, then from the owners to the new LLC. Needless to say, in one of these steps, you can be hit with a ton of taxes — sales tax, use tax, transfer tax, and so on. And if the transfer isn't done properly, the business can even get socked with unnecessary capital gains taxes. Some of these taxes are federal and some are state, but the one thing they have in common is that they can be pretty hefty if you don't watch out.

Taxes can be especially burdensome if your old business owns real estate. Regardless of whether the property is already in your name and contributions to the LLC are tax free, most states still impose transfer taxes. You should have your attorney and accountant assist you through this process because they know the specific laws for your state and can guide you.

The CD that accompanies this book contains a number of IRS and tax forms that you'll find useful.

Getting around the contractual stuff

So, you've managed to sort out the tax stuff and arrange your conversion so that you don't have to dish out too much dough. You do the conversion and . . . . ouch! You get served with a lawsuit from one of your vendors stating that you voided your contractual obligation and owe them a lot of money. And guess what? They're right.

If you look at the fine print on the contracts that your company has signed over the years, some of them say that the contracts can't be assigned or that that they'll be terminated upon the termination of the company that entered into the contract. This means that after you convert and terminate your old business structure, you may have some problems with the people or companies you were contractually obligated to.

Some common contracts that may be affected are

- ✔ Lease agreements for office space
- ✔ Equipment lease agreements
- ✔ Bank loans
- ✔ Personal loans
- ✔ Contracts with vendors
- ✔ Employee agreements

In some cases, you'll need to renegotiate the contract or buy your way out of it — which can cost you a lot of money. It's a good idea to speak with an attorney before starting any negotiations. I've found that the money spent on attorneys in these cases is money well spent.

 If you can't get out of the contract, you may want to consider just leaving your old company active so the contract doesn't have to be terminated. Whether this can be done really depends on the contract, the type of business entity you are currently using; and your attorney's opinion on the matter. You can also consider merging your old company and your new one, with your new company being the surviving entity. I discuss this in the "Looking at ways to minimize taxes" section later in the chapter.

Knowing How to Convert from Each Entity Type

After you've decided to take the plunge and convert your business to an LLC, how do you get started? How can you possibly transfer *everything* over to a brand-new entity? I understand your hesitation. You can't jump into a conversion without proper planning. Without forethought, the entire process can be incredibly troublesome and costly — especially if you have quite a few assets or lots of contracts. However, conversion shouldn't be put off either. After all, you'll need to do it eventually, and what better time than the present? Say you were to postpone the process for two years . . . your business (and your conversion problems!) will have probably quadrupled!

Conversions aren't necessarily hard to do, but the process varies greatly depending on how your business is currently structured. For instance, the time, money, and paperwork will normally be a lot more extensive when converting your corporation to an LLC than when you are converting your general partnership. The process for transferring assets will be different when transferring from a sole proprietorship to a new LLC than from a limited partnership.

There are four different business structures that most commonly convert to LLCs (for the basics of each of these structures, check out Chapter 2). They are

- ✔ Sole proprietorships
- ✔ General partnerships
- ✔ Limited partnerships
- ✔ Corporations (including S corporations)

I have divided this section according to these categories so you only have to read about your entity type to get the information you need as you start planning your conversion strategy.

If your business is laden with assets and contracts, I definitely recommend that you work closely with your accountant and attorney during the conversion process.

Converting from a sole proprietorship

Considering that the most common, albeit dangerous, method of operating a business is as a sole proprietorship, I'm going to bet that you're running a sole proprietorship as we speak. Although sole proprietorships are easy and cheap to start, they offer zero liability protection, and they give your customers and employees little confidence in your business acumen. Plus, you'll never be able to even think about raising capital or finding investors.

If you're currently operating as a sole proprietorship, you must form an LLC immediately. Luckily, converting from a sole proprietorship to an LLC is a pretty effortless, tax-free process. Your business assets should currently be in your name, so transferring them is easy. You won't need to file any conversion paperwork with the Secretary of State's office — just create an LLC as you normally would (see Chapters 6 and 8 for more information on creating and filing your articles of organization), and then use your current business capital as your initial investment in the new LLC.

If you are currently operating as a sole proprietor, it's imperative that you check to see whether your state allows single-member LLCs. Otherwise, before you can convert, you'll need to find a partner. Look in Appendix A to see whether your state allows single-member LLCs. Regardless, because LLCs are structured to be partnerships, it's probably a good idea for you to find a partner anyway. Even if you only give him a small percentage of the company, the peace of mind that you'll get will be well worth it. I go into more detail about this in Chapters 5 and 10.

If you want to convert your sole proprietorship to an LLC, here are the steps you need to take:

1. **Make a list of all the assets that your business currently owns (especially real estate) and all contracts, insurance policies, leases, and loans that your business is liable for.**

2. **Take this list to your attorney for his advice or contact the other parties with whom you're doing business to determine whether you can transfer the agreement as is to the new entity.**

   Often creditors will simply want you to remain as a personal guarantor and won't mind transferring the contract to the LLC. Others, such as leasing companies or vendors who may have an interest in getting you to renegotiate the contract, may feel differently, however.

3. **Create and file your articles of organization with the Secretary of State's office.**

   You can find detailed information on how to do this in Chapters 6 and 8. Make sure to file all required licenses and permit applications as outlined in Chapter 8.

4. **Acquire a tax identification number (also called an *EIN*, which stands for Employer Identification Number) for your new business.**

   This can be done on the IRS Web site at `https://sa2.www4.irs.gov/sa_vign/newFormSS4.do`.

5. **Open a new bank account that is for your business only.**

   You need new checks, an endorsement stamp, deposit slips, and a new debit card in your LLC's name. After the account is set up, you can transfer the funds from your existing business to the new LLC by writing a check from your personal account to your LLC account.

6. **If you have any contracts with your clients, redraft them so the contracts are with your LLC and not with yourself.**

7. **Update your company name and logo to include "LLC" or "Limited Liability Company."**

   Make sure to change your letterhead and business cards. Not only does this make you sound more official, but it's also legally required in most states.

8. **Create an operating agreement for your LLC (see Chapter 9) and update your company business plan to include any formalities that you want to take place (for example, holding annual meetings).**

9. **Transfer your assets into the new LLC by "contributing" them to your LLC in exchange for an ownership percentage.**

   I talk more about this in the "Transferring your assets" section near the end of the chapter.

After you are up and running under your new LLC, you must be careful not to revert to your old ways. You should include "LLC" after your company's name and should always sign documents as a representative of the company. The biggest danger you have to look out for is mixing your personal and business funds. That was okay when you were a sole proprietorship, but now that you are an LLC, it's a big no-no.

When bringing on a partner, there is a good chance you will be hit with some taxes, especially if the partner is only contributing services or if he is coming in at a time when the company has substantial business loans or other liabilities. I go over the details of these sorts of tax snags in Chapter 13.

Converting from a general partnership

Converting from a general partnership to an LLC is even easier than converting from a sole proprietorship. Why? Because you already have a partner! LLCs are set up to be partnerships, so it's always easier when they are operated that way.

By the way, that reminds me . . . before you can convert your general partnership operation to an LLC, all of the partners must unanimously agree to the decision. No, you can't convert without them knowing it! They will most likely have to sign off on it anyway.

After you have everyone on board, you can then go through the process of forming your LLC and transferring your assets. Although it isn't the most exciting pastime, the conversion process isn't as bad as you think because the IRS considers general partnerships and LLCs as "partnerships" with no difference between the two. So, very few changes need to take place as far as the IRS is concerned. Your partnership can have the same tax year-end (there is no interruption), and it can continue to be taxed as a partnership with the same year-end filings due as before.

Now, in most cases, a conversion from a general partnership to an LLC is a *nontaxable event,* so you won't get hit with a big tax bill at year's end. All you have to do is contribute the assets of your current business to the new LLC in exchange for membership shares. To avoid tax penalties, you must not change the ownership amounts in the new LLC. So if you have four partners in your general partnership who each owns 25 percent, then your LLC must have the same four partners with each owning 25 percent and being distributed 25 percent of the profits and losses. I go over this in detail in Chapter 10, but for now, just keep in mind that you can't change things up.

Keeping the ownership and distribution percentages the same is the only way to avoid a taxable event when changing an existing partnership into an LLC.

Converting from a limited partnership

If you are currently operating as a limited partnership, in most cases it would make perfect sense to convert to an LLC. Limited partnerships and LLCs are very similar except for the fact that the partners in an LLC are *all* shielded from any personal liability. In a limited partnership, only certain partners — the *limited partners* — are exempt from any personal liability.

Because the limited partnership and the LLC are such similar entities — they are both considered partnerships in the eyes of the law — a conversion is simple. The IRS has made it so that a conversion from one partnership entity (say, a limited partnership) to another partnership entity (say, an LLC) is a *nontaxable event*. You can transfer the assets from one entity to another without having to worry about getting a huge tax bill at the end of the year.

You and your partner will both need to decide to convert the partnership to an LLC. Unless you want an irate business partner pounding on your door, you probably shouldn't act unilaterally. If there are more than two members, check your partnership agreement to see what percentage of members needs to agree to the conversion. If your partnership agreement remains silent on the issue, then you should play it safe and make sure that all members agree.

If you want to change the ownership percentages among partners, then you or one of your partners may be hit with a pretty hefty tax bill. You should definitely speak with your tax advisor so she can assist you in structuring the deal while avoiding any impending taxes.

As far as the IRS goes, you need to file for a new tax identification number. Because your LLC's profits and losses can be reported on your personal tax returns, just like in a limited partnership, you can maintain your same tax year.

Some states actually have a state filing that facilitates the conversion. This is normally called a *certificate of conversion* or *articles of conversion*. I go over this in the "When your state does allow statutory conversions" section later in the chapter.

If your state doesn't facilitate a conversion — for instance, it doesn't let you file a certificate of conversion — you'll need to do the conversion yourself. The easiest way to do this is to form a new LLC and have the partners exchange their membership interests in the limited partnership for the same amount of membership interests in the new LLC. Now, the only owner of the limited partnership is the LLC. Because the limited partnership needs to have more than one owner, it must be liquidated and dissolved. The assets then go directly to the single owner — the LLC.

Now, you will still be required to transfer all of your contracts, loans, leases, and other agreements to your new LLC. This is probably the trickiest aspect of converting your entity. However, because limited partnerships and LLCs are so closely related, most creditors, individuals, and companies that you have contracts with should be pretty understanding. Before doing the conversion, sit down with your attorney and go over any contracts, mortgages, or leases that may look like a problem.

Converting from a corporation

LLCs are a relatively new entity, so if you've been in business for a while, you are probably operating as a corporation. Corporations are often ideal entities for running a business. However, if you are looking for pass-through taxation without having all of the different restrictions associated with being an S corporation (see Chapter 2 for information on S corporations), then an LLC is the right entity for you!

Before you begin the conversion process, or any major process for that matter, you must have a shareholders' meeting and make sure that you have a quorum and the required vote of the shareholders before proceeding.

When you convert your corporation to an LLC, you need to amend your company's business plan to account for the company's new structure. Keep in mind that the requirements to maintain an LLC are less than those of a corporation. All of the corporate formalities you have to go through with corporations, such as annual meetings, aren't required for LLCs.

Considering the tax impact

Unfortunately, converting from a corporation to an LLC can be problematic. Assuming that your state doesn't allow a *statutory conversion* (a document that you file with your Secretary of State's office), you'll need to liquidate and dissolve your entire company in the process. (I go into more detail about this in the "Navigating Through the Conversion" section.) This can lead to a pretty huge tax burden.

You see, corporations are taxed at two levels — the corporate level and the shareholder level. You'll often hear this referred to as *double taxation.* Because of the two levels of taxes, when you liquidate the company, first your corporation will be forced to pay corporate taxes, then, as the money is distributed to the shareholders, the shareholders will be required to pay capital gains tax — on both federal and state levels.

After the shareholders have the assets in their hands, they can invest the money and/or the assets into the LLC in exchange for membership shares. But by this time, I'd be surprised if they had half of their assets left after all the double taxation headaches!

Looking at ways to minimize taxes

The first way that you may be able to save taxes when converting a corporation to an LLC is by forming a brand-new LLC and doing a standard merger. A *merger* is when you combine two existing entities into one surviving one. All states have laws regarding mergers, so you'll have to research whether the laws of your state allow two different entity types (a corporation and an LLC) to merge into one with the LLC being the surviving entity. Some states provide no guidance at all, and in this case, your attorney is the best person to direct you through the proper procedures. Merging your corporation into an LLC is a great way to avoid sales and transfer taxes that are associated with moving assets from one entity to another.

If you don't want to go through the hassles of a merger, you may want to consider keeping just your assets in your corporation. I am a firm believer in separating your company assets from your operating business anyway. That way, if your operating business (in this case, your LLC) were to get sued, your assets would be protected in a completely different entity.

For example, if you own a local pizza company and you want to convert your corporation into an LLC, you would set up your new LLC, transfer your contracts, and convert your business operations over to it. However, you would leave your stoves and other equipment in the corporation. At the end of the day, your corporation would become a leasing company and lease the equipment to your operating LLC. This way, if one of your customers gets food poisoning and sues your company, your assets are protected in your old corporation.

If your corporation is in a tax-free state, such as Nevada or Wyoming, you may want to lease the assets to your operating LLC at a standard lease rate. This way, that profit won't be distributed to you at the end of the year and subject to your personal income and self-employment taxes; it will be safely sitting in a corporate bank account free from hefty state corporate taxes and franchise fees. What a great way to save up to buy more assets and equipment!

Navigating Through the Conversion

So you've decided that converting your current entity to an LLC is the right thing to do, and you're ready to get started! The details of the conversion differ slightly depending on which type of entity you're converting from, but for the most part you still have to do the same thing — form the LLC, create a plan, and transfer the assets and contracts. I cover two conversion processes in this section:

✔ **The "liquidate and form" process:** You have to liquidate your current company, transfer the assets to the owners (if you are currently a limited partnership or a corporation), then dissolve the old entity, form a brand-new LLC, and transfer the assets from the owners into the new LLC.

✔ **The statutory conversion:** If this conversion is allowed in your state, I recommend you go this route. With a *statutory conversion,* you can just file a short document with your Secretary of State's office that automatically converts your current limited partnership or corporation into an LLC. This option is not available for sole proprietorships and general partnerships.

You know that old adage, "Don't change horses midstream"? Remember it if you're considering changing your accounting methods. Upon the conversion, keep your accounting method the same. For instance, if you are on a cash-based system, don't switch to an accrual-based system. In the IRS's eyes, this could "accelerate the income," which means taxes, taxes, and more taxes! If you really want to change your accounting method, wait until the conversion has been completed, and then have your tax advisor assist you.

When your state doesn't allow statutory conversions

You can find out whether your state allows statutory conversions by calling your local Secretary of State's office. I provide this information for you in Appendix A. If your state doesn't allow statutory conversions, you have to take these steps:

- ✔ **Form a brand new LLC.** When you form your LLC, you need to do it just as I describe in Chapters 6 and 8. Nothing fancy required.

- ✔ **Check all of your loans for a "due on sale" clause that may become effective upon the conversion.** If you see this clause, you may be required to pay your entire loan if you transfer it. This could force you to refinance, and if the interest rates aren't good, this can cost you a lot of money in the long run. You can normally work with your bank to avoid this scenario.

- ✔ **Revise any contracts that your current entity is party to so the contracts reflect your new entity name.** In this case, you may want to work with your attorney, because some of the people you are in contractual arrangements with may see this as an opportunity to get you to renegotiate the contract before transferring it.

- ✔ **If you are currently operating as a sole proprietorship or general partnership, check whether your business name is available for use.** If it's taken, you may have to form your LLC under another name and then file a *fictitious firm name statement* (or *DBA,* which stands for "doing business as") at your county clerk's office.

- ✔ **If you have any current fictitious firm names, transfer them to your new entity.** The same goes for other intellectual property, such as trademarks, copyrights, and patents.

- ✔ **Check to see if your insurance carrier requires a new premium after the conversion takes place.** Often, insurance isn't transferable from one entity to another, so you may run into some snags if you don't find out ahead of time.

- ✔ **Check to see whether you must publish a notice of dissolution or conversion in the local newspaper.** Some states require that you give notice to the public when you are doing a conversion. You can contact your Secretary of State's office or your registered agent to find out whether this is required in your state.

If you have a sizeable amount of contracts and/or agreements (such as mortgages, employment contracts, lease agreements, loan documents, and license agreements) that your business is a party to, you should collect all of them and take them to your attorney. She can review each document and determine whether there are any dire consequences to a conversion. She can also renegotiate any contracts that need to be replaced with your new entity. (A word of caution: This may be a relatively costly process.)

When your state does allow statutory conversions

If you have a corporation or limited partnership, then you may be able to save yourself a little bit of hassle and file a certificate of conversion at your Secretary of State's office (a process called *statutory conversion*). In most states, this certificate of conversion doesn't do too much. It simply tells the world that your business has converted. However, the assets, contracts, loans, and leases don't automatically transfer over. Unfortunately, you still need to do a lot of the dirty work! The upside is that you have a valid reason for transferring your contracts and loan documents to a new name and entity type.

To find out whether your state allows statutory conversions, simply call your Secretary of State's office and ask whether there is a filing you can do to convert your limited partnership or corporation into an LLC (statutory conversions don't apply to sole proprietorships and general partnerships). If so, you can either have your registered agent do the required work for you, or you can normally download the forms off of the Secretary of State's Web site (I provide Web addresses for you in Appendix A).

Even when you are doing a statutory conversion, you'll need to form your LLC from scratch. In Chapters 6 and 8, I go into detail on how to create and file your articles of organization. After those are filed, you have to do a couple of things to complete the conversion.

In most states, such as Nevada, you file three things to convert your business from a limited partnership or corporation to an LLC:

- ✔ **Plan of conversion:** You have to create this document because it lays out exactly how everything will be moved from one entity to another, what the new articles of organization are going to say, how the new entity is going to be structured, and so on; however, only some states require it to be submitted to the Secretary of State's office. I recommend that you involve your attorney in the process of creating your plan of conversion.

✔ **Articles of conversion:** Normally, this is just one or two pages with some basic information, such as the name and entity type of the old and new entities, the updated company addresses, and the date that the conversion is to be effective.

✔ **Articles of organization:** These are the articles that create your new LLC. In Chapters 6 and 8, I go into detail on how to create and file these articles. Go through the same process as you would for a regular LLC and just include the articles of conversion and the plan of conversion.

All of these filings are relatively simple and intuitive. The most difficult document is probably your plan of conversion because of the amount of detail involved. The plan of conversion is not only legally required in most states when doing a statutory conversion, but it's also a good idea for you to have one for the sake of having a blueprint to go by. As I'm sure you know, things can get chaotic in business, and balls can be dropped. A plan of conversion keeps everything on track so the conversion runs smoothly and without a glitch, or even worse — a day of missed work!

These filings shouldn't be too expensive. I suggest figuring in the cost of filing the articles of organization (which is listed by state in Appendix A) plus a couple hundred dollars.

When you are going through the conversion process, you must be diligent to document *everything*. You can't let anything slip through the cracks. Just consider what would happen if you are sued and audited — are you comfortable with how organized and thorough your records are?

What to Do After the Conversion

It's official. Your business is a limited liability company. Congrats! So now what happens? First, you must amend all your official documents — your licenses, permits, and registrations — with your new name and entity type. Even if you are using the same name as before, you must be careful never to refer to your company without having "LLC," "L.L.C.," or "Limited Liability Company" after the name. Most states legally require this anyway; however, if you're ever taken to court, you'll be able to prove that you were operating as an LLC when transacting business.

Some of the common licenses and permits that you'll need to update or refile are:

✔ Your tax identification number

✔ Your state business registration/license

✔ Your sales tax permit

✔ Your DBA (fictitious firm name) filings

✔ Your city and/or county business license

✔ Any professional licenses or permits

After your official documents are amended, you must prepare a brand-new operating agreement for your LLC. Don't assume that you can use your corporate bylaws or your current partnership agreement as your operating agreement — you shouldn't. Your new operating agreement can be adapted from these agreements; however, you need a document that is specifically tailored to your brand-new LLC. Go through the steps in Chapter 9 to create your custom operating agreement.

Transferring your assets

After the LLC is set up, you must begin transferring the assets. As I describe in the section "The Drawbacks of Conversion" earlier in this chapter, this can be an expensive proposition in some cases — especially if you're transferring assets from a corporation where you may have to pay some pretty hefty taxes on them once you take them into your possession. This entire process can be taxing (literally!). Earlier in the chapter, under the "Looking at ways to minimize taxes" section, I go into some ways that you can alleviate the tax burden.

After the assets are out of the old company and in your hands personally, you can invest those assets into the new LLC in exchange for membership shares. LLCs make this process pretty easy. Contributing assets to an LLC is a tax-free event, so you don't have to worry about that. However, you should still work with an accountant or attorney to help make sure the process goes smoothly from beginning to end.

While you are going through the process of transferring assets and moving operations from one entity to another, you should work closely with your tax advisor and small-business attorney. Although you may find the suggestions in this book useful, you need to coordinate the actual execution of the conversion with a professional who knows your business.

Dissolving your old entity

After your new LLC is set up and all of the assets and contracts have been transferred, you can begin winding up the affairs and dissolving your old business structure.

In some states, before a partnership can be terminated, it must publish a *notice of termination* in a local newspaper. This public notice may even be required before the conversion can be effective. To find out whether this is the case in your state, call your Secretary of State's office. I put a list of contact information for every state in Appendix A.

If your old entity was a limited partnership or corporation, then you must file a *certificate of dissolution* (also called a *certificate of cancellation*) with the Secretary of State's office. This terminates your old entity in the eyes of the state and keeps old ghosts, such as company creditors, from haunting you. An officer, director, or member of the company must sign off on it, and it can only be filed after all of the company's owners approve. To make sure the dissolution is legal and thorough, you should be sure to hold a meeting, document the meeting minutes, and have all owners sign the company resolution to dissolve. In Chapter 11, I show you how to properly hold meetings and prepare meeting minutes.

Before you can file a dissolution with the state, you must make sure that the company is in good standing with the Secretary of State's office and that no fees are due. You must also make sure that the company has paid its taxes. If the entity isn't in good standing, it's likely that the certificate of dissolution will be rejected.

If your previous business structure was a sole proprietorship or general partnership, then you don't need to complete any special filings. You just need to make sure that you don't accidentally revert to your old ways and put contracts, notes, correspondence, and debts in your own name.

Chapter 8

Making Your LLC Official: Filing with the State

In This Chapter
▶ Filing your articles of organization with the state
▶ Applying for your state and local business licenses
▶ Obtaining permits for your business

*F*iling your articles of organization with the Secretary of State can be an exciting process. After you receive your file-stamped articles, that's it, you're in business! You'll most likely start thinking about all the things you need to do to get your business up and running: marketing your business, hiring employees, renting office space.

I know this time can be chaotic, but you need to take a couple of days and make sure you start off on the right foot with the federal, state, and local governments. You need to complete other applications and filings for things like business licenses before you can begin operations. That's what I discuss in this chapter.

When it comes to filing your articles of organization (which I show you how to do in the next couple of pages) and your applications for your various licenses, the task may seem overwhelming at times — especially if you are in a heavily regulated industry. But keep your chin up. If you stay organized and use the last sections of this chapter to figure out what licenses you need, you should be able to get all of your applications submitted within a couple of days. After you submit everything correctly, you can sit back and wait for your approvals to start rolling in.

Filing Your Articles

If you're interested in the how-to's of filing, then you've probably created your articles of organization by now. Therefore, why wait? Let's get 'em filed!

After all, your LLC can't come into existence until it's been approved by the Secretary of State. Just think of the date that your articles of organization are stamped with as your company's official birth date. If you're ever asked what your date of organization is, you'll refer to this date (called the *formation date*) — not the date that you draft the articles, nor the date that you received the filed articles in the mail. Along with your filed articles, you should receive a company charter that shows the date of formation.

In the following sections, I go over the step-by-step process of filing your articles of organization.

Until your articles of organization are actually filed at the Secretary of State's office and the formation date has been set, you and your partners are fully liable for any business debts that arise before this time. It's as if you are operating as a general partnership (see Chapter 2). If you get sued in this time and lose, nothing stops the winner of the lawsuit from taking your home and emptying your personal bank accounts.

Submitting the filing

So you have your prepared articles of organization in hand (see Chapter 6), and now you're ready to file them. Please, *please* take the time to do a bit of research to make sure you file your articles properly. When you follow the filing steps to the letter, you save yourself a lot of time and headaches later because your filing won't be rejected. From my personal experiences of working with Secretary of State's offices, I can't tell you how often they get filings and have to reject them for silly reasons — the fee amount is incorrect or the organizer only sent in one copy . . . . The list goes on and on.

To file your articles, the first thing you need to do is to go on your Secretary of State's Web site (I've provided the Web addresses for each state in Appendix A) and determine a few things, such as

- ✔ What fees are required?
- ✔ Whom do you make the check out to?
- ✔ Can you pay with a credit card?
- ✔ Are you allowed to fax the copies in?
- ✔ How many copies are required?
- ✔ Where do you mail the documents to?
- ✔ Are any cover sheets required to be submitted with the articles?

After you've answered these questions and double-checked your filing against the state's filing procedures, you should make a copy of the articles (for your own files), put a copy of the articles and anything else the state requires in an envelope (Don't forget to include the fee to the state! You can view the filing fees in your particular state in Appendix A.), and mail them. I always recommend sending your filing packet by a service that requires the recipient to sign for the package.

Waiting (and waiting and waiting) on the approval process

You're eager to put your business plan into action. Your first official day of work with your new company is planned out in your head. And of course, the one thing holding you up is the government.

After you've sent in your articles and payment, the Secretary of State's office can generally take as long as it wants to file your articles of organization. Don't be alarmed if six weeks later you still haven't heard back. Some states, such as California, can take up to three months if you file by mail.

In some cases, you can file the articles of organization in person and get moved much further ahead in line. If you can't file personally because you're in a different state, you can always have your registered agent do it for you. (See Chapter 5 for details about registered agents.) For other ways to speed up the approval process, see the next section.

After the Secretary of State's office has approved your articles, you'll receive your file-stamped articles back in the mail. Attached to your filed articles, you'll normally receive a *company charter.* This one-page document shows the all-important date of formation. The charter and the file-stamped articles of organization are your proof that your business is formed as an LLC in your state.

When you don't want to hurry up and wait: Fast-forwarding your filing

Some states will actually put your filing at the top of the pile! Depending on the state, you may be able to expedite the processing of your articles of organization. Some states give you the option of getting your articles back within 48 hours, 24 hours, or even the same day!

When submitting expedited articles, you should label the outside of the envelope with "Expedited Handling Required." It's also a good idea to put a sticky note on your document that says the same thing.

Although this seems like a perfect scenario, beware that the fee for this quick turnaround can range from an extra $10 to hundreds of dollars — call your Secretary of State's office or visit its Web site (listed in Appendix A) to find out the exact cost. Also, keep in mind that if your articles of organization aren't perfect and are rejected as a result, you're still required to pay the expedited processing fee.

Dealing with a rejected filing

When you receive a large envelope from the Secretary of State's office and you open it, expecting to see your filed articles, but instead see a rejection-of-filing notice, your heart will sink. It's a bummer when your articles are rejected — especially when you can't wait to get your business up and rolling.

Although this can be a setback, don't get too down about it. Nothing bad will happen. You just need to fix the problem and resubmit your documents. The rejection notice should tell you what the problem is. If the notice isn't specific enough, call the number listed on the form for your Secretary of State's office and ask them for more information.

The worst part of a rejection is that a small error can be time consuming to fix because you may need to wait at the end of the line. For instance, if your documents took three weeks to be reviewed by a clerk the first time, then after you resubmit them, they may go to the bottom of the pile, and you'll have to wait another three weeks to get them looked at. (Of course, you can always take the expedited route if your state offers it. See the previous section for the skinny on this.)

The Secretary of State may reject a filing for any number of reasons. Here are a few mistakes applicants make and how you can avoid them:

- **The name you want to use conflicts with another LLC (or other entity) that is formed in that state, or a name that has been reserved.** In this case, you just need to choose a new name. If you don't want to do that, you can contact the competing firm and try to get a letter from them giving you permission to use their name, but this is usually a long shot.

- **The name is considered misleading.** The name may have forbidden words, such as "banking," "financial," and so on. You can do two things in this situation:

    - You can go to the department in your state that regulates that industry and get approval for the wording from them. (You'll probably have to jump through a lot of hoops.)

    - You can change your company's name.

✔ **Your filing fees could be incorrect.** In this case, just write a check for the additional filing fees and resubmit your documents. Or, if the state returned your old check to you, void it and send a new one for the correct amount.

✔ **You may not have specified a registered agent.** This is a common error. Often when individuals form an LLC, they don't know what a registered agent is or does, so they leave this section blank. But you won't have this problem because you can read Chapter 5 for more information on these folks and then fill in the appropriate section on the form.

✔ **A provision is missing.** In this case, you most likely prepared the documents yourself, and you missed a *provision* (a section of the document that deals with a particular topic) that is legally required to be in the articles of organization. In this case, just add the provision to your articles (you can create a fresh draft so they look nice) and resubmit them.

✔ **You are missing a cover sheet.** Some states require cover sheets to be submitted with the articles. In this case, obtain the cover sheet from the Secretary of State's Web site, fill it out, and resubmit your articles with the cover sheet.

Filing Your Initial Report and Other Legal Requirements

So, you thought that you'd just file your articles of organization and you'd be finished, right? Not so fast. You aren't quite in the clear yet. After you file your articles, you have to do a couple of things to make sure you remain in compliance with the Secretary of State's office. I give you the rundown in the following sections.

Although this may seem like a trivial thing, if you don't file your initial report, your LLC could go into a *revoked status* relatively quickly. Often, the state doesn't even tell you that your company has been revoked; you may not even find out until you've been sued and realize that you don't have the LLC protection that you thought you had!

Starting with your initial report

In addition to filing your articles of organization, most states require you to file an initial report, also called an "initial list of managers or members" or an "information statement." Depending on the state, the initial report lists information such as

✔ The names of your managers and their addresses

✔ The name of your registered agent and your registered office address

✔ The members who own the LLC

Keep in mind that whatever you include on your initial report is *public record,* which means that anyone in the world can see it.

You'll most likely have to file this report annually or biannually, depending on the state. These subsequent reports are normally called *annual reports.*

The fees for the initial reports can be hefty — sometimes as much as the fee for filing the articles of organization. Also, unlike the articles of organization, where there can be a separate *organizer* (a person who files your articles but otherwise has nothing else to do with your company), a manager or member of the LLC needs to sign the initial report.

Filing public announcements in Arizona and New York

Two states — Arizona and New York — require you to file a public announcement of your articles of organization in a newspaper or other daily or weekly publication.

If you're setting up an LLC in Arizona, follow these steps to file the public announcement:

1. **After filing your articles of organization with the Arizona Corporation Commission, you must publish the entire text of your articles in a newspaper of your choice (as long as the periodical is published at least weekly and has at least 5,000 or so subscribers) for three consecutive days within 60 days of your filing date.**

2. **File your *affidavit of publication,* given to you by the newspaper, with the commission within 60 days.**

The affidavit of publication tells the state that you submitted your articles for print.

3. **Your LLC goes into effect only after the affidavit of publication has been filed.**

If you're setting up an LLC in New York, follow these steps for the public announcement:

1. **After filing your articles of organization with the New York Department of State, your articles must be published in two separate newspapers once per week for six consecutive weeks.**

Your county clerk's office will choose the newspapers that your articles will be published in.

2. **After publication, the newspapers will give you a signed affidavit of publication.**

3. **File the affidavit with the department of state within 120 days of the LLC's filing date.**

So, do you need to file an updated report and pay a filing fee whenever the information changes? Not really. In most states, you're only required to file the report on its due date (normally on the anniversary of the LLC's filing date). Not only does this save fees, but it's also a good way for LLCs to protect their owners' privacy. You see, if an LLC lists certain members during the time that the annual report is filed, it can add or change the original members of the company after the report has been filed (see Chapter 10 to learn how to transfer membership interests). No other report needs to be filed until the next annual or biannual due date. For more information on annual reports, see Chapter 11.

Business licenses: A necessary evil

Most states require that all businesses apply for a standard *business license.* This is the "letter of approval," so to speak, that you need to legally conduct business within the state. The state tax board uses the licenses to keep track of all enterprises that are responsible for paying state and sales or use taxes.

Believe it or not, in addition to the state license, you may also be required to file for a city and/or county license, depending on where you live. If your business is located within city limits, you need to obtain a license from the city; if outside, you must obtain your license from the county. Depending on where you live, you should contact your county clerk's office or the city's business license department and ask which local licenses and permits you need to obtain. Keep in mind that you'll most likely be required to pay an annual fee.

When it comes to business licenses, each state is somewhat different as far as what details it wants. Normally, you can expect a business license to request such information as

- ✔ Business name
- ✔ Business address
- ✔ Type of ownership
- ✔ Kind of business
- ✔ Formation date
- ✔ Federal tax identification number (see the section by the same name later in this chapter)
- ✔ Business activities
- ✔ Expected income
- ✔ Names and addresses of managers/members

To find out where to obtain the business license application and where your application must be filed, check the Secretary of State's Web site for the state you filed in.

If the ownership of your business changes, most states require that the new owners apply for a new business license under their name, even if the business name stays the same. Moving your business to a new address also usually requires a new business license application. Essentially, you just refile the form with the updated information. If a change doesn't significantly alter the structure of the business (such as adding or dropping a member who only owns a small percentage of the LLC), you normally don't have to file a new application. However, some states require you to submit a letter to the business license department describing the change that took place. The department uses the information to update your business license.

Applying for a sales and use tax permit

If you're selling tangible items, then you're required to collect sales tax from your customers and then pay the government. What is a *tangible good?* Although the definition may vary slightly between states, you can pretty much classify a tangible good as being any item that may be seen, weighed, measured, felt, or touched, or is in any other manner perceptible to the senses. Real estate is excluded.

What if you aren't selling tangible goods? What if you run a dry-cleaning service or a dog-grooming facility? Aren't you in the clear? Well, in some states, you are. Unfortunately, in many states, you are still most likely required to go through the process of obtaining a sales and use tax permit.

The board of equalization directs pretty much all small businesses to apply for a sales and use tax permit. You see, state governments prefer that individuals aren't the ones deciding whether they are liable for paying sales and use tax. The government prefers that a seasoned tax collector take over the job.

Most states call the department that collects the state taxes the *board of equalization.* (I have no idea what that means or why they decided to use such a dumb name — I suspect they decided that "the board of tax collectors" didn't sound so friendly. All I know is that a lot of people pay this department a hefty chunk of dough every quarter.)

To collect sales tax on the products you sell to your customers, you need a sales and use tax permit. What's the difference between sales tax and use tax? I'll explain.

> ✔ **Sales tax** is imposed on all retailers (anyone who sells tangible goods — not services — in the state). Retailers are required to pay and report sales

taxes to the board of equalization, and they have the option of collecting sales tax reimbursement from their customers at the time of the sale.

✔ **Use tax** is imposed on you when you purchase something from out-of-state vendors and use, consume, or store the item in the state. Use tax also applies if you lease the item. Ha! And you thought you were avoiding tax when you bought that fancy TV off of eBay.

You are normally imposed a statewide sales tax and a local sales tax that differs from city to city. If your business isn't located in an incorporated city, then you'll be required to pay the county at its local tax rate. By combining the state and local tax rates, you come up with the amount of sales tax you can charge your customers.

Although applying for the state sales and use tax permit can seem like a hassle, especially if you're a service-based organization, I urge you not to fall short on your obligation. Apply once, and then file your annual sales and use tax reports right and file on time. If you can't do it, pay your accountant or incorporating company to do it. Just make sure it gets done.

Trust me, you don't want to go through the harrowing experience of having a state tax auditor set up shop in your office for two weeks so he can pore over each and every income and expenditure record, tallying up use tax on sticky notes you bought online and sales tax on small thank-you items you shipped to your clients. Not only will the auditor pull every single penny of unpaid taxes out of the woodwork, but the state will impose hefty fines on top of it all. Needless to say, not fun.

Special licensing requirements

If you are one of the lucky ones who decided to set up shop in a heavily regulated industry, such as health care, gambling, auto repair, or the law, then you're probably going to be required to obtain special licensing. If you own your own building, you have to comply with building codes and obtain special permits. If you deal with any sort of food products, then health-code regulations come into play. Now that I think about it . . . if you're in business at all, you should read this section. I'm sure you'll find one thing or another that applies to you!

In the following pages, I go over some common special licenses that you may have to obtain. All states are different, though, and I can't possibly list every single license required in every single state! Before starting business operations, you should give your state's licensing bureau a call. They should be able to point you in the right direction!

In most states, because you'll be filing so many documents with so many different state and local agencies, you'll be assigned a nine-digit *UBI* (Universal Business Identifier) *number* upon filing your state business license. This is so all state and local agencies can easily identify you. You use this number on all of your state and local filings. A UBI number is sometimes called a "tax registration number," a "business registration number," or a "business license number."

State-issued licenses

In addition to the basic licenses required for most businesses, you may be required to file for other licenses, depending on your state. Here are a few that you may be required to apply for:

- ✔ **Licenses based on type of product sold:** Most states require you to obtain a license if you're selling certain products, such as liquor, tobacco, lottery tickets, gasoline, and firearms. These licenses can be hard to obtain and are often heavily regulated.

- ✔ **Professional/occupational licenses:** If you (and/or your employees) will be offering services in a specialized area that requires certain skills or training, then you, personally, and each of your employees performing that service will be required to obtain a specific license before opening shop. Some occupations that often require licensing are

    - Medical care — doctors, dentists, and so on

    - Auto repair

    - Real estate sales

    - Contractors

    - Cosmetology

    - Tax services

    - Legal representation/attorneys

- ✔ **Licenses for other regulated businesses:** Every state has industries they like to control. These vary widely from state to state, which is one reason for you to do your research. Some industries that may require additional licensing include: jewelry manufacturing and sales, furniture sales, automobile repairs, carnival operators, tree trimmers, motorcycle sales, auto towing, dating services, swimming pool services, janitorial services, taxicabs, movie and television productions, dance clubs, and adult entertainment-related businesses.

Locally issued permits

Some licenses aren't regulated by the state, but instead are issued by the local government, such as your city or your county. Here are a few licenses to be on the lookout for:

✔ **Fire department permits:** For those businesses that attract a large number of customers, such as nightclubs, bars, and restaurants, the fire department must conclude that the location is clear of any fire and safety hazards.

✔ **Health department permits:** These permits are most often required for businesses that prepare and/or sell food, or any other business where the health of the general public is a primary concern.

✔ **Property use permits:** If you start a business that involves manufacturing, or if you decide to operate a retail-type business out of your home, depending on your location, you may need to obtain a *land-use permit* from your city or county's zoning department that says you can use the land for something other than residential purposes.

✔ **Building permits:** If you're constructing a new building or expanding or renovating an existing building, you will need to obtain a *building permit* from the city or county. Getting a building permit can take years, and you probably will have to submit a detailed set of plans to the department and work with your builder to gain approval.

✔ **Zoning permit:** Some cities require that all new businesses get a *zoning compliance permit* before they open. This proves that you aren't operating a business out of a location that is zoned for residential use only. Some locales are even more complicated. For instance, you may only operate a retail store out of a property that is zoned specifically for retail.

✔ **Home occupation permit:** If your business is home-based, you may be required to obtain this permit when you file for your business license. It allows the state to keep track of which employees are working in what type of environment and whether your family members are involved in the business.

✔ **Use and occupancy permit:** In most states, when you apply for your business license, you must also apply for a *use and occupancy permit* from the building department (or equivalent in your state). This normally results in the building inspector (and possibly the fire inspector) visiting your business location to get an idea of what sort of conditions employees will be working under. This person looks out for the interests of the people working at the location and checks for things such as fire hazards, life safety issues, code compliance, building permits, zoning issues, and so on.

Federally issued licenses

If you are in a heavily regulated industry, then a federal license in your area of expertise may be required. This lets the public know that not only do you know your stuff, but you are also a reputable company operating under the watchful eye of the government. Here are some industries that are required to operate under special federal-issued licenses:

✔ **Selling securities or providing investment advice:** You are required to be licensed by the U.S. Securities and Exchange Commission (www.sec. gov). If you are only selling *securities* (your membership shares in exchange for capital investment) and are looking for a small number of investors, you may be exempt. See Chapter 10 for more information on registration exemptions.

✔ **Interstate trucking or any other form of interstate transportation:** You are required to be licensed by the U.S. Department of Transportation (www.dot.gov).

✔ **Preparation of meat products or other food stuffs:** You are required to be licensed by the U.S. Food and Drug Administration (www.fda.gov).

✔ **Manufacturing of tobacco, alcohol, or firearms, or the selling of firearms:** You are required to be licensed by the U.S. Bureau of Alcohol, Tobacco, and Firearms (www.atf.gov).

✔ **Radio or television broadcasting:** You are required to be licensed by the Federal Communications Commission (www.fcc.gov).

✔ **Manufacturing, testing, and/or selling of drugs:** You are required to be licensed by the U.S. Food and Drug Administration (www.fda.gov).

If you require federal licensing before being allowed to open your business, consider having your small-business attorney guide you through the application process. The applications can often be lengthy, and you'll want to make sure you do everything correctly because whether you are approved or not can make or break your business.

Other pertinent requirements

Ha! And you thought you were finished! You're dealing with the government here, remember? Between the federal, state, city, and country requirements, the paperwork is never-ending. Regardless, there are two more things that all businesses *must* handle. The first is your federal tax identification number — you won't get very far without it! Second is your workers' compensation insurance — don't even *think* about hiring employees until this is taken care of.

Federal tax identification number

All businesses must obtain an *employer identification number* ("EIN" for short, but also called a "tax identification number," or "tax ID" for short) from the Internal Revenue Service. The IRS uses this number to identify your LLC when it pays its taxes. Over the years, the EIN has become an important number for the government, financial institutions, and other businesses to identify different entities. After all, an LLC in Georgia can have the same name as your LLC in California — how would Uncle Sam be able to tell them apart? Think of it as a sort of Social Security number for your enterprise.

Some attorneys, accountants, and incorporating companies may charge you an arm and a leg to obtain this number for you, but you're smarter than that. Forget paying anyone! You can obtain an EIN immediately online at www.irs.gov. Do it now! It will be virtually impossible to obtain credit, pay taxes, or even open a bank account without one.

Workers' compensation insurance

Workers' compensation insurance is required of any business that has employees. Workers' compensation insurance protects employees in the event that they get injured on the job and can't work or have medical expenses that need to be paid. This insurance is provided by private insurance companies but is required by law for each employee who works for you.

Filings for LLCs Operating in Multiple States

When you're operating in multiple states, you'll probably be required to go through the same filing process for each and every state you are doing business in. If you don't have a physical location in that state, some filings may not be required, such as building permits; however, others, such as initial reports and business licenses, are still necessary. If you aren't sure about the requirements of transacting business in multiple states, read Chapter 5.

Because all of these filings can be extremely time consuming when you're operating in multiple jurisdictions that you aren't familiar with, I recommend that you have your registered agent in those states handle these filings for you. (For more about registered agents, see Chapter 5.)

Submitting several initial reports

In all states in which you *foreign file* (registering to do business in states besides the one in which your LLC was formed), you need to file an initial report. You need to make sure that the information you submit in one state on your initial report is the same information that you submit in another state. When you're doing so many filings in other states, sometimes it is hard to remember that your LLC is still only one entity with one set of members and one federal tax identification number.

Obtaining multiple business licenses

If you are foreign filed in multiple states, you need to apply for your state and local business licenses. Determine what your local jurisdiction is (your city or county) by whatever your corporate office address is in that state. If you're using your registered agent's address as your corporate office address, then you'll use that zip code to find what local agency you'll need to register with. Your registered agent should have this information for you.

If you're selling tangible goods and will be paying sales tax, you definitely need to open up a separate bank account for that state. Keep your sales receipts for each state separate so you know which state to pay sales tax to.

Part III
Running Your Brand-New LLC

The 5th Wave   By Rich Tennant

"You can file as a limited liability company in this State, but you'll be subject to a 'Not So Fast, Buddy' franchise fee."

In this part . . .

After your entity is formed, you get into the real meat-and-potatoes stuff — namely, how to run your LLC. First and foremost, you'll have to create an operating agreement, which I show you how to do in Chapter 9. Your operating agreement is the backbone of your business, so it's important not to skip this chapter.

Then, in Chapter 10, you'll discover everything you need to know about the ownership of your company — called *membership*. Before you know it, you'll be printing off membership certificates, raising capital for business operations, and arranging hostile takeovers. Whoa! Hold your horses, Warren Buffett — I was just kidding about that last one!

In Chapter 11, I get into how to keep your company records so your LLC stays in good standing with your members, the government, and your customers. Then, in Chapter 12, I address the sad eventuality that nothing gold stays and explain what to do when you gotta close up shop and dissolve your LLC.

Chapter 9

ABCs of Setting Up Your Operating Agreement

. . . .

In This Chapter

▶ Knowing the ins and outs of the operating agreement

▶ Customizing your operating agreement

▶ Creating the finished product

. . . .

*Y*our *operating agreement* is the backbone of your business. It governs how you decide your company's important issues and how you manage your business's internal affairs. Should a cataclysmic event happen, such as the passing of one of your partners, you (and the courts!) will look to your operating agreement for guidance.

Like partnership agreements or corporate bylaws, your operating agreement is your organization's blueprint. Just think of your business as a house, and your operating agreement as the framing. It is a governing constitution, of sorts, for your LLC. It puts all of the managers and members on the same page in regard to how the company is to operate. The document itself doesn't have to be too long or drawn out — it simply delineates the relationships between the LLC and its members, managers, and the public (its customers).

You can easily customize your operating agreement by choosing different provisions that fit your business and wrap them all up in the format that I provide for you in this chapter.

What is an Operating Agreement?

Ever want to make up your own laws? Just disregard the ones that the government imposes on you and decide how you want to behave? I know it sounds too good to be true, but believe it or not, LLCs make that a possibility. You may never have gone to law school, but now you can single-handedly operate as the legislative branch of your own LLC. You see, LLCs are often allowed to use their operating agreement to "replace" state LLC law. For the most part, if you place something in your operating agreement that contradicts your state's LLC statutes, your operating agreement will almost always win in the event of a lawsuit or disagreement among members.

Although the articles of organization can be created pretty easily on your own (see Chapter 6), I encourage you to involve your small-business attorney in the process of creating your operating agreement. I provide most of the *provisions* (various sections of the agreement that deal with specific topics) in this chapter and even show you how to put your operating agreement together, but you may need some legal guidance regarding which provisions to include and how to structure your LLC. If anything, an attorney can provide a sounding board in your negotiations with your partners and, with his opinion, may make the process easier and less argumentative. Just make sure that your attorney is well versed in LLC state and case law, and that he doesn't make the document so complicated and dense that you and your partners can't easily understand it.

LLC operating agreements aren't required by most states, but if you ask me, you'd be a fool not to have one. After all, would you really want all of your partners, managers, and employees making up their own rules as they go along, without any preapproved structure and rules to abide by? See "Why have an operating agreement?" later in this chapter.

Examining what the operating agreement governs

Operating agreements generally don't get into specific issues such as minor employment matters and the day-to-day business operations (with the exception of major decisions and/or purchases). You won't look at your operating agreement to see what sort of commission structure you should impose on your new sales reps. Nor should you look at your operating agreement to tell you what credit terms or payment plans you can give to your clients.

Your operating agreement covers the bigger issues, such as large purchases, the decisions to take on debt, profit and loss distributions, selling membership shares, and assignment of duties. It paints the big picture as to how your entity is to operate. If you are a small business, creating an operating agreement may seem like overkill now, but it's necessary. As you grow, you'll need guidance, and you should be able to turn to your operating agreement. If you and your partners negotiate and decide on everything in the beginning, then you'll most likely experience less chaos and fewer disagreements when your company hangs in the balance.

Assigning manager titles and duties

Regardless of whether your LLC is manager-managed or member-managed, some managers will still need guidance. Forming your operating agreement is the perfect time for you and your partners to sit down and delineate all of the specific roles and titles that each manager will take on. For instance, one manager may be great at numbers and will take on the role of chief financial officer, while another manager may have a solid vision of the company and is the person to lead the others on the path to success — this person can be named president or chief executive officer.

Keep in mind that while managers are legally called "managers" by the state, they can have whatever titles they want. So don't think you're missing out on the title of president or CEO if you're forming an LLC!

Outlining members' rights

After you have laid down the law as far as managers are concerned, what about the members? Members have responsibilities also, and your operating agreement needs to specify their roles in the company. With LLCs, you can create your own rules, and, if you choose, you can limit or expand your members' powers.

LLCs can have different classes of membership, so all members don't have to be treated the same. Some members can get voting rights, while other members have to remain silent on all issues. Some members can also be managers and take charge of the company's day-to-day issues, while others can only watch from afar.

Also, don't forget that members have certain powers that are inherent to owning the company, such as deciding who manages the LLC and whether to accept new members. You can also make the issuance of membership shares to a certain member contingent upon the member fulfilling his duties.

Why have an operating agreement?

Although an operating agreement is optional and not required by law, you should never run your company without one. With all of the paperwork you already have to deal with, I know it's tempting to write this off, but don't. If you ever go to court, all of your documentation will be revealed, and the judge will likely look to your company's operating agreement for guidance in the event of a dispute. If you don't have an operating agreement, you leave yourself open to being judged by your state's statutes — which you have no control over — and you probably won't like the outcome. You want your LLC to be governed by *your* rules, not those created by a state legislator who has no interest in your business or, most likely, business in general.

The easiest way for me to convince you of the necessity of an operating agreement is to describe what it would be like without one. Here are a couple of scenarios of what could happen if you face problems in your business sans The Agreement:

- One of your members passes away, and his family wants to step in and take control of your business. Without an operating agreement with a provision protecting the surviving partners, you could end up losing everything that you have worked so hard for to a partner's relative who knows nothing about your industry.

- You and your partner, each owning half of the company, decide to give your partner's assistant 2 percent of the company for her loyalty and service. One day you come back from vacation to find that the company has been liquidated and dissolved in your absence. When you go to your attorney to see what can be done, you find out that because your LLC had no operating agreement that stated that all members need to agree for dissolution to occur, state law prevailed. Unfortunately for you, your state law says that a company can be dissolved with only a majority of the members agreeing. Your partner and his assistant outvoted you while you were away.

Although oral agreements may hold up in most states, I wouldn't rely on them in lieu of a written operating agreement. Oral agreements are not only subject to different interpretations by the members, but are often taken with a grain of salt by the court system. In other words, if two members disagree, the so-called "agreement" can be completely disregarded in the event of a lawsuit.

Operating agreements for single-member LLCs

Is your LLC a single-member LLC that is owned only by you? Although it may go against common logic that you need an operating agreement — after all, why would you need to create your own rules just for yourself? — it's even more imperative that you, the single-member LLC owner, have one. If you are ever taken to court, your operating agreement will ensure that your personal veil of limited liability (see Chapter 11 for more on the veil of limited liability) remains intact.

You see, a one-person LLC looks a lot like a sole proprietorship; therefore, anything you can do to look and act like an LLC (or even a corporation, for that matter) will prevent the courts from deciding that you are liable for the lawsuit as a sole proprietor would be. In other words, you want every piece of proof you can get that establishes your LLC as being a completely separate entity.

Making up the rules as you go can be *bad*

Imagine a game of *Monopoly* where all of the players played by their own rules. It wouldn't take long before chaos would ensue. Some players would be dishing themselves cash every time they roll the dice; others might send the other players to jail as they pass them on the board. When the time came for the players to justify their behavior, they would all say the same thing: "There are no rules, so shut your trap." or "Whaddya gonna do about it?!" or "Make me!" or . . . well, you get the picture.

But the business world isn't a game of *Monopoly*—there are consequences. If all the partners were to run around doing whatever they felt like doing without getting proper approval from the other partners, it could spell the end of your business. Yes, you could try to settle everything in court, but without a written operating agreement, the plaintiff could say that there was a verbal agreement. In that case, the judge has to decide who's right and who's wrong, and it could be very hard to tell which way the wind will blow. So, you gotta ask yourself — why go through that hassle?

After you and your partners agree on and adopt an operating agreement, everyone knows where their boundaries are. And when issues pop up, you have a guideline on how to deal with the situation. You can rest assured that your business is safe from all kinds of internal disputes that can land you in court.

Establishing Your Provisions

You pretty much have all the freedom in the world when creating your LLC; you just have to state what you want in the operating agreement. Your operating agreement is composed of different parts, which are called *provisions*. Each provision deals with a different topic relating to your company, such as how it is managed or how new members are admitted.

Unfortunately, people are often intimidated by all of the legalese, so they don't create the agreement for fear of saying something wrong or using incorrect terminology. If you feel this way, just remember that something is better than nothing. The agreement doesn't have to be perfect — just do your best. And, don't forget, you can always ask your small-business attorney for guidance.

To make things easy for you, this section includes some provisions that you can use when creating your operating agreement. For the most part, you can pick and choose which ones you want. First, I give you a good outline for the operating agreement, and then I follow with sections containing some details about parts of the outline. Again, you can pick and choose (as well as change!) the provisions in the document so they apply to your business. Here's your outline:

I. Organization

    A. Formation and Qualification

    B. Name

    C. Principle Office

    D. Governing Law

    E. Term

    F. Registered Agent & Office

    G. Purpose of the Company

II. Membership Interests

    A. Initial Members of the Company

    B. Percentage of Ownership

    C. Membership Classifications

    D. Management by Members (if Member-Managed)

    E. New Members

    F. Capital Accounts

    G. Liability of Members

    H. Transfer and Assignment of Interests

III. Allocations and Profit Distributions

    A. Allocations of Profits and Losses

    B. Distributions

IV. Meetings & Voting

    A. Notice of Meetings

    B. Quorum

    C. Meetings

    D. Voting

    E. Proxies

V. Management & Duties

    A. Election

    B. Delegation of Powers

    C. Compensation

    D. Indemnification

VI. Miscellaneous

    A. Books and Records

    B. Financial Records and Reporting

    C. Indemnification Clause

    D. Dispute Resolution

    E. Dissolution

Organization

You might as well just copy and paste the text from your articles of organization (see Chapter 6) and put it in this section of your operating agreement because, for the most part, that's all it is. The Organization section just reviews the items you already decided on in the articles of organization. You see, your articles were most likely signed and submitted by an organizer who, for the most part, has no actual involvement in your business. By placing this information in your operating agreement, you tell the world that all members and managers of the LLC are in full agreement with the terms outlined in the articles of organization that were filed with the state.

In this section, you should include such provisions as the name of your LLC (under the subheading "Name"), your LLC's main office address (under the subheading "Principle Office"), the state in which your LLC was formed in and whose laws your LLC will abide by (under the subheading "Governing Law"), how long your LLC is to remain in existence (under the subheading "Term"), the name and address of your registered agent in all states your LLC is transacting business in (under the subheading "Registered Agent and Office"), and, lastly, the purposes for which your LLC was formed (under the subheading "Purpose of the Company"). Of course, all operating agreements are different and these subheadings are interchangeable, so feel free to arrange your information however you like — as long as it's there!

View the sample operating agreement on the CD to see how the Organization section is laid out.

Membership Interests

It's mandatory for your LLC to have one or more members. Members are the owners of the company. An LLC without members is like a child without parents — it just doesn't work! Your members are usually the ones who invested their money or time in the business in the first place because they believed in the idea. When a lot of people have a lot at stake, emotions are bound to get involved, and people tend to act irrationally. That's why you need to create some guidelines from the get-go that clearly delineate what each member's responsibilities are and what they can and cannot do.

Also, many situations come up that can be fatal to the business if they aren't dealt with properly. These also need to be addressed in the operating agreement so that there is a contingency plan that allows the business to not just stay afloat, but also prosper. A few questions that need to be addressed in this section are:

- How can a member sell or transfer his membership shares?
- What happens when a member gets divorced, passes away, or goes bankrupt?
- What happens when a member wants to retire?
- How can the company take on more members, if needed?
- How can the company expel members?
- What sort of contributions are allowed?
- Are there multiple types of members?

In the next few sections, I dive into some of these provisions in more detail. I only address the provisions that are important to customize to your organization and leave the rest for you to copy from the operating agreement I have provided for you on the accompanying CD.

Normally, with other types of partnerships, the document that covers partnership interests and shares is called a *buy-sell agreement.* However, with LLCs, the buy-sell agreement is normally incorporated into the operating agreement. If you have many different rules and provisions for many different members, such as who can transfer membership shares and how, then you should create a separate buy-sell agreement for each member and have him sign it (Chapter 10 has more details on drafting buy-sell agreements). After all, no one says there needs to be one solution for everybody!

Initial Members of the Company

Unlike corporations, where the shares are completely transferable and the shareholders change often, LLCs generally keep the same members that they have from the start. Because of this, you can list the initial member information in the operating agreement. If your LLC has a lot of members, you may want to list them on a separate piece of paper and refer to it as Addendum A.

Here's the information you should include for each member:

- Their full name
- Their home address

> ✔ The type of contribution they made (cash, equipment, services, and so on) and its value
>
> ✔ Membership shares or percentage of the company that was issued to them
>
> ✔ What class of membership shares they were issued (if your operating agreement allows for multiple classes, as shown in the "Membership Classifications" section)

You may also want to have each member sign next to her name. This shows that they concur with the information stated in the operating agreement.

Percentage of Ownership

When discussing how much of an LLC you own, you generally specify what percentage of the company your shares represent. For instance, if you have ten shares and the sum of all of the members' shares (including yours) is 100, then you can safely say that you own 10 percent of the company. Even if your shares are nonvoting and everyone else's are voting (see the next section), you still own 10 percent. Here's a sample provision you can use:

> *A member's ownership of the Company is the total of his Voting Shares and Nonvoting Shares, together with all of the rights that arise from the ownership of such shares. The Percentage of Ownership ("Ownership Percentage") shall be calculated by adding together that Member's membership shares (Voting and Nonvoting) and then dividing this sum by the total of all of the Members' membership shares (Voting and Nonvoting).*

Membership Classifications

LLCs are flexible in that you can give your members as few or as many powers and responsibilities as you want. And all members don't have to be equal! You can classify membership shares by the powers and responsibilities associated with them. One common method (the one that I have outlined in the sample operating agreement) is to have one classification of shares that is voting and one classification that is nonvoting. If you only intend to issue one type in the beginning, but you want the option of issuing the other type of shares in the future, then you can specify this by using the different phrases "The company *shall* issue . . ." and "The company *may* issue . . ."

Here are a few sample provisions you can use:

> *The Company shall issue Class A Voting Membership Shares ("Voting Shares") to the members who vote (the "Voting Members"). The Voting Members shall have the right to vote on all company matters, as outlined in this Agreement.*

> *The Company may issue Class B Nonvoting Membership Shares ("Nonvoting Shares"). Nonvoting Shares hold no voting rights whatsoever, and members who only own Nonvoting Shares will have no right to vote on any matters. Members may hold both Voting Shares and Nonvoting Shares.*

Management by Voting Members

Some businesses have two kinds of partners: operating partners, who manage the day-to-day affairs, and silent partners, who keep their noses out of the daily goings-on. If this is how you've structured your LLC, with only one group of your members doing the managing, do you really want your silent, nonvoting members to be muddling in your daily operations? Not likely.

First, you need to make sure that your LLC is manager-managed (because not all members will have equal say in the management), and then set up two classes of shares. Remember, you can set this up however you want. For this example, I've used voting and nonvoting classes. Then you state that one class shall have full management rights and shall be managers, while the other class has no management rights at all. Here's an example of some provisions that you can draw from:

> The Voting Members shall manage the Company. In their capacity as Managers, they shall have the right to make decisions and vote upon all matters as specified in this Agreement, in proportion to their respective Ownership Percentage of the Company. Voting Members need not identify whether or not they are acting as a Member or a Manager when they take action.

> Nonvoting Members have no right to participate in the management of the Company, nor vote on any matters of the Company. No Nonvoting Member shall take any action or enter into any contract or obligation on behalf of the Company without the prior written consent of all of the Voting Members. Likewise, no Nonvoting Member shall perform any act that is in any way pertaining to the Company or its assets.

New Members

As your company grows, you probably will want to take on new partners. When and how you add these folks is an important element of the operating agreement that you should decide on at the LLC's conception. This section doesn't have to be lengthy, but the provision's wording will be determined by what you and your partners decide.

You may want to consider the following points when drafting this section of your operating agreement:

- Will new members have to make a contribution of any sort? If so, what types of contributions are acceptable?

- How do you determine the value of the shares of the company? This is important to figure out, considering that your company's value may have appreciated since inception. If your company is worth, say, $2 million, you don't want to take on a 50 percent partner with only a $100,000 contribution.

✔ Will the new member be required to sign a copy of the current operating agreement, wherein she agrees to be bound by its terms?

✔ Does the current members' vote have to be unanimous to admit a new member with full voting privileges, or is a majority vote enough?

Here's a sample provision you can use:

> *The Voting Members may issue additional Voting Capital or Nonvoting Capital and thereby admit a new Member or Members, as the case may be, to the Company, only if such new Member (a) is approved unanimously by the Voting Members; (b) delivers to the Company his required capital contribution; and (c) agrees in writing to be bound by the terms of this Agreement by becoming a party hereto.*

> *Upon the admission of a new Member to the Company, the capital accounts of all Members, and the calculations that are based on the capital accounts, shall be adjusted appropriately.*

Liability of Members

Although state law normally provides a default liability protection for the LLC's members, it's always good to throw in a provision that calls for it anyway. It doesn't have to be anything too lengthy. Here's an example of a limited liability provision that you can use:

> *No Member shall be personally responsible for any debts, liabilities, or obligations of the Company solely by reason of being a Member. All debts, obligations, and liabilities of the Company, whether by contract or not, shall belong solely to the Company.*

Transfer & Assignment of Membership Interests

By default, most LLCs don't allow membership shares to be freely transferred. However, they can be *assigned.* This means that I can give my membership shares over to my brother, but he won't actually own them along with all of the voting rights and other perks. He will only receive any distributions of the profits and losses that the membership shares get. Operating agreements often state that membership interests can be transferred upon the approval of all or the majority of the other members.

You can structure this section however you want. However, I wouldn't allow your membership shares to be freely transferred like corporate stock is. Here's why — one of the three things that sets LLCs apart from corporations is that the stock can't be easily traded. If you sidestep this little rule and look and feel too much like a corporation, you can lose your *charging order protection* (the idea that the LLC is protected from the members' debts and obligations; see Chapter 11 for a complete explanation). I would, instead, require all the members to vote on whether to allow the shares to be transferred.

In the Transfer & Assignment of Membership Interests section, you deal with a lot of pertinent issues that need to be sorted out before you proceed with business. These issues include such things as what happens when a member retires or if a member wants to resign. You'll most likely want to sit down with your attorney and have her help you and your partners decide how you want your company to run in the future. Some important subjects that you will want to address in this section of your operating agreement are

- ✔ When and how can a member resign?
- ✔ If someone resigns, does he get his contribution or capital back?
- ✔ What happens when a member passes away?
- ✔ What happens when a member retires?
- ✔ What happens if a member goes bankrupt?
- ✔ Can a member be expelled?
- ✔ How are membership shares transferred?

Also, you should add a provision that states what happens if a creditor successfully obtains a charging order against a member. A good trick of the trade is to include a paragraph in your operating agreement that states that, should a *charging order* (a court order that takes any profits that would be distributed to a member and gives them to the creditor instead until the debt is paid; see Chapter 11 for more details) be obtained on a member, the remaining members have first right of refusal on purchasing the member's shares at a portion of their fair market value.

First, you want to uphold the charging order protections:

> *If a creditor obtains a lien or a charging order against any Member's membership interest, or in the event of a Member's bankruptcy or other involuntary transfer of interest, this act shall constitute a material breach of this Agreement by such Member. The creditor or claimant shall only be considered an Assignee and will be limited to the rights of such. The creditor or claimant shall have no right to become a Member or have rights to management participation nor have the right to participate as a Member or Manager in any regard to the affairs of the Company. Said creditor or claimant shall only be entitled to receive the share of profit and losses, or the return of capital, to which the Member would otherwise have been entitled.*

Then, you want to state that the partners have the option of purchasing the membership shares at a discount:

> *The Members may unanimously elect to purchase all or any part of the membership shares that is subject to the charging order, bankruptcy, lien, or other involuntary transfer at a discounted price. The price shall be equal to one-half (½) of the fair market value of such shares. Written notice of such purchase shall be provided to the creditor or claimant.*

Allocations and Profit Distributions

Considering that all of the LLC's members have contributed a portion of the upstart capital — whether in the form of cash, equipment, or services — everyone should be due a portion of the business's profits. Generally, this amount should be proportionate to their ownership percentage or their *capital account*. After all, the more you invest into the company, the more you should profit, right?

One of the great benefits of operating as an LLC is that you don't necessarily have to distribute the company's profits and losses according to the members' percentage of ownership. You can vary the distributions however you like, as long as you make sure you can give the IRS a good reason for doing so (which doesn't include tax avoidance. You didn't think they'd let you get away with that now, did you?).

Allocations of Profits and Losses

An *allocation* is the amount of company profit and loss that is passed on to each member for him to report on his personal tax returns. How much is allocated to a member has no bearing on how much cash is actually distributed to a member. This can cause what is called *phantom income,* in which case you'll be forced to pay taxes on company profits even when cash was never distributed to you.

The IRS (very stringently, I might add!) allows allocations to vary from member to member — and not just according to their ownership percentage. Of course, it's customary to allocate profits and losses to each member in accordance with how much they actually own, but if you want to change it up, you can! Just make sure that you work with your accountant before doing this so she can help you avoid potential tax pitfalls.

For instance, some members may want to be allocated more losses than other members. Why? Well, they may have a lot of passive income from real estate properties and such that they want to offset. In this case, they can deduct the passive losses from the LLC from their passive income from their real estate endeavors. The remaining amount is what they are taxed on. You just have to make sure that if you're going to be messing with the allocations this way, you have some reasoning behind it that doesn't involve avoiding taxes.

Here's a standard provision that you can include in your operating agreement that allows you to vary the allocations whenever you and your partners choose:

> *The profits and losses of the Company shall be allocated to the Members in proportion with their individual ownership percentages. Should the Company wish to make special allocations, they must comply with Section 704 of the Internal Revenue Code and the corresponding regulations.*

Distributions

When the cash actually hits your pocket, then it becomes a *distribution*. Although all company profits have to be allocated to the members (for them to pay taxes on it), not all company profit has to be distributed — you can leave some in the business. And you can schedule your distributions whenever you want — they don't necessarily have to be once a year. You can make the payouts quarterly or even monthly if you like.

You should also specify in your operating agreement the *kind* of distribution that can be made. For the most part, you'll only be distributing cash to the members. If the company doesn't have the money to pay a member, then that member can't demand an asset in lieu of the cash. They'll just have to wait until the LLC has the money or the entity is dissolved.

Here is a sample provision that you can use:

> *Subject to applicable law and limitations elsewhere in this Agreement, the members may elect to make a distribution of assets at any time that would not be prohibited by law or under this Agreement. The amount and timing of all distributions of cash, or other assets, shall be determined by a unanimous vote of the Voting Members. All such Distributions shall be made to those Members who, according to the books and records of the Company, were the holders of record of Membership Interests on the date of Distribution.*

> *The Voting Members may base a determination that a distribution of cash may be made on a balance sheet, profit and loss statement, cash flow statement of the Company, or other relevant information. Neither the Company nor any Members shall be liable for the making of any Distributions in accordance with the provisions of this section.*

> *No Member has the right to demand and receive any distribution from the Company in any form other than money. No Member may be compelled to accept from the Company a distribution of any asset in kind in lieu of a proportionate distribution of money being made to other Members except on the dissolution and winding up of the Company.*

Make sure that your operating agreement contains a contingency plan for members who come and go in the middle of a fiscal year. Normally, the distribution that they receive is calculated according to the number of days that they held membership. You can create whatever formula you think works best for your situation.

Meetings & Voting

Chapter 11 has lots of information about holding meetings, taking votes, and keeping records. In the meantime, you need to figure out how and when you'll hold meetings, and what issues need to be approved by a majority of the members.

A few of the issues that you should make sure to touch upon in this section of your operating agreement are

- When holding a meeting, what sort of notice needs to be given to the members?

- What sorts of decisions require a meeting of the members and a vote to take place?

- How many members need to be at the meeting in order for a vote to be taken (that is to say, what's the quorum)?

- How are voting interests calculated? For instance, does every membership share get one vote, or do all members have an equal vote, regardless of their percentage of ownership?

- If a member is unable to make it to the meeting, will you allow her to vote by proxy?

Notice of Meetings

Before having a meeting, you gotta give notice! After all, how will everyone know when and where you'll be meeting? Notice is required for LLC meetings, not just because it's polite and considerate, but also because it keeps the members from purposefully withholding meeting time and location information from certain members to prevent them from showing up at the meeting and voting against their proposals. Here's a sample provision you can use:

> *If any action on the part of the Members is to be proposed at the meeting, then written notice of the meeting must be provided to each Member entitled to vote not less than ten (10) days or more than sixty (60) days prior to the meeting. Notice may be given in person, by fax, by first class mail, or by any other written communication, charges prepaid, at the Members' address listed in Exhibit A, attached. The notice shall contain the date, time, and place of the meeting and a statement of the general nature of this business to be transacted there.*

Quorum

Exactly what percentage of members it takes to hold a meeting is called a *quorum.* Quorums can be unanimous, a simple majority, or 75 percent of the members. It's entirely up to you. If you don't have the requisite number of voters at the meeting, whether in person or by proxy, then no voting can take place. A new meeting time and place must be scheduled, and you can then try again to get the members there. I know that getting members to a member meeting can often be like herding cats — especially when you have a lot of members. If this is the case, then you may want to make the quorum a simple majority. That way, it only takes half of your members to be on the ball to make things happen. Here's a sample provision:

> *Members holding at least fifty-one percent (51%) of the Voting Membership Interests in the Company represented in person, by telephone, or by proxy*

shall constitute a quorum at any meeting of Voting Members. In the absence of a quorum at any such meeting, the Voting Members may adjourn the meeting for a period not to exceed sixty days.

When drafting your operating agreement, you need to determine whether any decision or issues, regardless of quorum, require a unanimous consent of members. The minority shareholders often get the short end of the stick when it comes to voting on business affairs. To combat this, you can set up your LLC so that pertinent issues need to be approved by *all* members before they can be put through. This includes such issues as selling the business, offloading major business assets, acquiring a large amount of debt, or settling major litigation claims.

Voting

Not only do you have to determine what specific issues require a vote of the members, but you also have to determine how members get to vote (usually called their *voting interests*). You can structure voting interests two ways:

- ✔ **Allow each membership share to have one vote.** That means that if your membership shares represent 55 percent of the company, then you have 55 percent of the vote. This is the most common way to structure voting interests.

- ✔ **Give one vote per member.** This means that if you have 55 percent of the company, you will have one vote, which is equal to the member who owns only 1 percent of the company.

You also have to take into account that you may have different types of membership shares: voting and nonvoting (see the earlier section, "Management by Voting Members"). If this is the case, then only the voting shares receive votes — no matter how you structure it.

Here's a sample provision you can use:

Except as expressly set forth elsewhere in this Agreement or otherwise required by law, all actions requiring the vote of the Members may be authorized upon the vote of those Members collectively holding a majority of the Membership Interests in the Company. The following actions require the unanimous vote of all Members, who are not the transferors of a Membership Interest:

> *i. Making an Amendment to the Articles of Organization or this Agreement;*

> *ii. Absolving any Member from the obligation of making a capital contribution or returning money or property that was distributed to such Member in violation of law or this Agreement;*

     iii. Approving the sale, transfer, assignment, or exchange of a Member's interest in the Company and the admission of the transferee as a Member with full rights therein;

     iv. Purchasing, by the Company or its nominee, the Membership Interest of a transferor Member.

You may want to calculate each member's voting interest from the get-go and place it in the operating agreement where you state their name, address, and initial capital contributions. This way, when a vote takes place, the voting interests are already calculated, and the members have already approved and signed off on their individual voting interests.

Proxies

Say that you can't make the meeting but still want to vote on the issues that are being addressed. A common solution is to do a *proxy vote,* which means that you assign another person to vote in your place. If you have ever held shares of a publicly traded company, then I'm sure you're aware of proxy voting. You tell your proxy how you want them to vote, and they submit the vote for you. Otherwise, every time a Fortune 500 company that you own a share or two of holds a meeting, you'd be required to fly around the country to cast your vote.

If you want to allow your members to vote by proxy, you need to say so in the operating agreement. You can state whatever terms you like; however, a common provision is as follows:

     Proxies are only valid when signed by the Member entitled to the vote and must be filed with the secretary of the meeting prior to the commencement of voting on the matter in which the proxy is being elected to vote upon. Proxies shall become invalid after 11 months from the date of their execution unless otherwise stated in the proxy. Additionally, the proxy may be terminated at will by the voting member. The termination of such proxy must be submitted to the Company prior to the termination being effective.

Management & Duties

This section is especially important for manager-managed LLCs. If your LLC is managed by the members, as opposed to a separate manager or two, then all members have equal say in the management of the company. On the contrary, if your LLC is manager-managed, then you'll be bringing in an outside person (or group of people) who may not even be associated with the business. They don't even have to own a percentage of the company.

The *manager* is the person who runs the company. His actions determine whether the business succeeds or fails. He is a pertinent player in the game, and, for this reason, the members must choose wisely. The members must also retain control of the manager. If the manager screws up, the members need to have the power and authority to replace him on a dime. If you are a manager-managed LLC, this is probably the most critical part of the operating agreement.

Unless you plan on changing your managers out often, you'll probably want to place the names of the initial managers in the operating agreement. If there are more than a few, you can attach a separate piece of paper with the names and refer to it as Addendum A or B.

If you have multiple managers, you'll want to state in this section who is the Big Boss. You'll probably want to give the Big Boss a more official title like CEO, president, operating manager, Chief Yahoo . . . you get the picture. If you have other positions that you can place managers in, feel free to list them here. You may want to list things such as chief financial officer, treasurer, vice president of yadda yadda yadda . . . . Make up whatever you want; just make sure to include what that position entails, such as the limits of responsibility and the day-to-day duties.

Election

If you are in business for a while, you'll probably see a lot of people come and go. You see it happen with Fortune 500 companies all the time — they recycle leaders on what seems like a weekly basis. If you're like most people investing in a business, you'll want to make sure that if the people you put in charge aren't cutting it, you can kick them to the curb and find someone who can do the job better. Hey — it's your hard-earned money you're talking about. You wouldn't entrust it to some yackahoo, now would you?!

I didn't think so. That's why you need to sit down with your partners at the beginning and decide how you're going to manage your managers. If you want to give your managers some job security, you may want to state in this section that the managers stay in power for a one-year term; then the members have to vote to reinstate them. At this point, the members can choose someone more qualified if they want to.

If you're a little more cutthroat, you may want to write the provision so that the manager can be replaced at any time by a vote of the majority of the members. At that point, the members will elect a new manager or select someone to serve in the interim.

Here's a sample provision you can use:

> *The Company shall be managed by one or more appointed Managers. The name and address of the Managers of the Company can be found in Exhibit B, attached. The Members, by a majority vote, shall elect and appoint as many Managers as the Members determine shall be in the best interest of the Company, though no less than one.*

One manager shall be elected to take the position of Chief Operating Manager. The Chief Operating Manager shall be held responsible for managing the operations of the Company and shall carry out the decisions of the Managers.

Members shall serve until they resign or their successors are duly elected and appointed by the Members.

Delegation of Powers

The question will come up — "What can and can't we do as managers?" Although managers must use common sense to avoid stepping over their boundaries and making important decisions without consulting the members, the operating agreement must have a section that gives them guidance. This section tells them what decisions they can make on their own and what decisions require a resolution of the members. Here's a sample provision you can use:

The Managers are authorized on the Company's behalf to bind the Company to contracts and obligations, and to do or cause all acts to be done deemed necessary or appropriate to carry out or further the business of the Company. All decisions and actions of the Managers shall be made by majority vote of the Managers as provided in this Agreement. The Managers have in their power to authorize or decide the following:

   i. The employment of persons or institutions for the operation and management of the company affairs.

   ii. The execution of all checks, drafts, and money orders for the payment of company funds.

   iii. The delivery and execution of promissory notes, loans, or security agreements.

   iv. The purchase or acquisition of company assets.

   v. The sale, lease, or other disposition of company assets.

   vi. The granting of security interests in the company assets in exchange for capital.

   vii. The prepayment or refinancing of any loan secured by the company assets.

   viii. The execution and delivery of all contracts, franchise agreements, licensing agreements, assignments, leases, and subleases which affect the company assets.

For the most part, your managers can bind the LLC to contracts and other obligations. You can limit their powers in this section of the operating agreement. However, even if they act out of their authority, it doesn't necessarily void any contracts that they entered into. Ultimately, it's up to a judge to decide.

You may want to include a paragraph that states that any expenditures over a certain amount (say, $5,000) require an additional authority. This can mean that a vote of the members is required. Or perhaps more than one manager or member has to sign off on the expense.

Compensation

The managers' compensation isn't something normally decided by the managers — for good reason. Generally, most LLCs are structured so that before any high compensation or bonuses can be doled out, the members must take a vote, and the majority must approve. This is a great provision which can really keep company costs from spiraling out of control. It maintains a checks-and-balances system and is a great way to keep payroll in check. You can also throw in a sentence or two that states that the company is required to reimburse the manager for all expenses she incurred on behalf of the company. Here's a sample provision you can use:

> *Any Manager who renders services to the Company shall be entitled to compensation in direct proportion to the value of such services. Additionally, the Company shall reimburse all direct out-of-pocket expenses incurred by the Managers while managing the Company.*

Miscellaneous

As you now know, you can put anything you want in your operating agreement. You can make it as detailed or as basic as you like. I have laid out a basic format for your operating agreement, but you don't have to stick to it. You can organize your provisions however you want. Then you can put all of your leftover provisions — the ones that don't easily fit into the categories — under a Miscellaneous section.

Financial Records and Reporting

This section gives members the right to inspect all of the business's financial records. It should tell them where the financial records are held and what sort of financial reporting they can expect as members. After all, as a member, wouldn't you want to know what's going on with your investment?

A few specific things that you should include in this section:

- ✔ **Books and Records:** Here you should state that all company records shall be held in a corporate kit (see Chapter 11). Also state where the corporate kit is to be maintained — whether at the registered agent's office, the company's headquarters, or at the company's attorney's office. Here's a sample provision you can use:

    > *The Members shall maintain at the Company's principle place of business the following books and records: a current list of the full*

name and last-known business or residence address of each Member, together with their capital contribution and membership interest; a copy of the Articles and all amendments thereto; copies of the Company's federal, state, and local income tax or information returns and reports, if any, for the six (6) most recent taxable years and a copy of this Agreement and any amendments to it.

✔ **Accounting and the Company's Fiscal Year:** This provision states what the company's year-end is and also who the company bookkeeper or accountant is. You can choose whether to include this in your operating agreement. It's not vital, but may be nice to have, depending on your situation.

✔ **Financial Reporting:** It is common practice for the company manager to provide regular financial reports to the members. The type of financial reports (balance statements, profit and loss statements, and so on) and the frequency of which they are distributed should be noted here. Here's a sample provision you can use:

> *The complete and accurate accounting and financial records of the Company shall be held by the Managers at the Company's principal place of business. Such records shall be kept on such method of accounting as the Managers shall select. The Company's accounting period shall be the calendar year.*
>
> *The Managers shall close the accounting records at the close of each calendar year, and shall prepare and send to each member a state- ment of such Member's distributive share of income and expense — in the form of a Schedule K-1 — for income tax reporting purposes.*

Who is responsible for maintaining the company books and records? Will one person be in charge of this? If you have a larger company, everyone will most likely go about their daily business and not give a care in the world about dealing with the random record-keeping tasks that come up. You may want to assign one person to handle everything; that way, they are responsible for the job and can be held accountable if it isn't completed.

Indemnification Clause

Although all managers and members are provided a basic level of *indemnifi- cation* (a fancy word for "limited liability"), it's always good to restate it in your operating agreement. Essentially, you're telling the world that all of the LLC's managers, members, and employees are free from and are not responsible for the obligations and debts of the company. Like I said, this provision isn't required, but hey — it can't hurt! Here's a sample provision you can use:

> *The Company shall indemnify any person, to the fullest extent permitted by law, who is a party defendant or is threatened to be made a party defendant, pending or completed action, suit, or proceeding, whether civil, criminal, administrative, or investigative (other than an action by or in the right of the Company) by reason of the fact that he is or was a Member of the Company, Manager, employee, or agent of the Company, or is or was serving at the*

request of the Company, so long as the person did not behave in violation of law or this Agreement, for instant expenses (including attorney's fees), judgments, fines, and amounts paid in settlement actually and reasonably incurred in connection with such action, suit, or proceeding.

Dispute Resolution

Whenever a lot of people get together and work on a project for an extended period of time, disputes are bound to come up. Often, they come out of nowhere, blindsiding you at the worst times. Unless dealt with properly, they can seriously harm your business, and resolving them can take time and precious resources that your business needs to grow and prosper. To prevent these situations from occurring, you and your partners should be forward-thinking enough to add guidelines on how to effectively deal with disputes when they come up.

First, you should specify the state in which the disputes are to be dealt with. It can be incredibly expensive to handle lawsuits and disputes in states other than where your company headquarters are. Therefore, it's a great policy to make sure that all members are bound to taking legal action only in the state that your company is located in.

Second, you'll want to keep your disputes out of the courtroom. Lawsuits can be costly and, at times, debilitating. You should provide your members with a means to get their disputes handled in a friendlier, laid-back way. Specifically, you'll want to bind them to *mediation and arbitration* (a diplomatic way to handle disputes in which a third party hears both sides of the disagreement and then makes a decision about the outcome).

Here's a sample provision you can use:

> *The Members agree that in the event of any dispute or disagreement solely between or among any of them arising out of, relating to, or in connection with this Agreement or the Company or its organization, formation, business, or management, the Members shall use their best efforts to resolve any dispute arising out of or in connection with this Agreement by good-faith negotiation and mutual agreement. The Members shall meet at a mutually convenient time and place to attempt to resolve any such dispute.*

> *However, in the event that a member dispute cannot be resolved, such parties shall first attempt to settle such dispute through a nonbinding mediation proceeding. In the event any party to such mediation proceeding is not satisfied with the results thereof, then any unresolved disputes shall be finally settled in accordance with an arbitration proceeding. In no event shall the results of any mediation proceeding be admissible in any arbitration or judicial proceeding.*

Dissolution

The dissolution provision is an incredibly important one that you definitely should include in your operating agreement. Just because it's in the

Miscellaneous section doesn't mean that it should be taken lightly or disregarded altogether. All good things come to an end, and chances are that your LLC will be no different. Eventually, you'll have to go through the dissolution process. If you are in a short-term project, then this provision is especially imperative because it specifies how the profits and losses are divvied up among the members, and you'll want to make this section as detailed as possible.

First, outline what scenarios or actions will cause the company to dissolve. (For more information on the actions that can trigger a dissolution, read Chapter 12.) You also need to specify what percentage of members it takes to approve a voluntary dissolution. It's common to require a unanimous consent from all members — that way, no members can come back and dispute the dissolution, saying that they never approved it.

You should also outline the process for winding up the company's affairs. After the company is liquidated, what is the order in which people are paid? By law, you generally have to pay the company creditors first, but then what? You should check your state laws to see how much leeway you have. In most states, you are legally obliged to distribute profits according to the member's ownership percentages.

Putting It All Together

How you put your operating agreement together isn't nearly as important as what it contains. However, if you're going to take the time to create it in the first place, why not make sure it's organized and easily readable? It isn't hard to make your document look like a million bucks — or at least like the million bucks it probably would have cost to have an attorney draft it from scratch.

Achieving A+ form and structure

The operating agreement is laid out similar to the articles of organization (see Chapter 6) in that that there are articles, sections, and subsections, all designated with letters, numbers, and/or Roman numerals. For instance, the layout may look something like this:

Article I

Section A

1.

2.

3.

Section B

Or, something like this:

Article 1:

    Section A

        Subsection I

        Subsection II

        Subsection III

    Section B

        Subsection I

        Subsection II

        Subsection III

Article 2:

    Section A

If you use a lot of legalese or industry terminology, you may want to consider making the first article a "Defined Terms" article with a list of definitions so the reader understands what certain words mean as he reads through the document. After all, if he is binding himself to the contract, he needs to understand it fully.

Signing and ratifying

With an LLC, all of your managers and members should sign the operating agreement (if you are used to running a corporation, then this part may throw you off a bit). As attorney David LeGrand has told me over and over again, "Some of the worst client problems I have seen arose because not every member had signed the operating agreement, resulting in thousands of dollars of legal fees and lost time from disputes."

To protect against this, not only should each member (and manager, if manager-managed) sign off on the operating agreement, they should also sign off on their capital contribution, membership interest, and distributive shares that are listed in the agreement. If there are a lot of members, then you can include a signature page as a separate piece of paper.

You should also make sure that you hold a meeting of the members (and managers, if you like) and take a vote to approve the completed operating agreement. You should draft minutes of this meeting to further document that all of the members got together and approved the document. This way, if the document is ever contested in court, you can prove that the contesting member was there when the document was up for a vote and could have disputed the document at the time. This is why it's a good idea to have *all* of the members approve the operating agreement as opposed to a simple majority. (For more information on how to hold meetings and draft meeting minutes, flip ahead to Chapter 11.)

Now . . . put it away!

First, you may want to give copies of the operating agreement to each of the members and managers. This ensures that everyone is on the same page and each person is familiar with company policies and procedures. Second, you will want to keep the original safely tucked away in your company kit (see Chapter 11).

Before putting your operating agreement away, it's a good idea to run it by your company attorney to make sure that you aren't missing any pertinent information that is applicable to your company or industry. By drafting the operating agreement yourself and then having an attorney double-check your work, you do a lot of the legwork and save yourself a lot of dough, but you still get the professional finished product that you would have gotten if your attorney had drafted the entire thing from scratch.

Amending the Agreement

As companies grow and change, so should their infrastructure. If you are in this for the long term, then you'll probably reach a point in time when the operating agreement needs to be amended. How you amend your operating agreement is largely determined by the laws of the state that your LLC is domiciled in. If your home state says that your operating agreement can be amended by unanimous consent, then all members will have to approve the amendment for it to be made. All in all, you need to check your state laws. Some states say that it only takes a majority of the members to amend the operating agreement, while others permit the managers to amend the operating agreement if the articles of organization permit it.

When amending your operating agreement, you go through the same process as if you were amending your articles of organization (see Chapter 6). You'll hold a meeting of the members (see Chapter 11), present the amendment for a vote, then draft a resolution stating that all (or a majority) of the members resolved to amend the operating agreement. Then draft meeting minutes to this effect and keep the minutes and resolutions in your corporate kit. It's vital to have this proof that all members agreed on changing the operating agreement. If you're ever taken to court, you can prove that all members voted and signed off on the amendment.

Unlike when you amend your articles of organization, you don't need to file the amendments to your operating agreement with the state or local jurisdictions because your operating agreement isn't a public record. Your operating agreement is a private contract between the members (and managers) of the LLC. This means that your amendment is valid as soon as it has been voted on.

Chapter 10

Who Owns What: Deciphering Membership Shares

*I*n the eyes of the law, your LLC is a separate entity — almost like a separate person. But because it's not alive and can't breathe or think on its own, someone must do so on its behalf. In this case, the owners — that is to say, *you* — will make sure the business stays alive.

The LLC's members are the major decision makers. For the most part, the business's success falls on their shoulders. Even if they don't manage the day-to-day affairs, they still control who *does*. As far as I'm concerned, until membership in your LLC has been issued — in other words, until the LLC is actually *owned* by someone — the business doesn't really exist.

In this chapter, I show you how to take ownership of your LLC by issuing membership interests to you and your partners. I also go into detail on how to sell and transfer membership shares and deal with situations such as the death or divorce of a member. Then, I show you how to raise money by selling your membership shares in exchange for investment.

Interpreting the Terminology: Members, Interests, and Certificates

The legal term for the owners of an LLC is *members*. Some states have a specific definition for what a member is, while other states have no definition at all. Don't let this throw you off.

Think of the ownership of the LLC as a big pie, and each owner gets a portion. These portions are called the *membership interests* or *ownership percentage* (different states tend to use slightly different terminology, but they all mean the same thing). Often, when you issue membership interests, the entire pie must be consumed, so to speak. The pieces of this pie are normally called *membership units.*

For instance, if there is a total of 100 membership units in the company and you have 35 membership units, then you own 35 percent of the company. In other words, you have a 35 percent *membership interest* in the LLC. An easy way to calculate your membership interest is to divide your membership units by total number of membership units the company has issued.

The piece of paper that proves your ownership of the LLC is called your *membership certificate.* A membership certificate includes the name of the member, the date that the certificate was issued, the amount of membership interests, and the signature of one or two members and/or managers.

It's a strange thought — you can invest thousands into an enterprise, and all you get is a simple piece of paper. But that piece of paper gives you the one most important thing in business — control. Without that certificate, you have no say in how the LLC is run, how the money is spent, or how the company is

The reality of membership shares

Childhood friends Ed, Sal, and Greg have dreamed forever of opening up their own motorcycle shop. Although they all work odd jobs, they soon realize that together they could finally make this mere vision a reality. Ed owns an excess of equipment for building custom bikes, including the paint and specialty tools. Sal has full access to, but doesn't own, an old vacant warehouse, and Greg has saved $50,000 in his successful entrepreneurship. Together, they possess all the pieces to build their own custom bike shop, ESG Motorbikes.

They form an LLC and divvy out their membership shares. Although Greg is fronting the capital to get the business afloat (providing the largest set of funds), Sal and Ed aren't letting Greg overlook the value of their contributions, so after some persuasion, Greg finally relents and agrees to spread the shares out evenly at

33.3 percent. The LLC protects the members from losses that can't exceed what they invest into the company, but it seems Greg has much more at risk and might deserve a greater piece of the pie.

A couple years down the road, when the going isn't great, a private investor offers to purchase ESG Motorbikes for $100,000. Greg, having invested the most money, isn't too happy about this, but Sal and Ed outvote him and decide to sell. Sal and Ed will make a quick profit, but unfortunately for him, Greg's membership certificate states that he owns one-third of the company. Therefore, he is only entitled to one-third of the proceeds from the sale of the business. So now it seems Greg's risk in the venture may have exceeded his reward, while his buddies gained probably more than they should have.

structured. The business could be terminated tomorrow, and you would get nothing. That little certificate means everything in the world of business, so make sure you have one!

Believe it or not, in most states, membership certificates aren't actually required by law to be distributed to the members — the ownership breakdown can just be stated in the operating agreement. However, just because it isn't required, doesn't mean you shouldn't do it anyway. I recommend that each and every member gets a membership certificate as proof of their ownership.

Do a quick review of your state's laws regarding LLC ownership to figure out what terminology the state uses. I have provided contact information for each state in Appendix A.

Setting Up and Managing Your Membership

After you have filed your articles of organization and have created your operating agreement (see Chapter 9), you can stake your claim! You take ownership of the LLC by issuing membership shares to yourself and your partners. The percentage of the LLC that a member owns should be relatively proportional to the amount that he initially invests, be it money, equipment, or services. All of this is reflected in the buy-sell agreement that you and your partners will write up and the membership certificates that each member will receive.

In this section, I explain most of the basic rules of membership shares. After you've got that down and you know what your limitations are, I show you how to issue membership shares for the first time.

Looking at some membership rules

LLCs are really flexible entities where members are concerned. The laws give you a lot of freedom in how you can structure your LLC. Some examples of an LLC's flexibility are:

✔ **Most states allow members to make contributions in the form of services in exchange for membership interests.** *Services* are defined as time that the member puts into the organization. (This allows someone who has a talent you need to invest his time and skill instead of money.) Just make sure that if you allow services as a type of contribution, this is specifically stated in the operating agreement.

✔ **Distributions can be varied from member to member.** In other words, if you follow some very specific IRS rules, you can change the company's distribution of profits and losses to be different from the percentage of ownership. For example, if you and your partners choose, and you meet IRS criteria, you can own 10 percent of the company and get 50 percent of the profits and zero percent of the losses.

✔ **There can be an unlimited number of members.** Unlike some entities, you can have hundreds of thousands of members if you want! This is a huge benefit if you are looking to raise capital for your business.

Keep in mind, though, if you are a really small business, you may want to limit the number of members you bring on. Even if your LLC is managed by separate managers who aren't involved in the business's day-to-day operations, you'll still need the members to vote on important issues, such as selecting the managers and taking on sizeable debt. If your members are not easily accessible or you have too many, making a quorum or getting a majority of the members to vote can be an issue. Not to mention the fact that the more people who are involved in the decision-making process, the harder it is to reach a consensus.

✔ **The members can be non-U.S. citizens and even be other entities, such as corporations, trusts, limited partnerships, and LLCs.** Making another entity a member in your LLC is a huge benefit if you're trying to set up an asset protection plan where the LLC needs to be a subsidiary of another company. Also, if you are the only member in the LLC and you don't want to share any control, you can form another entity to be your second member. This way, you'll keep all the power, but avoid having to deal with the hassles of being a single-member LLC.

✔ **You can have different types (*classes*) of membership.** For instance, you can issue Class A membership, where the members can participate in the management of the LLC, and a Class B membership, where the members are only silent partners with no participation in the day-to-day operations. In most states, you can structure these classes however you want — just put it in the operating agreement. (I go into more detail on this in the next section.)

✔ **You can decide how members will transfer their membership shares.** Members can be restricted to transferring only the economic interest (the distributions), or they can transfer their full membership (voting rights, economic interests, and all) but only on a vote of the majority of the other members.

As you can see from this list, when I said that LLCs were flexible entities with regard to membership, I meant it! This amazing flexibility allows LLC owners to run many different types of businesses, from raising financing for a real estate deal to movie production to running a small business. Also, keep in mind that with an LLC, the members don't have to manage the company.

Instead, separate managers can be selected. These managers can be owners or non-owners. This is one of the main reason why LLCs are gaining popularity as an entity to raise capital with — you can fully manage the entity yourself, while your investors remain silent in the business's day-to-day activities.

If a person in the organization isn't given membership, then they aren't an owner. If they manage the LLC, they have a say in the day-to-day operations, but their position isn't necessarily permanent. The members decide who manages the LLC, and the manager's involvement solely depends on the members' approval. In other words, a manager who isn't a member is little more than a glorified employee.

Establishing membership classes

If the LLC is the most flexible entity around — allowing you to tailor it completely to your needs — it definitely lives up to its reputation when it comes to the ownership. You see, if you choose, your LLC can offer different classes of membership. *Membership classes* designate certain rights and rules for different groups of members. Often, these different classes are marked with a letter (Class A membership, Class B membership, and so on).

Now, what can you do with these different classes? Anything! With membership classes, you can give some of your partners more voting rights than others. Or the rules regarding the transfer of the membership shares can be different among members. You decide. Hey, no one said life is fair! Your LLC needn't be either.

Meeting the minimum number of members (No, your dog doesn't count)

LLCs are set up to be partnerships. Therefore, you need a partner! I know a lot of you want to fly solo — but trust me, you don't want to go there! Although it's possible in many states to operate as a single-member LLC, it isn't a good idea.

If you are intent on having 100 percent control over your entity, you can gift a small percentage of shares to a close friend. That way, you still have the majority vote, which means complete control over the LLC.

If the thought of having a friend involved in your business makes you cringe, or if you don't have anyone whom you can trust, you have another option. You can form a corporation and make it your partner in the LLC. This may seem like a lot of work, but you can use the extra corporation to protect your assets even further. If you are serious about flying solo and protecting your assets, this move may be the best one.

To establish membership classes, you create one set of rules and procedures for the Class A membership and another set for the Class B membership. For instance, you can create different classes of membership for the operating partners, the investors, and the employees. Their control in the company can be limited according to their respective positions. You can also use membership classes as an incentive for investors to contribute more money to the business. After all, it only makes sense that the investors who contribute the most money should have more influence in the company than those who barely invested at all.

After you have decided what you want your different membership classes to be, you include them in your operating agreement (I show you how to do this in Chapter 9). You also include the information on your membership certificates. You usually do this by putting the class (such as "Class A," "Class B," and so on) on the front of the certificate. Then, you put a *legend* — a paragraph stating the class restrictions — on the back of the certificate.

When creating classes, if you want to allow some of your members to manage, but not all of them, then you need to make sure that your LLC is designated as manager-managed. In most states, if you designate your LLC as member-managed, then all members are equal managers in the business, regardless of the classes set forth in your operating agreement. For more information on manager-managed versus member-managed LLCs, see Chapter 4.

Creating a buy-sell agreement

A *buy-sell agreement* outlines the rules regarding members voluntarily or involuntarily transferring their membership. It also explains what the members should do when a member retires, goes bankrupt, becomes incapacitated, or passes away. Normally, if your buy-sell agreement covers all members in the company, then you just include these provisions in your operating agreement. But with LLCs, you don't have to hold everyone to the same standard. If you want, you can have individual buy-sell agreements for each of your members.

A buy-sell agreement prevents situations like the following two:

✔ Your best friend and long-term business partner dies in a skiing accident. You are devastated. When you think it couldn't get worse, his nephew, his only heir, decides that he has the right to step in and take control of the business. Legally, you and your partner had no agreement in place that provided for a situation such as this one. When you show up at court to provide your defense, you are empty-handed. Meanwhile, the little scamp is acting like a tyrant and undoing all of your years of hard work.

✔ You and your brother start a pet shop and put it in a member-managed LLC. When the two of you get into a quarrel, he finds the only person in the world who doesn't like puppies and sells her his membership shares. The next day, Cruella DeVille, your new partner, shows up for work and starts making changes. She fires your best employees and spends the company money like there's no tomorrow.

A buy-sell agreement must cover

- How much money a member's membership shares are worth

- Who controls the member's shares if she leaves the LLC for any reason

- The reasons why someone may be admitted as a member and issued membership shares

- What happens to a member's shares when the member departs or withdraws

  - The LLC or the other members can purchase the shares

  - The shares can be sold to the general public

- The process of transferring membership shares

- What happens if a member declares bankruptcy or divorces

The buy-sell agreement is usually a component of the operating agreement when all the members have to follow the same rules and regulations. However, you don't have to put your buy-sell agreement in your operating agreement. If different members are subject to different rules and regulations (for instance, a certain set of members can't transfer their shares, while the rest can), then you need a separate buy-sell agreement for those members. In this case, you would have individual buy-sell agreements, instead of a company-wide one that resides in your operating agreement. (Chapter 9 shows you how to create an operating agreement.)

When you issue your membership shares, you must create a buy-sell agreement at the same time. Otherwise, a buy-sell agreement that you create after issuing membership shares may not be retroactive and cover all members and any future transferees. If you've already issued your membership shares and now want to create a buy-sell agreement, make sure that

- All of your members vote on it.

- The agreement specifically states that it covers all *current* LLC members.

Determining profit and loss distributions

First, let me describe what *profit and loss distributions* actually are. At the end of every year, whatever income (profit) the company generated during its operation passes on (or is distributed) to the owners' personal tax returns,

When special allocations make sense

Eric decides to partner up with his best friends Martin and Adam. They have been thinking about setting up a film production company since they were kids and have decided that now is the time to jump in. Martin and Adam will be putting in the upstart capital ($30,000 each), and the three of them will be sharing equally in the work.

Eric, knowing that it wouldn't be fair for them to split the profits equally, works out a deal with Martin and Adam. Each partner will own one-third of the company, so they all have equal voting power and control over the company, but Martin and Adam will receive 100 percent of all company profits until they have been paid back their initial investment plus 20 percent. Martin and Adam agree and they decide to form an LLC — the only entity that allows them to distribute the profits not according to the percentage of ownership each member has.

almost as if it were their personal income. They report this on a Schedule K that they attach to their Form 1040 that they file every year. The same goes with the company's expenses and losses — they are also passed on to the LLC's owners.

Normally, the amount of profits and losses that are passed on is determined by the amount of the company they own. For instance, if you own 20 percent of the company, then you will be allocated 20 percent of the company's profits and 20 percent of the company's losses. When you don't distribute the profits and losses according to the percentage of the company that a person owns, it's called a *special allocation* of the profits and losses.

But it's not just a free-for-all out there regarding company profits. To prevent fraud, the IRS doesn't let you decide how to allocate profits however you want. If it did, members with the most personal income would make sure they received all of the LLC's losses to offset the income they made from other ventures. For instance, unless you have a good reason, one partner can't receive 100 percent of the losses, while another takes 100 percent of the profits. You have to be able to substantiate your decision. In other words — you can't play with the profit distributions for tax-evasion purposes — you must have a real reason behind it.

Want to always be guaranteed that you can change your distributions of profits and losses at a moment's notice without getting nailed by the IRS? Well, there is a way. The IRS provides guidelines for determining whether special allocations are okay. You can put certain language in your operating agreement and do some simple things to protect yourself from any tax troubles. Here are a couple of ways to make sure you're covered:

- ✔ **The partners' *capital accounts* (how much equity each partner has in the partnership) should be carried on the books according to the IRS regulations.** Don't worry — this isn't as difficult as it seems and is nothing out of the ordinary. For more information on this, speak with your tax professional or read the regulations regarding capital accounts under Section 704 of the Internal Revenue Code.

- ✔ **The operating agreement must specify that upon termination and liquidation of the LLC, the members will receive the profits according to their capital accounts.** If a member's capital account is in the negative (that is, she owes money to the company), then that money must be paid back when the company ceases operations or before the member sells her membership share in the company. Look at your equity as a loan that must be paid back if the investment isn't profitable.

As your company distributes profits and losses, accepts contributions, and the assets appreciate and depreciate through the year, you'll need to adjust each members' individual capital account. Because this is a complex process unless you're well educated in accounting, you should work with your company accountant so he can adjust each member's capital account. You'll also want to reissue the membership so it properly reflects each member's new percentage of the company.

Setting up a single-member LLC

If you're planning on being the only member of your LLC, watch out! LLCs were designed to be *partnerships.* Therefore, the IRS only agreed to accept LLCs if they followed some simple partnership rules — the main one being that you have an actual *partner.* And no, it can't be your cat or your dearly deceased Aunt Peggy.

Unless you are completely diligent in your record keeping and dot every *i* and cross every *t*, single-member LLCs (SLLCs) lack a lot of the basic liability protection that an LLC offers. And this protection is one of the LLC's fundamental benefits. The IRS doesn't even consider an SLLC a partnership (after all, there aren't any partners!). SLLCs are taxed as sole proprietorships, and you pay the company taxes on a Schedule C, Profit or Loss From Business, attached to your personal tax return.

You know what an SLLC is called in IRS terms? A *disregarded entity.* And disregard it, you shall. Without the basic limited liability, why even go through the hassle of forming an LLC in the first place?

Still being stubborn and don't want to share your ownership with someone else? Don't fret. I've got you covered! If you don't mind extra paperwork, you can be the only owner of your LLC and keep your limited liability. It might be somewhat tedious, but you'll get your way!

Some states don't even *allow* single-member LLCs. If you are unfortunate enough to be located in one of these fussy states, you can just file your LLC in another state, such as Nevada or Wyoming, then register to transact business in your home state (see Chapter 5 for more on choosing a state to file your LLC in).

If you are a single-member LLC and deemed by the IRS to be treated as a *disregarded entity,* you lack the dual liability protection that a partnership offers (see Chapter 2 for details). Therefore, if you claim a home-office deduction (IRS Form 8829, Expenses for Business Use of Your Home), your home *could* theoretically be considered a business asset and could be seized if you lose a lawsuit.

Although the law doesn't automatically offer it to single-member LLCs, you *can* still demand the liability protection that an LLC or corporation offers. This isn't easy, though, because you must be rigorous in making sure that everything is filed correctly, and you have to go above and beyond to treat your entity as though it were truly separate from yourself.

To keep the liability protection in your SLLC

- ✔ **Be diligent in keeping your business assets and cash flow *completely* separate from your personal assets and cash flow.** You must have documentation to this effect.

- ✔ **Sign all of your filings as owner, on behalf of your LLC.** Never sign any business documents without this designation.

- ✔ **Add your federal EIN number and your LLC's filing number (provided by the Secretary of State) to your Schedule C.** Adding your LLC's file number makes your LLC look much more legitimate and can deter those looking for a lawsuit.

- ✔ **Act like a corporation.** This involves complying with all corporate formalities, such as meetings of the members and managers, keeping extensive minutes, and passing resolutions. Just because only one person is involved in your entity, don't think you can get out of these tasks. It may seem silly to have a meeting with yourself, but it's necessary to document all decision-making affecting the company.

- ✔ **Elect corporate tax treatment on IRS Form 8832, Entity Classification Election.** When electing corporate tax treatment, you are automatically saved from being considered a proprietorship, and none of the above rules need to be followed.

Do you still want to be the only owner of the LLC, but are afraid of the risk of operating as a single-member LLC? Don't worry, you have some other options.

- ✔ You can form another entity to act as a second member of the LLC.

- ✔ You can choose someone whom you trust to act as a secondary partner.

The person or corporation that you select as the second member doesn't have to own that much interest in the LLC — you only need to issue another party a small percentage of membership to avoid being considered a single-member LLC.

One plus one equals one. Don't believe me? A husband and wife who are the only members of an LLC are considered one unit; therefore, the LLC is a single-member LLC.

If you choose to have a single-member LLC, then be aware that you probably can't take advantage of the charging order protections that LLCs offer (which I explain in Chapter 11).

Adding and Withdrawing Members

When you are jumping head first into business and then working flawlessly with your partner, you may think that it's silly to discuss the prospect of a change in ownership. After all, you and your partner work incredibly well together, and everything is moving forward seamlessly — there's no way the ownership will ever change!

Listen, I know that you may think it's bad luck or a touchy subject to come up with a contingency plan when things are running so smoothly, but when else are you going to do it? When the you-know-what hits the fan? Not a good plan! Not to mention that a change in ownership doesn't necessarily have to be the result of some argument or other sort of falling-out. A change in ownership can occur for myriad other reasons, good and bad.

It's somewhat more difficult than you might expect to transfer an LLC's membership units.

> ✔ An LLC is considered a *partnership* by the IRS, and one of the primary things that sets a partnership apart from a corporation is that the ownership isn't freely transferable.

> ✔ Your state believes it's imperative to protect the partners in a business from showing up for work one day and finding out they have a new partner who they now have to find a way to work with.

Ultimately, the laws are designed to protect *you,* and these little guidelines make LLCs the phenomenally superior entities that they are.

You see, the fact that ownership is not freely transferable really works for you when you lose a lawsuit and the plaintiff is about to seize your ownership of the LLC. Because the LLC's shares aren't easily transferred, the plaintiff can't seize the actual shares. He can only seize the profits (and losses!) that you receive from your interest in the company. You can use this little rule to your advantage to stay out of lawsuits. I go over this in detail in Chapter 2, but for now, keep in mind that these rules work *for* you more often than they work against you.

All of the rules regarding adding and withdrawing members can be laid out in your operating agreement. You want to make sure that the required provisions are there, because if your operating agreement or buy-sell agreement doesn't address an issue, then state law decides. If you require a vote of the members before a membership share can be issued or transferred, then your operating agreement or buy-sell agreement should state what percentage of members must approve the transfer. Will you require a unanimous decision among members, or will a simple majority do? You decide.

Doing the membership shuffle

No one should be stuck in an investment that isn't working out for them, just like no owners should be stuck with partners whom they don't like or agree with. You may need to remove (technically called *withdraw*) a person from your LLC team when

- ✔ A member passes away
- ✔ A member retires
- ✔ A member becomes severely ill or incapacitated
- ✔ A member goes through a divorce
- ✔ A member goes bankrupt
- ✔ The other members are unhappy with one member
- ✔ A member needs cash and wants to sell his membership
- ✔ A member wants to gift his membership to someone close to him
- ✔ A member has his membership units seized
- ✔ The owners want to bring on an additional partner

Sometimes you may want to add members after your LLC is already established. Some reasons include

- ✔ You want to raise additional capital to take your LLC to the next level. In exchange for his investment, you want to offer the member a piece of the pie.

✔ You have a member-managed LLC, and the workflow is becoming too great. You want to bring on another owner who can contribute her experience and expertise to take your business to the next level.

✔ Your employees have worked hard for your company over the years. As a way of repaying them, you want to issue them a small percentage of ownership.

Make sure that all actions on behalf of the members of the company, especially those concerning adding and withdrawing members, are clearly documented in the company minutes. Recording these changes shows a history of the company procedures and will be invaluable if any actions are contested or if the company is taken to court.

Giving new members their share

When a new member joins your LLC, how do the profit distributions work? Assuming that you are distributing the profits according to the ownership, you would pay her a percentage of the profits based on her ownership shares and how long she has been a member during the current fiscal year.

For example, if a new member, owning 10 percent of the LLC, is admitted to the LLC on July 1, does she get 10 percent of the profits at the end of the year? Of course not! Your accountant can assist you in your exact calculations, but in this case, if the total profits distributed are $100,000, then the new member will receive 50 percent (for the half of the year she was a member) of the 10 percent (her ownership share) for a grand total of $5,000. After that distribution has been made, the remaining $95,000 can be distributed according to the other members' percentages.

Make sure that you have outlined this provision in your buy-sell agreement, especially if you allow members to come and go. Can you imagine the outcome if a member were to buy in on December 20, take a huge chunk of the distributions for that year, then sell out on January 2? Trust me, it's happened, and the only way to prevent that situation is to make sure your operating agreement or buy-sell agreement clearly states that distributions are calculated according to the number of days of the year that the member has been admitted to the entity.

If a member is contributing a piece of property or equipment in exchange for membership shares, her tax basis may change (especially if the item carries a mortgage or other debt). This is called a *return of capital* in IRS terms and can be a good thing in the long run, trust me. The member should hire a qualified small-business accountant or CPA to keep track of her tax basis.

Speaking of taxes, whenever a new member contributes money, property, equipment, or any other type of asset, the IRS doesn't consider any gain or loss taking place by the member or the LLC itself. It is considered an *equal-value exchange* in IRS terms. This means it's a tax-free transaction; even though you report the transfer on your tax return, the IRS takes no money out of your pocket.

When a member wants to leave

When a member withdraws, two things can happen to the person's membership shares

- ✔ The withdrawing member will sell her interest to another member or a third party.
- ✔ The withdrawing member will want the LLC to buy her interest back from her.

First, the LLC should attempt to purchase the membership interest itself. After this has been done and the member has relinquished her shares to the LLC, the other members can reconfigure their ownership percentages. For instance, if three members each owned 33 percent of the company and one member decides to sell her shares back to the LLC, then the remaining two members will each own 50 percent of the company.

Make sure you outline the specifics of this process in your operating agreement or buy-sell agreement. If you don't do this, in some states, the LLC may have to pay the member the value of his initial contribution, or worse, the value of the membership shares he wants to get rid of. Obviously, this could be a problem if the LLC doesn't have that sort of money lying around.

In other states, the complete opposite may happen, and the withdrawing member may have to pay damages to the LLC to cover the losses that the LLC incurred by her withdrawal. As you can see, the laws vary widely, and the best way to control what happens in the event of a member withdrawal is to state what you want in your operating agreement or buy-sell agreement.

If the member wants to sell her shares, the most common way to handle this situation is to give the other members *right of first refusal.* This means that the other members have the option of purchasing the membership shares at their *current value* (the total value of the LLC divided by the percentage of membership shares being sold).

If no members purchase the shares, then the withdrawing member has the right to sell them to the general public. If someone who is not a member buys the shares, the incoming member won't have full rights in the LLC; she'll only have *economic rights,* which means she gets the profit and loss distributions, but has no right to vote or manage the LLC. However, the other members can vote to allow the incoming member the rights that were previously denied her. At that point, she becomes a full member.

When you just gotta say goodbye!

Say you gave membership to an employee, and six months later, you catch him stealing from the till. You and your partners are furious, and you decide that the only option is to fire him. Unfortunately, he still has the membership that was given to him. Considering that you and your members want to cut ties with the thief, you consult your buy-sell agreement.

Luckily, you see that you were smart and included a provision that allows for the expulsion of a member. You and your members take a vote and send a letter to the excommunicated employee letting him know that he is being expelled as a member of the LLC and will receive the value of his shares in a structured payment plan that suits the company. This is all in accordance with the buy-sell agreement that he signed and received a copy of when he was issued his shares.

If the member withdraws during the fiscal year, it's usually up to the withdrawing member and the incoming (new) member how to work the distributions. In most cases, I would advise you to pay the distributions to the new member and let him then pass on the profits and/or losses that are due to the old member. If you want to be nice, you can calculate the distributions on a per-day basis and pay the old and new members their individual shares.

When it comes to hiring, firing, and retiring managers, state law is usually silent on the issue. So you need to have provisions in your operating agreement that discuss how managers will be retained and replaced. If the LLC is manager-managed, the operating agreement should state that the members get to vote every year on whether to replace the current manager. The members should also be able to take a special vote to expel the manager at any time, if need be. Managers should also be admitted in much the same way — with a vote of the members. As for the manager withdrawing, you have to choose whether to allow it, and if you do allow it, what penalties will be assessed. This should also be placed in the operating agreement.

What to do when a member passes away

Although you can decide on your own how your LLC behaves upon a member's death, you should know that no matter what, the law protects the remaining members. Because membership shares of LLCs are considered personal property, those shares will go through estate and probate much the same as the other assets of the deceased. The membership shares will be distributed according to his will or estate plan. Therefore, you can easily end up with a new partner.

The plus side is that, if your operating agreement is worded correctly, the beneficiary of the LLC membership interests has no real power in the company, only an economic interest. So the beneficiary can only receive the portion of profits and losses that his membership shares entitle him to. When it comes to voting, he has no say. When it comes to managing, he must remain silent. He can only become a full partner if the other partners take a vote and agree.

Now, this isn't necessarily the status quo in all states; therefore, it's important to add a provision in your operating agreement that outlines what happens if one of the members dies. You may also want to add a provision that states that the LLC has the right to buy back the shares within a certain timeframe.

Transferring membership shares

You normally can't automatically transfer your membership shares like you can when you own stock in a corporation. You must first assign them, which means that whomever you assign the shares to doesn't have voting and/or management rights. They can only receive the distributions. Upon a vote and agreement among the majority (or whatever you set in your operating agreement) of the members, then the member can be transferred the shares in full, meaning he will no longer have any restrictions to his membership.

When approving a transfer of membership, most state laws don't require a unanimous vote — just a majority. You can put whatever you want in your operating agreement as long as a majority vote is required.

Not all states make a distinction between transferring membership shares to members and transferring to nonmembers. However, the IRS doesn't require that all members consent when it comes to transferring to other members. Make sure to have a provision in your operating agreement that goes over this.

When the transfer has been complete, don't forget to reissue the membership shares of the LLC to reflect the transfer and, just as important, collect and cancel the old certificates.

Although you can set up your operating agreement to allow membership interests to be freely transferred (like stock), you should avoid this. By allowing the ownership of your company to be freely transferable, you become less like an LLC in the eyes of the law and more like a corporation. This can be a big issue when someone sues you, and you ask for charging order protection (see Chapter 11), a benefit that is exclusive to partnerships such as LLCs.

Regardless of whether you want your membership to be freely transferable, the feds may not like that idea. In their opinion, any membership shares that were purchased under a registration exemption such as those listed later in the chapter, will be considered *restricted securities.* This means that they can't be offered or resold without the resale taking place under an available exemption. Otherwise, you must register the securities with the SEC and that is definitely a process you won't want to stray from — I promise.

If you or your partners really want to transfer your membership shares and have obtained approval from the other members, then all you will have to do is transfer the membership in accordance with one of the exemptions that I detail in the next section. Also, make sure that the state laws allow for the same exemption; otherwise, you risk getting in trouble with the locals.

Selling Membership Shares for Dough

Before you can open your business, you most likely need money. More often than not, the upstart capital for a business comes from the founders and people willing to finance it for a piece of the action (otherwise known as *investors*). Therefore, raising money is a vital aspect of any up-and-coming business. The good part is that, unlike sole proprietorships or general partnerships, LLCs can actually sell portions of the ownership — the membership shares. Membership shares are normally given to investors in return for cash, property, or other assets. You can also give them to employees or contractors in exchange for their services. This is a great tactic to use if you're just starting out and don't have a lot of money to pay employees.

In some states, you can give *promissory notes* for future money, property, or services that someone intends on contributing. That way, you can issue the shares first, and then the person can make his contribution. You can always note in your operating agreement that if the individual doesn't live up to his promises, his shares are confiscated.

One of the reasons LLCs are quickly becoming the entity of choice for raising money is because they provide unmatched limited-liability protection for everyone involved in the business (see Chapter 14 for more on limited-liability protection).

When setting up your LLC and creating your operating agreement (see Chapter 9), make sure to list all of the members, their membership interest, and all of the contributions received from them. This isn't always necessary, and the information can be changed later with the members' approval; however, I strongly recommend that you follow tradition and keep these pertinent facts in the operating agreement.

Although you don't have to issue membership certificates, I always recommend them. They add legitimacy to the investment, and investors like to have them. If your operating agreement includes restrictions about transferring the membership, then you should print a notice of these restrictions on the actual certificate. This notice is commonly called a *legend*.

In the following sections, I go over federal and state laws regarding investments. Then, I show you ways that you can get around the detailed process of registering your offering with the federal and state securities commissions. These are called *registration exemptions.* You should remember that term because these exemptions will be your lifeline when navigating the securities law minefield.

Knowing the laws when it comes to securing investments

So, you know that an LLC is the best entity to use when raising capital. Now the question is whether you legally can. After all of the hard work of finding investors, you're nearing the finish line and just need to cut a deal, right? Unfortunately, you may not be able to just take their money. Special *securities laws* protect the innocent from bad investments, and you must comply with these laws before legally raising financing. I know it seems like a pain in the neck — and it is — but trust me when I say that you do *not* want to mess with securities laws. The penalties for noncompliance are steep and include huge fines and jail time.

Most people think of securities laws and the Securities Exchange Commission (the SEC) as only applying to large public corporations trading on exchanges like NASDAQ and NYSE. Not so! If you sell shares of your small business or real estate property to the general public, then the securities laws apply to you.

To make matters even worse, not only do you have to comply with federal laws — which are regulated by the SEC — but you also have to follow state laws. State laws are called *blue sky laws.* The term *blue sky* originated from a judge who said that the advertisement of a certain stock had "about the same value as an area of blue sky." When setting up your financing plan, you need to take state and federal laws into account.

Federal securities laws

The federal government considers anything to be a *security* if an individual or entity invests cash, property, services, or other assets into a business and isn't involved in the business's management decisions. This means that whenever you accept any form of contribution for your membership shares, you are dealing in securities. Ha! And you thought you had to be some bigwig Fortune 500 company to do that!

Two major pieces of legislation control all U.S. securities: the United States Securities Act of 1933 and the Securities and Exchange Act of 1934. Both pieces of legislation have their own sets of rules and regulations and have been amended numerous times over the years. These acts were set up to protect the investor, but also make the act of complying with them too difficult for most small businesses. First of all, the process of registering your securities with the Securities and Exchange Commission is not only a lengthy one but also comes with some enormous expenses, including registration fees, CPA fees, attorney fees, underwriting fees . . . The list goes on and on.

So, what's a small business to do if it can't afford the huge costs of raising just a little bit of money? Well, the Feds got smart, and they now allow registration exemptions for businesses that want to raise a limited amount of money and don't mind being limited to some pretty strict rules. These are called *exemptions,* and I get into them in more detail later in the chapter.

State securities laws (also known as blue sky laws)

If you want to advertise your investment nationally or find investors from all over the U.S., then you have a long road ahead. It isn't as simple as just registering your securities with the state that your LLC was formed in; you have to register your securities in every state that you seek and/or find investors in. Because the laws differ from state to state, registering your securities in multiple states can be very time consuming and very expensive — especially if you have a securities attorney doing all of the research and filing.

There is a way to get around this, but it will still take some good old-fashioned research on your part. You can use the registration exemption to get around having to register your offering with every state securities commission.

Registration exemptions actually started with the federal government. Because it's so difficult to register securities with the SEC, the feds decided to cut the average small-business owner or real estate investor a break and let them raise money without too much red tape. The problem that occurred, though,

Securities laws protect you and the economy

Believe it or not, the securities laws in place help make the United States the economic superpower that it is today. Before the United States Securities Act of 1933 was created, the stock market was a pretty rogue business. There were no regulations, and anyone investing in the market was definitely doing so at their own risk (and risky it was!). It was common for criminals to create fictitious companies with the sole purpose of taking the common man's life savings and heading for the border. It's because of these dishonest practices that when many of these seemingly legitimate companies failed to report any earnings, the great Stock Market Crash of 1929 rocked the nation. When the U.S. dove into the resulting Great Depression, lawmakers knew that something had to be done. With lessons learned, the Securities and Exchange Commission was thus born, and laws were drawn up that protect the innocent man from fraudulent investments.

is that companies were easily able to navigate the federal securities laws but were still getting hung up in all of the red tape created by state securities commissions. Registering your securities in one state is difficult, and then add to it all of the states that you intend on finding investors in. There aren't enough painkillers in the world to cure that headache!

So, to help out the small businesses and real estate transactions that don't raise a large amount of financing (between $1 million and $5 million), the Uniform Commission of State Laws with the blessing of the SEC tried not only to put all of the states on the same page, but to offer registration exemptions that matched those of the federal government.

The resulted was a set of provisions titled the *Uniform Limited Offering Exemption* (or ULOE), and the federal government offered them to the states on a silver platter, begging them to copy and paste that set of securities laws into their own state statutes. The idea was that if you comply with the federal registration exemptions, then you're automatically in compliance with the state securities laws. Some states agreed, but others only copied part of the code. Therefore, you and your attorney must go through each state's code to see whether that registration exemption is available in your state, and if so, what the specific rules are.

If you want to file under the ULOE, you can get the SEC Form D document at www.myllc.com/dummies. Basically, the ULOE took the federal registration exemptions 505 and 506, made a few simple variations, and then handed them over to the states, ready for the taking. Just remember: Run things by a qualified securities attorney before filing!

You are required to register in *every* state that you advertise your investment in or take investment from, not just the state that your LLC was formed in.

How the laws apply to you

One of the first ways to legally get around securities laws is to make sure that when you raise capital, the membership shares you offer aren't considered securities in the first place. The best way to determine whether securities laws apply to your organization is to take a good look at how the management will be structured after you raise the financing.

- ✔ If the investors have a full and equal say in the management of the company, then the securities laws do *not* apply.
- ✔ If the LLC is managed by separate managers or the investors have limited managerial powers, then the securities laws *do* apply.

I like to think that there are a few loose rules to determine whether you will be selling securities. If any one of these rules applies to your LLC, then you are automatically required to comply with securities regulations.

✔ Your LLC is manager-managed.

✔ Your LLC is member-managed, but some or all of the investors are junior managers and don't have a full say in the business's day-to-day operations.

✔ Your LLC has hundreds of members. Even if they all have a say in the company's management, there are too many to realistically manage the day-to-day operations.

✔ You are widely advertising the investment and looking for multiple investors.

Now, beware! These guidelines are loose and based on federal interpretations of the law. When it comes to states, the laws and the interpretations of what a "security" is differs greatly. For instance, states such as New Mexico, Ohio, Vermont, and Alaska consider *all* membership shares to be securities, whether the LLC is manager-managed or not.

If you are just looking to raise a little bit of money, then I suggest that you find an investor or two who may have good input in the business operations. This way, you can avoid a lot of the securities laws, but your investor can also be an asset in terms of knowledge and experience.

When you want to create a member-managed LLC, make sure that the articles of organization and the operating agreement both specify that each member is equally responsible for the operations and success of the LLC. There should be no centralized management, like corporations, where the shareholders elect directors, who then elect the officers, who then manage the LLC. Avoid that structure and instead get used to managing as a team. All members must collectively be in charge of the major decision making and have the power to select or remove key employees. (See Chapter 4 for how to set up a member-managed LLC.)

If you transfer your membership shares to someone, such as a family member, as a gift, the securities laws do not apply. However, this can only happen once — you may not make multiple gifts of unrestricted membership shares!

Securities registration exemptions

So, when all is said and done, you have decided that you still want to sell membership shares as securities. You don't want your investors to have control over the operation of the business; you just want them to sit back and be silent partners. That's okay. As a matter of fact, because the federal government knows how difficult, costly, and time consuming it can be to register your securities with the SEC, it has provided some exemptions that mostly apply to small businesses or small projects that are looking to raise a small amount of capital.

Now, what I list here only applies to federal exemptions, so you'll still need to look at each and every state in which you intend on selling your securities and determine which laws apply to you and whether you can meet their criteria for an exemption from registration.

At this stage in the game, I recommend working with a securities attorney who is familiar with conducting searches on securities laws in multiple states. To save money, you may be able to work out an agreement with the attorney in which you take on some of the workload yourself. Just make sure that, no matter what, the attorney specializes in securities laws. A regular business attorney normally won't cut it.

In the following sections, I outline the federal exemptions available to small businesses. Remember, most states offer some variation of the Rule 505 and 506 exemptions. You should check the laws yourself or contact a securities attorney who can check for you.

Rules 504, 505, and 506 are called *Regulation D Exemptions* because they all belong to Sections 3 and 4 of the Securities Act. If you're using a Rule 504, 505, or 506 offering exemption, you must read and follow some corresponding general rules. These are Rules 501, 502, 503, 507, and 508. You can find these at www.myllc.com/dummies.

Intrastate exemption

The *intrastate exemption* seems better than it is. It requires that you find investors or members only in the one state that your LLC operates. There are a few problems with this:

- ✔ All of the members of the LLC must be in the same state where the LLC has its business operations.

- ✔ The LLC can't advertise for investors in any state other than the one where it has its business operations.

- ✔ The LLC can only operate in this one state. This is the worst rule of all and where most people get disqualified. This means that anything related to your business can't be done in any state other than your home state. You can't market to people out of state, and you can't have customers in or purchase supplies from other states.

In a day and age where the world keeps getting smaller and smaller every year, it becomes increasingly impossible for most companies to raise money under this exemption. However, if you're a small mom-and-pop business that only operates locally, this exemption may work for you — just make sure that you don't do any business out of state. Also, keep in mind that you'll still be required to file an exemption with your state's securities commission. To do this, file the SEC Form D (which I have uploaded at www.myllc.com/dummies) with your state securities commission. Just make sure to clear everything with a qualified securities attorney before doing so.

Rule 504 exemption

If you're looking to raise less than $1 million, then you are automatically exempt from having to register your securities with the SEC. This is the *Rule 504 exemption.* In general, you can't advertise the investment opportunity, and you aren't required to make any specific disclosures about the investment. However, all of this must be done within a 12-month period. After that time, you must register the securities with the SEC or find another exemption.

After you first sell some of your securities, you have to file a Form D, which includes some basic information about the company, such as the names and addresses of its owners and stock promoters. You can download a Form D from www.myllc.com/dummies.

You can only use this exemption if your LLC isn't selling any other securities that are registered with the SEC. For instance, if your LLC has another class of membership that is being offered for $50 million and is registered with the SEC, the same LLC can't use this exemption to raise under $1 million.

The federal exemption code that most states have adopted doesn't cover Rule 504 exemptions. If you choose to sell securities under the Rule 504 registration exemption, then you should contact a qualified securities attorney who can assist you in all of the states you'll be selling your securities in.

Rule 505 exemption

If you plan to raise less than $5 million, you may be able to use the *Rule 505 exemption.* It has a few more limitations than the Rule 504 exemption, but this is natural considering that you're raising more money. First, you can't use *general advertising* (any advertising that is targeted to the public at large, such as newspaper ads, TV ads, and so on) to sell your securities. Also, you can only have a maximum of 35 regular-Joe investors; although, you can have as many accredited investors as you like.

What's an *accredited investor?* It's a person or institution that meets certain financial criteria. These investors are well-off enough to suffer the financial hit of a bad investment. They normally have a net worth of more than $1 million. They generally are more educated about investing and can make better decisions on where to place their money than the average person.

When selling to *non-accredited investors* — the regular Joes — you must adhere to the SEC rules regarding investment disclosures. These disclosures outline the risks inherent in the investment. You must be completely forthright and disclose everything that the SEC requires you to. Your attorney can help you write disclosure statements that comply with both federal and state laws.

Like the Rule 504 exemption, you can't take longer than 12 months to raise your funds. Also, to use Rule 505, your company must have CPA-certified financial statements, which can be quite costly since the Sarbanes-Oxley laws took effect.

Rule 506 exemption

Rule 506 is the golden rule that most companies raise funds under. When offering securities under the *Rule 506 exemption,* you are doing what is called a *private placement,* and you can generally raise as many funds as you like. The guidelines for Rule 506 are very similar to Rule 505. Here, you're also limited to 35 Joe-schmo investors, but you can still sell to an unlimited number of accredited investors. Again, like Rule 505, you can't do any general advertisement of the investment. However, if you sell any securities to non-accredited investors, you must make very specific and comprehensive disclosure statements regarding the investment to all investors.

To streamline the process of a Rule 506 offering, many companies issue what is called a *private placement memorandum* (or PPM, for short), which adheres to the SEC guidelines on what needs to be disclosed regarding the investment. If you ever come across investment opportunities that aren't listed on the stock exchange, you will most likely see them in this format. Or you may see what is called an *executive summary,* which is just a summary of the PPM that teases your interest in the investment. After you're interested, you will most likely be given the full PPM.

A PPM is normally a complete business plan, 30 to 50 pages long, put into a special format that includes certain disclosures, such as who is involved in the business and the risks that are inherent to the investment. I encourage you to be completely forthright when drafting your PPM. Most smart investors will look for these disclosures and, believe it or not, will be a lot more confident in the investment when they see that the company is being very open and honest about the risks involved.

You can always purchase a template for a private placement memorandum online. However, you may want to have your attorney draft it for you, even though the cost may be in the thousands. Most templates only comply with federal laws, and your attorney will have to make sure that your PPM and your financing plan comply with the blue sky laws (state laws) as well. Not to mention, your presentation will end up looking much more professional to prospective investors.

Regulation A exemption

If you plan to raise less than $5 million, you may want to consider offering your securities under the *Regulation A exemption.*

With a Regulation A offering, you aren't limited to the number of Joe-schmo investors you bring on board. You will still need to do a *private placement* (a long-winded form that is comprised of your basic business plan and some hefty disclosures about the investment); however, Regulation A allows you to advertise the investment in more ways than a Rule 505 or 506 exemption does. For instance, you can use radio or mass mailing to advertise your investment. Also, when registering under a Regulation A exemption, you can advertise your investment before having prepared a private placement memorandum, so long as you don't take in any money. This allows you to test your response rate before incurring the cost of creating all of your disclosure and financial statements.

As part of the disclosure, you must show financial statements; however, they can be unaudited if no audited statements are available.

Chapter 11

Record Keeping and Maintaining the Charging Order

*R*ecord keeping is the most important aspect of LLCs and often the least understood. I would say that the majority of LLC owners in the United States don't keep their company records properly, usually because they don't know what to do. For most people, the entire concept of recording meeting minutes and drafting resolutions is foreign. Because of all of the confusing vocabulary and the lack of reference materials on what exactly needs to be done, most people just avoid the task altogether. And who can blame them?

You need to take the time to read this chapter and find out how to properly record your decisions and organize your company records. Then you can peruse the accompanying CD in this book for the documents you need. Otherwise, if you ignore your record-keeping obligations, you'll no doubt end up in front of a judge with a confused look on your face as he orders the liquidation of your personal assets to settle a petty lawsuit. At that point, it's too late to get your records in order. You never want to be caught back-dating corporate documents at the last minute — it only gets you into more trouble. You must be diligent about dotting your *i*'s and crossing your *t*'s. It's not nearly as difficult as you think, and in this chapter, I give you the tools you need and the steps you must take.

Keeping Your Limited Liability: Why It's Important

Record keeping is just that — the keeping of the records. However, you can also think of it as the "keeping of the limited liability," because without maintaining your records properly, you lose all the benefits of operating as an LLC.

All of the hoopla about LLCs generally stems from one thing — the liability protection that they offer. LLCs actually offer two types of liability protection:

- ✔ A standard *veil of limited liability* — similar to what corporations offer their shareholders — that protects the members from the LLC's debts and obligations
- ✔ A *charging order protection* that protects the LLC from the members' debts and obligations

If you're going to own and operate an LLC, you need to understand what these layers of liability protection are and how to maintain them. In the following sections, I give you a brief overview of each type and explain what you need to do to keep each layer of liability protection intact.

Limited liability: It goes both ways

First and foremost, you must understand that LLCs offer the same basic liability protection that corporations do. In other words, unless you personally guarantee something, you aren't responsible for any of the business's debts, judgments, or obligations. If your business gets sued, you can rest assured that your house, your car, and the money in your bank account are safe and protected.

With corporations, though, the limited liability protection only goes one way. It protects the business owners from the debts and lawsuits of the businesses, but it doesn't protect the business from the owner's personal lawsuits. If a business owner gets sued personally, his stake in the corporation is considered a personal asset and can be taken away from him. If the business owner has a majority of the business's stock, then the entire business can be liquidated and the money can be taken.

But LLCs are different, and this is the reason they are the entity of choice. LLCs are considered partnerships, and under the partnership law that governs them, a debtor can't just seize the membership shares of a partnership like she can corporate shares — this would put the other partners in a bad position. The law states that partners can't be forced into an unwanted partnership — this would cause the business's innocent partners to suffer.

What this means in real life is that a creditor can't take the LLC membership shares from the partner in legal trouble; she can't have a vote or say in the business; she can't have a role in managing the company. She can simply receive profit distributions to those membership shares. Nothing more. This is called a *charging order protection,* which I go over in detail in the next section.

Piercing the veil of limited liability

Like corporations, LLCs offer their members a *veil of limited liability.* This is the main thing that separates LLCs from general partnerships, which offer the owners of the business no liability protection at all. (Chapter 2 talks about what a general partnership involves.)

The best way to understand the term *veil of limited liability* is to think of your liability protection as a piece of fabric, a veil that protects you and your personal assets from your business's litigious predators. The term specifically refers to the protection that the LLC provides your personal assets if a lawsuit is filed against the business.

Whenever this veil of protection is breached by a creditor of the LLC and your personal assets are seized, this is called *piercing the veil.* In short, the limited liability, perhaps the most important attribute of an LLC, has been lost.

The one and only way to keep your veil of limited liability intact is to keep perfect records in accordance with your state's laws. You must keep a close eye on your company's record-keeping practices. Not only is properly keeping records a practical solution for keeping all partners on the same page, but it shows the courts that you are a serious business, and it motivates them to treat you like one.

To pierce your veil, the creditor has to add you, as an individual, to the lawsuit against your company. In the complaint, she will seek to impose personal liability on you, the owner, for the business's debts or wrongdoing (in other words, she'll plead the court to pierce the veil of limited liability). Then the creditor has to prove to the court that the veil of limited liability should be pierced. If the creditor proves that the veil should be pierced, the court will make you personally responsible for the judgment. This means that the creditor can seize and liquidate your personal assets to settle the claim.

Under most circumstances, the court will pierce the veil of limited liability and hold the owner responsible for the debts if the creditor can prove one of six things:

✔ **Your LLC is an *alter ego*.** This means that the LLC wasn't treated as an entity separate from its owner — the LLC's only job was to do the owner's bidding, without actually operating as a business. In this case, the creditor must establish that the owner failed to separate his personal financial affairs from the entity's financial affairs, and/or he failed to keep proper records and follow established formalities (see the "Maintaining Company Records Properly" section for more information).

✔ **The LLC was undercapitalized.** If you don't put money into your LLC, then how can you say that it's an operating business and that you aren't just using it to protect yourself from creditors? You can't. This is why you must invest in your business when you purchase the membership shares. This is the easiest way to satisfy this requirement. After all, if your business doesn't have even a little money, the judge may find this a good reason to pierce the veil and hand over your personal assets to settle the lawsuit.

✔ **Your LLC is actually a sole proprietorship.** Single-member LLCs aren't too different from sole proprietorships. They both have pass-through taxation, and they both have one owner and very few reporting requirements. Single-member LLCs are even classified as sole proprietorships by the IRS. The problem here is that sole proprietorships offer no limited liability whatsoever. So, to maintain a basic level of limited liability, the best thing to do is to just take on a partner. Even if your partner is a friend or a corporation that you control, and only owns a small percentage, this prevents the LLC from being classified as a sole proprietorship.

✔ **Your LLC is in "revoked" status.** The department that you file your articles of organization with — usually the Secretary of State's office — will require you to file an annual or biannual statement. (I go into more detail on annual statements of information later in this chapter.) If you miss your filings, eventually your LLC will go into a *revoked status.* This means that your company is no more, as far as the state is concerned. In other words, the state gave your LLC life, and it can take it away — especially if you miss filings and don't pay your state fees. If you're sued when your LLC is in a revoked status, the judge can disregard the LLC's liability protections and hold you personally responsible for the judgment.

✔ **Your records are incomplete.** The law is vague when it comes to the record-keeping requirements of LLCs. Don't assume that if there is no law, no record keeping is required. If you only file your articles of organization and keep no other records of company activities, a judge can determine that you're operating as a general partnership and pierce the veil of limited liability. To avoid this, stay on the safe side by carefully following all record-keeping requirements that I outline in this chapter.

✔ **Your LLC has been dissolved.** A lot of events can trigger the dissolution of your LLC. The most common is that your LLC went past its duration period, and you never renewed it by amending the articles of organization and/or the operating agreement. For more information on dissolutions, see Chapter 12.

Piercing the veil of limited liability is one of the most frequently litigated issues involving small businesses. If you get a creditor persistent enough to sue your LLC, you can be confident that she'll attempt to pierce your veil. After all, it costs nothing for her to add you to the lawsuit. So you must make sure all of your ducks are in a row *before* you ever hit the courtroom.

If you're doing business in a particular state and haven't registered to transact business there or aren't in good standing, don't worry too much — your limited liability is still intact. Your status in the state that you originally filed in (your *domicile*) is what matters. However, make sure that you catch up on your filings before heading into court.

What is a charging order?

After a creditor obtains a judgment against you for a certain amount of money, she can request that the judge grant her what is called a *charging order.* In a corporation, your personal creditors can obtain your shares of stock and can sell them, transfer them, and do whatever else they desire with them — the shares are theirs. With an LLC, all the creditor gets is a charging order. A charging order is a special court order which says that if any profits are distributed to you, they must go to the creditor instead until the debt is paid. With a charging order, the creditor gets no rights in the business and has no say. She can just hold on — quietly — and wait to be paid.

Charging orders are so protective to the members of an LLC that if an attorney sees that a savvy business owner has protected his business assets in an LLC, he will often try to settle or refuse to sue altogether. Charging orders are a pain in the butt for creditors because they are so restrictive that a creditor basically just sits there, bound and gagged from making any decisions regarding the company, and waits for the other partners to pay her — should they choose to.

Because the managers decide if and how much profit is to be distributed to the members, the managers can actually withhold distributions from all members, and the creditor receives nothing. The managers can still take their salaries, as usual, of course.

The most vital element of record keeping is your operating agreement, to which I have dedicated all of Chapter 9. Unless you're in one of the few states that actually requires creditors to obtain charging orders by law, then you must provide for them in your operating agreement. If you don't and you get sued, then state law can prevail, and your company can be taken away from you in the blink of an eye.

Thirteen states provide for charging orders in the statutes (therefore, you don't need to provide for them in your operating agreement); they are Arizona, Arkansas, Connecticut, Delaware, Idaho, Illinois, Louisiana, Maryland, Minnesota, Nevada, Oklahoma, Rhode Island, and Virginia. Keep in mind, though, that even if you are operating in one of these states, I encourage you to put the charging order protections in your operating agreement. Review Chapter 9 for detailed instructions on how to do so.

Why creditors hate charging orders

In order for a creditor to obtain a charging order for your LLC, she must be granted one by the judge who is handling your case. The charging order gives the profit distributions you receive from the LLC to the creditor until your debt is paid. This would seem like a viable solution for most creditors, right? Think again! From a creditor's perspective, this seemingly great scenario can be a nightmare! Creditors normally avoid charging orders like the plague because

- ✔ **The creditor can't force the LLC to make any payments to her.** The LLC's managers decide how much money is distributed to the members and to which members it is distributed.

- ✔ **The charging order doesn't allow the creditor to have any voting rights, make any management decisions regarding the LLC's operations, or add or withdraw other members.** This means that the creditor holding the charging order can't make any executive decisions — especially those that involve distributing company profits to her!

- ✔ **If the operating agreement allows for it, the LLC's managers can refuse to distribute the earnings.** How is this bad for the creditor? Well, the creditor is still required to pay income taxes on these profits as if they were received. This is called *phantom income* and a way that a lot of savvy LLC owners (like you) pass on their income tax burdens to their creditors instead of their cash.

A creditor who obtains a charging order on your LLC membership shares doesn't become the full owner of them. Instead, she becomes a *transferee* or *assignee* who is only entitled to the profits (and the income taxes!) of the LLC, but isn't allowed to vote or take any role in managing the company — she can't even force a payment of the profits!

The negotiating power of a charging order

The best way to get rid of a creditor is to hold tight and not distribute any profits to her. This way, because the creditor is considered a substituted partner in the LLC, she is still required to pay income taxes on the profits she should have received. Instead of making money, she will be spending it, and you will have forced her into a much better position to negotiate.

How to get rid of a creditor with a charging order

Does a creditor have a charging order against your LLC interests? If so, here are a few ways to make her life a nightmare and encourage her to settle:

✔ Increase your and your partners' salaries (make sure that the salaries remain in line with similar positions in your industry). Your intention is to make sure that you'll have an income and that very little profit is left in the company to be distributed at the end of the year.

✔ Amend your operating agreement to allow the company to retain the profits and to minimize the profit percentage that is distributed to you (which would be going directly to your creditor).

✔ Every six months, send your creditor a letter stating how well the business is doing and that you are making sure she is prepared to pay the taxes on the profits at the end of the year.

✔ At the end of the fiscal year, send the creditor the K-1 which states her percentage of the income generated by the LLC (income which is being retained by the company and won't be distributed). Along with the K-1, send a letter advising your creditor that she is required to pay taxes on this income.

✔ Send a letter to the IRS requesting an audit of the creditor because you want to be tax compliant and you want to make sure that all taxes have been timely paid and are up to date.

✔ Send the creditor a copy of the letter sent to the IRS with an additional copy of the K-1.

✔ Repeat this process until the creditor is so saddled with IRS debt and headaches that she proposes a settlement.

This may seem to be a harsh way of getting rid of a creditor, but I assure you it's common practice. The attorneys that I work with on a day-to-day basis use this strategy all the time with our clients. If you are unclear about anything, though, you should definitely have your attorney assist you!

Unfortunately, while you are doing this, you and your partners can't take any profits either. However, you can pay yourself a salary and take company loans instead. After all, it won't be for too long! In the meantime, the creditor has no say about it because she has no management control over the business. If you can still pay yourself, why bother distributing membership shares in the first place? After all, wouldn't you want to just sit tight and make the creditor pay for all of your income taxes on the profits instead? Come to think of it, doesn't it make you almost *want* to have someone obtain a charging order against your LLC?!

After a creditor has a charging order against your LLC and you have put them in a tight spot where she is dishing out the dough to the IRS (on your behalf!), you'll be in a much better negotiating position. At this point, you should try to settle the judgment debt or just convince her to drop her collection efforts. Regardless, your business is still intact, and that's what matters. If you were operating as a corporation or other type of entity, this wouldn't be the case.

Ways to protect your charging order

The worst thing that can happen to you is to think that your assets are protected, when they really aren't. To make sure that, no matter what, your LLC holds up in court and a charging order can be applied, you must do a couple of things:

- ✔ **Before a lawsuit, distribute profits regularly.** When suing you, if a creditor sees that your LLC doesn't distribute profits regularly to its members, a creditor can petition the courts to allow her to foreclose on the member's shares. This means that if state law allows, and the courts agree, the creditor can become the new legal owner of those LLC membership shares and have all the rights and powers that you once had. After your creditor has obtained a charging order, you can *then* stop distributing the profits.

- ✔ **Have at least two members in your LLC.** This one is important. LLCs have this special charging order rule to protect the innocent partners in the business. If the business has no other partners, then the creditor can apply to have the charging order circumvented and can seize your company right out from underneath you. I also recommend that the other member is not your spouse. If you have no one else whom you can trust to act as the other member, then you can always form a corporation to serve as the second member. And remember — that other member can own a very small percentage.

- ✔ **Classify the LLC as manager-managed.** If you classify your LLC as member-managed instead of manager-managed (see Chapter 4 for more details), then any creditor who obtains the assets may be able to manage the LLC to the same extent as the owner. Even if all members will equally manage the business, I suggest that you still classify the LLC as manager-managed and name each person, individually, as a manager of the LLC.

- ✔ **Elect pass-through taxation.** Theoretically, an LLC that looks and acts like a corporation can be treated as a corporation by the courts. This is the one drawback of electing to be taxed as a corporation as opposed to sticking with the pass-through taxation that is the default for partnerships. For more information on pass-through taxation, see Chapter 2.

Maintaining Company Records Properly

One of the most debated aspects of LLCs is how much record keeping they are required to do. They definitely don't have the strict record-keeping requirements of corporations, but the laws about what record keeping is necessary are pretty vague. However, to be safe and not put yourself at risk of having your veil of limited liability pierced (see the "Piercing the veil of limited liability" section earlier in the chapter), you should keep detailed records of all of your company activities and go through many of the same formalities that corporations do.

Throughout the following sections, I go over all of the pertinent record-keeping requirements, including

- ✔ Storing your records in a special customized company kit
- ✔ Maintaining your membership roll
- ✔ Keeping your tax and financial records organized
- ✔ Holding regular meetings with the other members and managers of the company
- ✔ Drafting resolutions which document your major company decisions
- ✔ Documenting your corporate activities in the meeting minutes

I know that this all seems incredibly time consuming, but believe it or not, this stuff isn't that difficult! Your company records don't have to be perfectly drafted in complex legalese either. Even if you write and sign your company resolutions on the back of a napkin and hold your company meetings with your partner at the local bar — it's still better than nothing and will most likely still hold up in court. The point I'm trying to get across is this: Just get it done!

Completing the company kit

Although it's not necessary or required by law, a *company kit* can be a god-send. It will keep everything organized for you and cover your butt if you end up in court. With it comes your *company seal,* which in most states *is* required by law. Your company seal is a little device that imprints your company name and formation date onto paper. It's often used to show that a document is a true and original copy that was verified by the company.

The kit is not very complicated. It's normally a nice binder that is closed by either a zipper or in a slipcase. The kit allows you to easily carry your corporate records from place to place. If you intend on meeting with banks or private investors for capital, you will definitely want a corporate kit. It's the only truly accepted method of presenting your company documents in an organized and professional manner.

Don't order your corporate kit through your attorney or incorporating service — you will pay a premium price. Instead, order it online from a corporate kit supplier. My company uses CorpTech Supply (www.corptech supply.com) — all kits are completely customized and are shipped the same day you order (two-day shipping is included in the price). Most of their kits are $59.

When ordering from a kit supplier, your company kit should come with the following:

- ✔ A professional binder that either zips closed or is enclosed in a matching slipcase, and is customized with your LLC's name on the spine
- ✔ A seal customized with your LLC information
- ✔ Custom-made, numbered membership certificates printed with your company name
- ✔ A complete set of index divider tabs. The actual tabs may vary, but they should include articles of organization, operating agreement, and membership certificates.
- ✔ Some blank template documents including a sample operating agreement, some sample meeting minutes, and a sample membership issuance agreement
- ✔ A blank membership roll
- ✔ Perhaps some business licensing information that is applicable for your state

After you receive your kit, you should keep the following documents in your company kit:

- ✔ Your state-filed articles of organization and company charter
- ✔ Your operating agreement
- ✔ Your company meeting minutes and resolutions
- ✔ Your membership roll
- ✔ Any cancelled membership certificates
- ✔ Your federal tax ID number and filing
- ✔ Your business licenses and state filings
- ✔ Any foreign filings that you have made in other states
- ✔ Your company's registered agent information for each state

If your attorney is forming your entity, he must supply you with a corporate kit. This is the standard practice and is the only professional thing to do. Some attorneys try to save money and make their own corporate kits out of plastic binders that they buy at the local office supply store. Those attorneys also don't often supply their clients with company seals. If your attorney does this, you should consider where else he may be shorting you on value.

Creating a membership roll is very simple. You just take the blank form that you received in your company kit and fill in each member's name and address. Next to this information, put the amount of membership shares each person has. Make sure to update the roll every time your LLC's membership changes. Some states even require that you supply your registered agent with an updated copy of your membership roll. That way, if any of your members wants to view the membership roll, they can arrange to do so with your registered agent.

Staying up-to-date with annual reports

Shortly after you file your articles of organization, you must file a statement of information (also called an *initial report,* depending on the state; see Chapter 8). This filing normally states such information as your managers and/or members, their addresses, your corporate headquarters, registered agent and address, and so on.

In most states, you are required to file this form every year, in which case it becomes known as the *annual report.* Some states, like Alaska, only require you to file this form once every two years. The fees that go with these filings vary from state to state. Check Appendix A for your state's annual fee.

Always file your annual report on time. In most states, if you fail to file this form once, you'll go into a "default" status until the filing is made. If a full year passes and you still haven't filed the form, your LLC will then be *revoked,* which is a similar to being forcibly dissolved. Not good.

If you are sued while you are in revoked status, piercing the veil of limited liability is easy. After all, your LLC doesn't even exist in the eyes of the state. The annual filing is the first step to protecting your LLC — if you fail at this step, then you shouldn't even bother with the rest.

Tracking tax filings and financial information

Your tax returns and financial reports show the backbone of your business. These records undeniably prove that your LLC is an operational business. Because they are backed up by bank statements and receipts, they are taken very seriously by the courts as testimony to the intricacies of your business.

You need to hang on to your pertinent tax records and financial statements for seven years. These tax records show the courts that your company is, financially, a separate entity — in other words, you and your LLC don't share a bank account. Your financial information proves that you have been actively engaging in business and not using the entity as an extension of yourself (also called an *alter ego*).

Your operating agreement (see Chapter 9) should designate what sort of financial reports the members have access to and how they can go about viewing the records. Tax returns, balance sheets, and profit-and-loss statements should be kept at your corporate office in case one of the partners wants to view this information. Also, in the event of a lawsuit, you will most likely be required to hand copies of this information over to the plaintiff.

Let's Keep in Touch! Holding Regular Meetings

What would a business be without meetings? You know — those boring snooze fests where the only thing that is usually accomplished is a mutual sense of frustration? Yeah, those. But, at least you can skip out on them from time to time (which really means every time). After all, it isn't like they are legally required, right? Wrong. The government has managed to make everyone's least favorite pastime an actual legal requirement. Luckily, the government is pretty lax when it comes to LLCs (as opposed to corporations), and therefore, meetings only need to take place once a year and before making important decisions that affect the fate of your company.

There is a plus side, however. What the law *doesn't* state is *where* the meeting must take place. And anywhere it does take place, you can deduct the travel expenses. Umm . . . Hawaii, anyone? Tahiti, perhaps? Aruba? It doesn't matter if it's just you and your business partner. Or, if a corporation that you own is the only other partner, then it'll be a lonely party of one on the island.

The most important aspect of the meeting is the meeting minutes. *Minutes* are the detailed records of what took place at the meeting. Larger companies have secretaries who record the discussions as meeting minutes while the meeting takes place. The minutes of smaller companies just record any issues that were brought up in the meeting and any decisions that were made (called *resolutions*). Minutes serve as a record that all partners in the business got together to discuss the issues at hand and that all major decisions were approved by a majority of the partners.

Deciding when to meet

Corporations are required to meet annually to go over corporate business. However, LLCs aren't obligated to have set meetings unless the LLC's operating agreement requires them. I recommend that you provide for yearly meetings in the operating agreement. I believe it's important for all of the partners to get together with the sole purpose of discussing infrastructure and business affairs. It's also a common practice for LLC members to reelect the managers at these annual meetings.

In addition to the annual meeting, you should call a meeting if

- ✔ A legal or tax issue needs to be addressed, approved, and recorded
- ✔ Membership shares are to be issued or transferred
- ✔ There is a change in management or managers need to be elected
- ✔ Assets need to be sold
- ✔ Major purchases need to be made
- ✔ Leases or other debts need to be incurred
- ✔ The company is to be dissolved
- ✔ The company's name changes
- ✔ Any other pertinent decisions need to be made that require the consent of all of the partners

Assembling the members for the meeting

In order for it to be worth your while to hold a meeting in the first place, you have to have what is called a *quorum*. A quorum is the number of members it takes to pass a vote and should be stated in your operating agreement. If it's not stated there, the state law prevails. Some states require a simple majority of the members (51 percent); other states require three-quarters. Without the proper number of members showing up at the meeting, a vote can't take place.

For instance, if your LLC's operating agreement states that the quorum is a majority of the members, and four of your ten members show up, then a quorum is not present. You would need to have six members for a quorum. Otherwise, nothing can be resolved by a vote.

If getting all of your members together for a meeting is like herding cats, then you may want to allow your members to vote by proxy. A *proxy vote* is cast by a person (a *proxy*) on behalf of a member who can't attend the meeting. The member will tell the proxy how they want their votes represented. Proxy votes count toward meeting a quorum.

Like most non-Fortune 500 companies, you most likely can't afford to hire a special proxy voting service. If you want to allow your members to vote by proxy, you can send out cards or a sheet of paper that describes the issues up for debate and allows the member to check how they want to vote. After they have marked their response, they send in their card to the proxy, who represents them at the meeting.

Is it hard for you to get all of your members in one place? You can have your meetings in cyberspace! There are a lot of different software solutions for online meetings. Some sites that facilitate this are www.gotomeeting.com and www.webex.com.

Just a minute: Holding the meeting and recording minutes

As much as you dread the idea, you know you have to call a meeting. I'm sure you've spent more hours than you'd care to count attending seemingly pointless meetings called by your colleagues. You want your meetings to be a valuable use of time, and you want everyone to leave the meeting feeling as if something worthwhile was accomplished. There is a way to do this.

Say your Uncle Joe wants to get involved with your business and is even willing to make a sizeable investment in exchange for some membership. You approach two of your five partners, and they agree that it's a good idea. It's time to call a meeting.

Here are the steps that you will take:

1. **Loosely gather information from your partners on what would be a good date and time for the meeting. Then prepare a notice of meeting and send it to all partners.**

2. **Prepare a meeting agenda with all of the items that you would like to resolve. Make a copy of the agenda for all partners in attendance.**

   In this case, you include an agenda item to discuss whether your Uncle Joe should become an investor.

3. **At the meeting, appoint a chairperson, who conducts the meeting, and a secretary, who documents the votes and the resulting decisions that are made.**

4. **The chairperson calls the meeting to order — the meeting has begun.**

5. **The secretary determines whether a quorum is present. (See the "Assembling the members for the meeting" section for an explanation of a quorum.)**

6. **If any unfinished business was tabled at the last meeting and needs to be addressed at this meeting, the secretary reads the minutes of the last meeting.**

   All issues that are being carried over from the last meeting are addressed first.

7. **The managers present their reports on how the company is operating.**

   This is not required, but a lot of your silent partners will appreciate it, I promise.

8. **Go over the agenda items one by one and discuss them. Then take a vote of the members. Make sure to write down what was discussed!**

   The notes you take during the discussions and votes will become the minutes.

9. **Adjourn the meeting.**

10. **The secretary drafts the minutes of the meeting — in the proper format (you can find an example on the accompanying CD) — and sends them to all of the members for their signatures.**

   If there are too many members, the secretary can sign the minutes herself.

Resolutions to be on the lookout for

When an item has been voted upon and approved by the quorum of members, it's called a *resolution*. Here are some common resolutions that you may have to put in your meeting minutes:

- ✔ Resolution for the treasurer to open and use LLC bank accounts along with a designation of authorized signers
- ✔ Resolution for adoption of a fictitious firm name (a "DBA")
- ✔ Resolution for the approval of a contract
- ✔ Resolution for the lease of property by the LLC
- ✔ Resolution for the purchase or sale of real property by the LLC
- ✔ Resolution for the LLC to elect corporate tax treatment

Basic forms to get you started

On the accompanying CD, I have included some fill-in-the-blank minutes and resolutions that you can use for guidance. These are

✔ Notice of meeting

✔ Waiver of notice of meeting

✔ Certification of mailing of notice

✔ Meeting agenda

✔ Minutes of the initial meeting of the LLC

✔ Minutes of the annual meeting of the LLC

✔ Approval of LLC minutes

✔ Membership subscription agreement

✔ Written consent to action without meeting

✔ Resolution for the acquisition of an independent audit of the LLC's tax and financial records

✔ Resolution of the LLC's fiscal tax year

✔ Resolution to amend the LLC's articles of organization

✔ Resolution to amend the LLC's operating agreement

✔ Resolution designating membership distributions

✔ Resolution approving additional capital contributions by members

✔ Resolution admitting a new member

✔ Resolution allowing the transfer of membership

✔ Resolution approving the LLC's purchase of the membership shares of a withdrawing member

✔ Resolution appointing LLC managers

✔ Resolution approving salaries and bonuses of key employees

Chapter 12

Knowing Your Exit Strategy: Dissolutions and Extensions

In This Chapter
▶ Reviewing the reasons your LLC can go kaput
▶ Knowing how the dissolution process works
▶ Avoiding the tax traps that dissolutions can cause

All good things come to an end — your LLC is no different. Sometimes things just don't go as planned and you decide that you need to close up shop. Other times, legal technicalities get in the way and you are *forced* into what is called a *technical dissolution,* which I explain in greater detail later in the chapter. In legal terms, the termination of the LLC is called a *dissolution,* or in some states, a *termination.*

Dissolving doesn't necessarily mean that you are giving up your business. In some cases, you're just dissolving on paper or for tax purposes, but it doesn't affect your day-to-day business operations. Other times, you *will* be shuttering your services and calling it quits. Whatever your reasoning, you need to make sure that you do it right. The devil is in the details — if you don't cover all of your bases before dissolving, you can end up with a hassle later on.

When terminating your business operations, a proper dissolution allows you to tie up all the business's loose ends so it quietly fades away with its paperwork in order and all of its affairs wrapped up. A dissolution wreaks less havoc in the long run and keeps your previous business dealings from coming back to haunt you. It allows you and your partners a fresh start to pursue your next big idea.

Before dissolving your LLC, I advise you to thoroughly review this chapter and get with your members and create a detailed plan. This way, you're all on the same page and there are no arguments later. After you have created this plan, get your accountant to take a look at it and advise you of any major tax consequences that may occur. If you change your plans at any stage, run them by your accountant to make sure that you aren't walking into a huge tax trap.

Help! It's Melting! Examining the Reasons Your LLC May Dissolve

One of the big things that sets LLCs apart from corporations is that they weren't originally meant to have a *perpetual existence*, meaning that they aren't supposed to operate indefinitely. LLCs weren't designed to be long-lasting entities, and because of this, they are much easier to wrap up and dissolve than other entities. This is one of the reasons why LLCs are the best bet around for short-term projects, such as movies or real-estate deals.

Here's a list of common reasons why your LLC may dissolve, which I cover in detail in the following sections:

- ✔ Your business isn't working out — management is deadlocked over an issue, or the company isn't profitable — therefore, the members decide unanimously to terminate the LLC.

- ✔ One of the members (if state law provides for this) directly or indirectly terminates the company. In most states, it only takes one member to trigger a dissolution. He can do this by:

  - Being kicked out by the other members (in other words, *expelled*)

  - Passing away

  - Going bankrupt

  - Retiring and choosing to resign as a member

  - Going insane or becoming incompetent in some way

- ✔ The IRS or the courts order you to dissolve your LLC. This is commonly caused by a bankruptcy or if your business is caught red-handed in criminal acts.

- ✔ You have reached the set dissolution date for your LLC as stated in your articles of organization.

- ✔ You have sold or transferred more than 50 percent of the company within a 12-month period, and you're subject to a tax termination.

- ✔ You fail to file your state reports and the Secretary of State terminates your LLC.

- ✔ The articles of organization or operating agreement states that the LLC is to dissolve when a specific event occurs, such as the sale of a patent or technology. After that event occurs, let the dissolution begin.

- ✔ You are a licensed professional, such as a physician or an attorney, and you lose your license. If you are operating under a professional LLC, there is a good chance your LLC will need to be terminated.

You just want to dissolve: At-will dissolutions

Business is hard. Really hard. If you're tired of struggling and have decided to throw in the towel, don't beat yourself up about it — you're not alone. One in ten businesses don't make it past their first year. And because you had the foresight to set up your businesses as an LLC, it should be relatively painless to close the doors.

If you used an LLC for a short-term project, such as film financing or a real estate deal, maybe the project has run its course, so you dissolve the operation and split the cash among the members. Simple as pie.

Some states only require that three-quarters of the members need to vote for a dissolution in order for it to happen. If you own one-quarter or less of the LLC, it could easily be dissolved under your nose! You can protect against this by specifying in your operating agreement that it takes a unanimous vote of the members for a dissolution to occur.

Now, the complications arise when one member wants to dissolve and the others don't. Or it's split fifty-fifty. Unless you have specified otherwise in your operating agreement, most states dictate that when one or more members decide to resign, the remaining members still have the option of continuing on with the company. I go over this in more detail in the next section.

The at-will dissolution is relatively simple to perform. If all the members are on board and no legal proceedings are looming over the LLC, terminating the company is easy. I cover the process in the "Undergoing the Dissolution Process" section later in the chapter.

Considering that LLCs are separate from their owners, they can file bankruptcy separate from their owners as well. This means that your company can handle its debts through bankruptcy without your personal credit being affected. When an LLC wants to file bankruptcy and call it quits, it files for Chapter 7 bankruptcy. When an LLC wants to file bankruptcy but stay in business (called a *reorganization*), it files Chapter 11 bankruptcy. If you are a single-member LLC, you may be able to file a personal bankruptcy. When filing for bankruptcy, you must work with a qualified bankruptcy attorney who can assist you in doing it legally and without any tax consequences.

Disassociating yourself from the LLC doesn't dissolve it. Even if you are a single-member LLC, selling or assigning your membership shares to someone isn't considered a dissolution. An LLC is an entity separate from yourself. The LLC is still in existence; it's just that now the other person owns it and all of its assets.

I know that sometimes people ignore things, hoping that they go away. But if the company isn't doing well, you can't sell it, and your heart isn't in it anymore, then you should definitely take a couple of days and do a formal dissolution. When you file everything properly and go about paying the debts as best you can, nothing can come back to haunt you later. The extra peace of mind that you get from going that extra mile will be worth it, I promise.

Being left in the dust by a member

There are a zillion reasons why a member might leave his membership behind. Some will make you sad (he passes away or loses his sanity); some will make you jealous (he retires); and some will make you irate (he empties the bank account and heads for Mexico). But regardless, you still have to address these matters because they can cause your LLC to dissolve if you aren't careful.

If a member experiences any of the following, your LLC is in jeopardy of dissolving:

- ✔ Death
- ✔ Retirement
- ✔ Resignation
- ✔ Bankruptcy
- ✔ Expulsion

It doesn't matter what percentage of the LLC the member owns; she could own only 2 percent, and, in some states, single-handedly dissolve the LLC. When working with partners, you need to protect your interests. You don't want to work hard to build your future, only to have it torn down by some minority partner. This is where the operating agreement becomes vital.

Although most states have laws that allow the members to continue the LLC, you don't know what the specifications and technicalities are. With LLCs, you can make your own rules, so make sure to specify in the operating agreement that the remaining members can vote to continue the LLC if one of these matters befalls a member. Then take it a step further and specify whether the decision to continue should be unanimous, or if a three-quarters or majority vote "yes" is enough to continue the LLC. Remember, these decisions affect you *big time*. You need to make these judgments; don't trust your state laws.

If the remaining member (or members) just doesn't want to deal with the company anymore, then she should go through the formal dissolution process that I outline in the "Undergoing the Dissolution Process" section later in the chapter.

When expelling a member is the only choice

Chris, Alex, and Brad, best friends from college, decided to form a Web design and hosting company that caters to small businesses in New York City. Things were going great for a couple of years, the business was making money, and, while not wealthy, the guys could cover their living expenses. Around the third year in, things took a turn for the worse. Brad started partying all night at the clubs and got hooked on drugs and alcohol. His life started to spiral out of control, and Alex and Chris were concerned. They tried to talk to Brad, but he got defensive, and it only made things worse between them.

After a few months, Brad had run out of money. He started using his company credit card to pay for his late-night escapades. The guys decided to take Brad off the bank account, but because the LLC was member-managed, he just put himself right back on. He was dragging the company down, and after not being able to make payroll, Chris and Alex realized that their only

solution was to expel him from the company. They wanted to do this the legal way, so they took their operating agreement to their attorney and had a powwow. Their operating agreement and state law stated that they could expel a member if he was incapable of operating the business.

The guys then sat down with Brad for lunch and gave him the hard news. They passed him a letter that documented that they had used their collective 66 percent of the company to expel him. They included a cashier's check that covered his initial contribution and his portion of what the company was worth. Chris and Alex had to take out a business loan to cover this, but they knew that it was their only hope of saving what they had worked for. Brad protested, but he legally had no recourse. Alex and Chris tried to remain friends with Brad, but after many unsuccessful interventions, they eventually parted ways.

The laws on LLCs vary widely from state to state. For instance, in South Carolina, if a member invested a total of $10,000 for 5 percent of the business, she can demand that $10,000 back at any time during the course of business. If she can't get it back — for instance, if the company is tight on cash at the moment — she can legally dissolve the LLC all by herself simply by filing articles of dissolution with the Secretary of State. Even if she only owns 5 percent of the business! The members can't say anything about it. For this reason, it's imperative that you specify in your operating agreement and/or buy-sell agreement, the company policies on dissolving. See Chapter 9 for more help on this.

After a member leaves the LLC and you have decided to continue operations, make sure that you redistribute the membership shares accordingly among the remaining members. You should distribute new membership certificates to the remaining members and document the new ownership percentages in the company minutes.

'Cause the IRS says so

Believe it or not, the IRS can actually dissolve your entity. Well, sort of. It's not a full dissolution, so to speak — it will be what's called a *tax termination*. Your LLC will still keep on kicking, and the Secretary of State's office will definitely keep sending you invoices and reports that you need to file. A tax termination just means that, in the eyes of the IRS, your LLC has dissolved and distributed all of its assets to a brand-new LLC (which, as far as you are concerned, is really just the same LLC as you were using before).

So, what does it take to trigger one of these so-called tax terminations? One of two things can happen

- ✔ Your LLC suddenly stops conducting business for a lengthy period of time.
- ✔ You sell or transfer 50 percent or more of the membership of the LLC within a 12-month period.

The latter of the two is the most common. If you stop doing business, the IRS waits until you actually liquidate and distribute the cash to the members before considering it a termination.

In the event of a tax termination, your *tax election* is dumped and a new one must be made. Remember when you chose to be taxed like a corporation for a couple of years until you got your business up and running? Well, that's a tax election. When you elect to be taxed as a corporation, you are sort of blocking yourself in because you can't change your tax election for five years (see Chapter 13 for more on tax elections).

Because tax terminations ditch that entity classification election, you can reorganize your company if you decide you want to be taxed like a partnership and don't want to wait for five years. The easiest way to reorganize your LLC is to have a corporation be a member of the LLC. When you want to trigger a tax termination, you just form a new corporation and transfer the LLC's membership to that entity. Assuming you transfer more than 50 percent of the membership, this is a quick and easy way to change from corporation tax status back to a partnership tax status.

If your LLC has been tax terminated, you don't need to file new articles of organization or even acquire a new tax ID. Really, you don't have to do much of anything except consult with your company accountant so he can work out the tax issues, if there are any. However, you and your partners may have to recognize a gain or a loss on your personal federal tax returns. Therefore, you may want to just head to your accountant's office to have a little chat. Nothing big — just so he knows what's going on and can plan for it.

The history of the fictional dissolution

By now, you are probably wondering why on earth going through this process of dissolutions when you plan to keep the company going is even necessary. I know that it makes zero sense, but it's just one of those formalities that happens when our federal and state governments are a little too slow to adapt to the constantly changing nature of business. Let me explain. When Wyoming first decided to allow the illustrious LLC, the IRS had no idea how to tax it. It was sort of like a corporation (liability protection for all) and sort of like a partnership (the profits and losses pass through to the owners). Because it looked like a corporation, yet still wanted to be taxed like a partnership, the IRS decided that at the LLC could choose from four corporate characteristics. It could only choose two, though, because otherwise it would be too similar to a corporation and could not be taxed like a partnership.

These four corporate characteristics are limited liability, centralized management, perpetual life, and free transferability of ownership. Lawmakers felt that the two most important facets were the limited liability and the centralized management

(LLCs can have separate managers) and therefore set up the following regulations to differentiate the LLC from corporations:

✔ There must be a limited duration; in other words, it can't "technically" continue on for the rest of eternity like corporations can.

✔ Membership shares cannot be freely transferred.

In response to this, most of the states decided to add their own laws which alleviated some of the pain of having to dissolve so soon after forming the LLC. They added in their statutes that, should the members vote and agree, they can choose to continue the existence. Now do you understand why I call it a "fictional dissolution"? Even though during the formation you have to choose a termination date, you don't really ever have to dissolve!

Because of this obviously "fictional" dissolution requirement, the IRS has started to ease up its restrictions. Thankfully, it now allows corporations to have pass-through taxation like partnerships (S corporations) and limited liability companies to elect to be taxed like corporations.

I know tax terminations can be incredibly confusing. Just sit back, 'cause the whole dissolved/not dissolved thing happens pretty instantaneously. It's strange, I know, but don't forget — it's the IRS we're talking about here!

After a tax termination has occurred, you need to elect a new tax year. You do this by filing IRS Form 1128. You can download a copy at www.myllc.com/dummies.

If you get hit with an unexpected tax termination, don't fret! They are usually completely tax-free events. Just make sure that your accountant knows what's happening.

You've reached the set dissolution date

When LLCs were first created, one of the big things that set them apart from corporations (and thus allowed them to have the favorable pass-through tax status) was that they didn't have a *perpetual existence*. Luckily, the IRS has smartened up to their absurdity, and this is no longer the case. However, this explains why you have to put a *duration*, or a dissolution date, in your articles of organization in most states. The most common is a 30-year duration. That means that 30 years after the initial formation date, the LLC has to dissolve.

Although the IRS has moved forward, most states still require your LLC to be limited in its lifespan. Well, if you have any sense at all, you most likely don't want to spend 30 years building a company only to kill it off after it has reached critical mass on the success scale. You don't have to! Luckily for you, you can specify in your operating agreement that the members of the LLC can choose to continue the business past the proposed dissolution date — which is why this is called a *fictional dissolution*. And unless you decide it's time to pack up and move on, there's no good reason why you wouldn't choose for the LLC to carry on with operations.

Later in the chapter in the "It Just Keeps Going and Going: Using an Extension to Avoid Dissolution" section, I show you how to extend the life of your LLC when a dissolution date is looming.

If you have reached the end of your duration and your termination date is near, make sure that you act fast! Most states require that you and your partners get together and vote on whether to continue the business within 90 days of the termination date.

It Just Keeps Going and Going: Using an Extension to Avoid Dissolution

Business is going great, and before you know it, you're hit with a dissolution. Lots of things can trigger an unwanted dissolution, which I discuss in the "Help! It's Melting! Examining the Reasons Your LLC May Dissolve" section earlier in the chapter, but how do you get out of a dissolution when it occurs? You do what's called an *extension*. This is where the operating agreement comes in handy. Your operating agreement allows you to decide what happens in the event that you are faced with an unwanted dissolution. If your operating agreement doesn't address this situation, you'll fall victim to the state's rules.

Chapter 9 covers how to create or amend an operating agreement. Go through the steps there and amend your operating agreement so that it specifies that you can continue the LLC by a vote, instead of dissolving.

After your operating agreement is set up properly, you can take the following steps when faced with an unwanted dissolution:

1. **Hold a meeting of the members.**

2. **Take a vote on whether to dissolve or continue the LLC.**

3. **Make a record of the resolution that was made by the members.**

4. **Put that resolution in the company minutes.**

For more details on all this voting, meeting, and minutes stuff, head over to Chapter 11, where I explain the ins and outs of each of the steps above.

Keep in mind that if your dissolution date is looming, you'll want to take these steps as early as possible and extend the life of your LLC before it actually passes the dissolution date.

If you are voting to extend the life of your LLC because of a dissolution date in your articles of organization, you'll have to vote to amend the articles (which I explain how to do in Chapter 11) and then file the amendment with the Secretary of State's office.

If, however, your LLC is facing dissolution because a member died, resigned, or experienced one of the other events listed in the "Being left in the dust by a member" section earlier in this chapter, the member who created the dissolution event normally doesn't get a vote (unless you state otherwise in your operating agreement) when the other members vote on whether to continue the LLC. Therefore, if you have three members, and you own 40 percent, while the other remaining member owns 30 percent, and it only takes a majority to approve the continuation, then you have the majority and can take the vote all by yourself.

Upon the occurrence of one of these dissolution events, you don't have much time to get your act (and the members!) together. You often must take a vote and resolve to continue the LLC within 90 days of the triggering event!

Undergoing the Dissolution Process

With all of the things to do, it almost seems harder to dissolve an LLC than it does to form one in the first place! It makes sense though, considering that after years in business, your LLC may have a lot of baggage, so to speak. It's like a divorce — the longer you have been married, the more stuff there is to sort out. My goal in this section is to take you through the dissolution steps, one by one, so you can file your two-page dissolution form with the Secretary of State's office and know that you are completely protected from anything coming up in the future and biting you in the butt.

Everyone must go through a three-step process when dissolving an LLC:

1. **Acknowledging the end is here.**

   This is simple — the LLC is legally forced to dissolve, or the members vote to discontinue the business. Either way, coming to terms with the fact that the company is going to be dissolved and coordinating the logistics of it is what this first step is all about.

2. **Winding up the affairs.**

   This is probably the longest and most arduous process of them all. The longer you have been in business, the harder this step may be because of the sheer amount of paperwork, creditors, clients, and business associates that you have acquired over the years. Here, you make all of your last filings and liquidate the company. You then distribute the assets: first paying creditors, then any members the company owes money to, then you return the investments of the members, and finally distribute the profits according to each member's percentage of the company.

3. **Terminating the company.**

   This part is probably the easiest — it's all just filing paperwork. Before doing anything, you want to make sure that you are in good standing with the Secretary of State's office. You can't file a dissolution until you are caught up with your previous years. Why? Because they want your money, of course! Then, if you are operating in multiple states, you'll want to withdraw from those states. I show you how to do this later in the chapter. After you have withdrawn from all of the states that you are foreign filed in, you must file articles of dissolution in your home state.

 Read your state statutes regarding dissolutions. You can find a list of state Web sites in Appendix A. If you don't like your state's laws and guidelines, then I urge you to create your own rules and stick them in your operating agreement. I show you how to do this in Chapter 9.

In the following sections, I cover the most important dissolution processes in detail. For now, though, this checklist gives you an idea of the baby steps you should follow within the bigger steps I outlined earlier. The list also includes the paperwork involved to successfully dissolve your LLC:

✔ Hold a meeting of the members and vote to terminate the LLC.

✔ Liquidate all LLC assets.

✔ Make final federal tax deposits — IRS Form 8109B.

✔ File final quarterly or annual employment tax forms:

- Form 940, Employer's Annual Federal Unemployment (FUTA) Tax Return

- Form 941, Employer's Quarterly Federal Tax Return

- Form 943, Employer's Annual Tax Return for Agricultural Employees (if necessary)

- Form 943A, Agricultural Employer's Record of Federal Tax Liability

✔ Issue final wage and withholding information to employees — IRS Form W-2.

✔ Report W-2 information to the IRS — IRS Form W-3.

✔ If necessary, file the final IRS Form 8027, Employer's Annual Information Return of Tip Income and Allocated Tips.

✔ File federal tax returns:

- Form 1040, U.S. Individual Income Tax Return

- Form 1065, U.S. Partnership Return of Income

- Form 1065 (Schedule K-1), Partner's Share of Income, Credits, Deductions, etc.

- Form 1120 (Schedule D), Capital Gains and Losses

✔ Issue payment information to subcontractors — IRS Form 1099-MISC.

✔ Report information from 1099s issued — IRS Form 1096.

✔ Report business asset sales — IRS Form 8594.

✔ Report the sale or exchange of property used in the LLC — IRS Form 4797.

✔ File final employee pension/benefit plan — IRS Form 5500.

✔ If necessary, report the exchange of like-kind property (1031 exchange).

✔ Cancel all state and local business permits.

✔ Cancel all fictitious firm name filings.

✔ Transfer all intellectual property (domain names, patents, state and federal trademarks, and so on).

✔ File the last state tax return.

✔ Pay all franchise and corporate tax fees for the current year.

✔ If necessary, obtain a certificate of good standing with your state tax bureau.

✔ Send notification of dissolution to vendors/creditors.

✔ Publish a notice of dissolution in the local newspaper in each jurisdiction you have transacted business in.

✔ Pay/reject all creditor claims.

✔ Pay all debts that are owed to members, including distributions that were never made.

✔ Distribute any remaining profit to the members according to their ownership percentage.

✔ Pay any back fees that are owed to the Secretary of State in each jurisdiction you are transacting business in.

✔ Withdraw from all states in which you are foreign-filed.

✔ File articles of dissolution with the Secretary of State.

✔ If necessary, notify your customers of the dissolution.

All in favor: Taking the vote

Unless you really want to make your partners angry and probably end up in court, you won't want to go around like some rogue operator, terminating the company all on your own. You need approval. You and your partners need to sit down and agree on the approximate date that you want to terminate your company. You should then come up with a plan on how you are going to go about doing it.

If your termination date is upon you, and you and the other members have decided not to continue the company (see the "You've reached the set dissolution date" section earlier in the chapter), then taking a vote is optional. Normally, you can just start the dissolution process.

However, if you want to dissolve the LLC before the termination date — assuming that it's your decision to make and you aren't being forced into it — then you'll need to take a vote of the members. Make sure to check out what your operating agreement says about dissolutions. For instance, it should go into what percentage of members must vote to dissolve and what the process is. If your operating agreement is silent on the issue, then your state's laws will automatically govern your dissolution. Call your registered agent or your attorney for assistance — they should know this stuff by heart.

After you have all of the members together, you can vote to dissolve your LLC. When taking a vote, make sure to hold a proper meeting, keep meeting minutes, and then create a resolution that records your vote. I go into detail on how to do this in Chapter 11. This way, the other members have no recourse should they change their minds afterward. In other words, they can't say that you did it without their permission!

Settling your debts: Paying creditors

Most states require that you notify your creditors in the event of a dissolution. However, even if it isn't mandatory, you should still do it. During the dissolution process, the more of a paper trail you create that shows you attempted to pay your creditors, the less recourse they have in the future.

Members have limited liability and are protected from the LLC's creditors. But this doesn't mean that you can just liquidate the company, take the money, and dissolve. If you have debts, they must be paid before any member sees a penny. Otherwise, the creditor may be able to go after you and your partners for any money that you took that may have belonged to them.

If your LLC is faced with a dissolution, but the members decide that they want to continue on with business, then the creditors don't need to be notified that you're not dissolving the LLC. As a matter of fact, if you send a notification, it may just cause a lot of confusion.

Giving them notice

Before doling out the cash to your creditors, you should send them a notification letter. The purpose of the notification letter is to allow creditors to send their claims. The good thing about this is that if they fail to send their claim by the cutoff date (usually 120 days), then they can't make the claim after the dissolution has occurred. You just may be a lucky duck and have lazy creditors who never send their claims in.

The notification letter should contain the following information:

- ✔ A statement that you intend to dissolve, including an approximate dissolution date, if you have one.

- ✔ What information you want the creditor to give when they send in the claim (invoice numbers, dates, and so on).

- ✔ The deadline by which claims should be submitted. I know it's tempting to make this a very short amount of time, but if you make it too short, the notice may be disregarded by the courts. The standard deadline is 120 days — you should probably just stick to that.

- ✔ A paragraph that states that any claims received after the deadline won't be honored.

- ✔ The person and mailing address to which the creditor must send the claim (normally your registered agent's address).

When sending a notification letter, make sure to send it via certified mail. You need to have a receipt that proves you sent it.

You don't necessarily know who may think that you owe them money. I recommend sending this letter out to all companies and individuals that your LLC has used as a vendor or independent contractor in the past.

Handling claims

Now, after you have received a claim, you have the option of either accepting it or rejecting it. If you choose to accept it, keep in mind that everything is negotiable. You can often settle the claim for less than the total amount. Just make sure that once you settle a claim, you pay it.

Before paying your creditors, you need to liquidate all of the LLC's assets. The amount of cash that your company has after liquidation determines how much the creditors get paid. Whatever is left after the creditors have been paid gets paid to the members.

If you choose to reject a claim, you will have to do so at your own discretion. Will this creditor seek recourse? If you think the creditor will be a problem, talk to your attorney to prepare for any actions the creditor may take after the company has been dissolved. When you reject a claim, you should write a letter to the creditor stating that you are rejecting it. If possible, and if your attorney thinks it's a good idea, you should give a brief explanation as to why you've refused the claim.

Covering your bases

So, what about the creditors you don't know about? It's always what you don't know now that can hurt you later. One of the most powerful moves that you can do when dissolving your LLC is to publish a notice in the local newspaper. With this notice, you can let creditors know that they have a certain timeframe in which to send claims to be considered. I know, I know . . . how many companies actually read these ads with itty-bitty type in the newspaper? Very few probably. However, this shows that you did your due diligence and is usually enough to satisfy the courts.

If you are registered in multiple states, you should probably publish this notice in every state that your LLC conducts business in. This can be time consuming, so I recommend that you get your multistate registered agent to help you.

Who's due what: Paying members

After you have liquidated your LLC's assets (that is to say, sold them) and settled all of its debts, you can focus on paying the members. The IRS recommends a specific order in which members are paid, and unless your operating agreement states otherwise or the members have taken a vote and created a resolution, you should probably stick to the status quo.

Generally, the first to be paid are those members who are owed distributions. For instance, if the LLC recognized a profit, but for some reason didn't distribute that money to a member (say it needed the cash for something else), then that member should be paid what he is owed. Also, if a member has made a loan to the company, then that member should be paid back.

After the members have been paid what they are owed, the remaining money is used to refund the members for their initial contributions. This may seem strange, but it's true. The money that you invested will actually be returned to you before receiving any dividends.

Did your investment in the company only consist of services? Well, services have a value too! Get with the rest of the members in the company and decide what the value of your services was worth. You can look at current pay scales in your industry as a guideline. For instance, if you worked for free for the company for one year, and your peers were paid $50,000 for that same year, then you can reasonably ask for $50,000 as payment for your services.

After all of the initial contributions have been returned to the members, the remaining money (if there is any) can be distributed to the members according to their percentage of ownership. Yes, according to their percentage of ownership. If you weren't distributing profits and losses in the past according to the member's percentage of ownership, this can be a bit confusing. But it's rather simple. If a member owns 30 percent of the company, she gets 30 percent of the remaining cash. Easy as pie!

As for taxes, as long as you are being taxed as a partnership, you'll just report this income on your personal tax return as you normally would.

Wrapping up the government affairs

Now that the creditors have been paid and the members have been reimbursed — and perhaps even given some extra cash — everyone should be happy (assuming there was enough money for everyone; otherwise, you may know some pretty grumpy folks out there). Now it's time to deal with the government — and that means paperwork. Lots and lots of paperwork.

First, are the tax forms. You have the federal, state, and local tax forms. First, your accountant needs to file your final federal and state partnership tax returns. To file your final federal return, you just file a normal return and check the box at the top which indicates that this return is a final return. If your state requires you to file a special LLC tax return, then you will also want to file a final version of this return.

There are quite a few other forms and returns that you must file. It would be virtually impossible to go over all of them in detail, so check out the dissolution checklist, which you can find earlier in the chapter. Make sure to go over this with your accountant. LLCs all differ somewhat, and you may have to make additional filings, depending on the nature of your business.

Now, before dissolving, make sure that your LLC is in good standing with your home state and all of the states that you are foreign filed in. Your registered agent should be able to provide you with your status in every state and also let you know the steps that you need to take to get back into good standing, if necessary. If you have failed to file your annual returns in many states, this could be a costly endeavor. After you are in good standing in all of the states that you are registered in, you can start the withdrawal and dissolution process.

Making it official: Filing the dissolution

After your affairs have been completely wrapped up, it's time to officially dissolve your LLC. When you terminate it with the state, its public status will be shown as *dissolved* or *terminated*.

If you are registered in multiple states, before dissolving in your home state, you need to withdraw from the other states that you are registered to transact business in. The *withdrawal process* is similar to the dissolution process and usually requires a nominal fee. Just keep in mind that you don't file articles of dissolution to withdraw from a state. States have separate forms for this purpose.

If you have a multistate registered agent, let her handle the entire withdrawal and dissolution process for you. It can be a big hassle to coordinate with many state agencies at one time, especially because they all have different timeframes that they process the paperwork in. Leave it to the pros who already have the relationships. It is definitely worth the extra fee.

It's important that you pay all of your taxes before filing the dissolution. Some states don't even allow you to file unless you have received a tax clearance. Your registered agent or accountant can usually help you resolve things with the state and local tax boards.

To make your life a little easier, I have included the dissolution form for each state on the accompanying CD.

You can also create your own articles of dissolution; just make sure to use the points on the state form as a guide for what needs to be included in your articles. Generally, articles of dissolution consist of

- ✔ The name of the company
- ✔ A list of the members of the company
- ✔ The reason the company is dissolving
- ✔ The date that you wish the dissolution to become effective
- ✔ Any information regarding unpaid taxes
- ✔ The members' signatures and the date the form was signed

You may also need to include a statement, signed by the managers, that states that the LLC has handled all of its liabilities, made the distributions to the members, and no lawsuits are pending (or if there are, a payment arrangement has been made for any judgments).

If you don't dissolve through your registered agent, you should let her know that you are dissolving your LLC and no longer need her services.

Some states have it backward and require you to file your dissolution papers before paying your creditors and winding up your affairs. In this case, talk to your registered agent, who should be well apprised of all state laws regarding dissolutions. She can let you know the proper order in which things must be done.

Dealing with the tax consequences

The tax consequences can be good and bad for the members when dissolving the LLC. Your accountant can go over these with you when you run your dissolution plan by her before dissolving. Remember that if your LLC isn't profitable, the losses can also be passed on to the members. This can offset other income and save you and your partners a lot of money in taxes.

Because your LLC is a pass-through entity, it doesn't have to deal with too many tax consequences. Just file Form 1065, U.S. Partnership Return of Income, on its behalf at the end of the year; the form is more of an information statement than anything else. All profits and losses are passed on to the members and are reflected on their personal tax returns on the Schedule K-1. If you are operating as single-member LLC, then you attach a Schedule C to your personal IRS Form 1040 instead.

If your LLC is canceling debt that the members were personally responsible for (for example, paying off bank loans and such), then the IRS treats this as income to the members, which can cause some unexpected tax burdens. This is one of the reasons why it's important to go over your dissolution plan with your accountant. You can read more about this rule under Section 108 of the Internal Revenue Code. We have included a copy for you at www.myllc.com/dummies.

Unfortunately, your state has you by the throat when it comes to dissolving. Often, they won't honor your dissolution until every penny of your state taxes is paid. If your state has a franchise fee, you need to make sure that you've paid it for the year before dissolving. In states such as California, this is based on the company's income and can be as much as $750 or more.

When your LLC has employees, there is a whole new level of consideration. You must make sure that you are caught up on your federal and state payroll taxes and your unemployment insurance. Again, your accountant is the best person to help you with this.

Part IV
Making Cents of Taxes and Protecting Your Assets

The 5th Wave   By Rich Tennant

"Here's what I think happened: He was wounded by Schedule A and B; then he was hit by Schedule D, which brought him to his knees. Then, as he was crawling to reach his calculator, he gets it square in the pocketbook by Schedule C, and that's what finally did him in."

In this part . . .

What's the point in reading a book on LLCs if it doesn't address the two things that LLCs are known and admired for — asset protection and tax savings. Limited liability companies offer excellent tax savings, which I address in Chapter 13. They're also commonly used for protecting your business and personal assets, which I cover in Chapter 14.

I devote Chapter 15 to LLCs and real estate — one of the most common investments that LLCs are used for. LLCs and real-estate investments were made for each other, and in this chapter, you'll see why. You'll also get some pretty nifty strategies on how to protect your investment properties better by using multiple entities.

Lastly, in Chapter 16, I go over estate-planning techniques that you can use in conjunction with LLCs. For anyone looking to plan their estate, this chapter is a must-read.

Chapter 13

LLCs and Taxes: Arranging the Best Scenario

In This Chapter

▶ Understanding pass-through tax status

▶ Filing your tax returns

▶ Saving taxes with your LLC

I know, I know — just the thought of taxes probably makes you want to throw this book across the room. But don't do it. This isn't the most entertaining chapter that you're going to read, but it will be quick and painless, I promise. Although taxes can be a pain in the butt, by educating yourself about them, you gain the upper hand and end up paying less. Just think, after reading this chapter, you'll be able to stride into your accountant's office with your head held high, and you'll have no problem discussing the tax basis of assets, tax reporting requirements for LLCs, and how you can avoid sending a chunk of change to the IRS.

LLCs can be taxed a multitude of ways, but I'd say about 90 percent of them just stick with the default pass-through taxation. And why not? It's a great way to be taxed! I touch on all types of taxation in this chapter, but I spend the most time discussing the pass-through tax status because it's the most common and the most unique.

If you are like most people, you'll be confused by the tax information at times. Don't let this get you down. You don't need to know everything — just enough for planning purposes and to have an informed conversation with your accountant. After all, accountants are there for a reason — use 'em! An accountant spends his days poring over tax law and dealing with the IRS. Although you should have a basic understanding of this stuff — which I strive to provide for you in this book — you should still use an accountant for the important stuff, such as distributing money to the members and filing the end-of-year tax forms.

Understanding LLC Tax Categories

The LLC has been gaining in popularity because it's the only major entity type that combines full limited-liability protection for all members and pass-through partnership taxation. For the most part, pass-through taxation is more straightforward than corporate taxation, and therefore, easier to figure out. You don't have any extra returns to file, and sometimes the members can personally benefit if the LLC has a bad year. Plus, you can transfer assets in and out of the company tax free.

Your LLC will fall into one of the following tax categories:

- ✔ **Partnership:** If your LLC has more than one member, it will automatically be taxed as a partnership and given pass-through tax status.

- ✔ **Sole proprietorship:** If your LLC has only one member (a single-member LLC), then it will automatically be deemed a *disregarded entity* by the IRS and will be taxed as a sole proprietorship.

- ✔ **Other:** If you want, you can elect a different type of taxation such as corporate taxation or even S corporation tax status (a different type of pass-through taxation) for your LLC.

I cover these approaches in more detail in the following sections.

Examining LLC pass-through tax status

All LLCs are created with a default tax status. It's like hair color — you're born with one color, but as you get older you can choose to change it if you want. The default tax status for LLCs is "partnership taxation" — a favorable form of pass-through taxation. *Pass-through taxation* means that the entity itself doesn't pay federal income taxes. Instead, the business passes the profits and losses on to the individual owners so they can pay the taxes on their personal tax returns. Not only does this save some paperwork hassles, but it also allows the members to offset some of their other income with the losses of the business, should it not be profitable.

Even though the LLC isn't required to file a tax return, the IRS wasn't going to let it get off that easy! LLCs still have to file a Form 1065, U.S. Return of Partnership Income, at the end of every year. Form 1065 is just an information statement, not a return. It lets the IRS know the amount of profits and losses that the company allocated to each member — that way the Feds can follow up and make sure they get their dough.

If you are currently operating as a sole proprietorship or general partnership, you are already familiar with the pass-through tax status of LLCs. Essentially, you are taxed the same — all of the business's profits and losses flow through to you, the owner, and get reported on your personal tax return.

A lot of people think that just because corporations can choose to have pass-through taxation (called an S corporation), that it's the same as an LLC. Close, but no cigar. LLCs and S corporations are dramatically different. For one, S corporations have more restrictions on who can and can't be an owner. Also, certain things like contributions are taxed differently. Don't make the mistake of forming an S corporation because you think it's the same as an LLC. Make sure to have a good long chat with your accountant to go over the merits (and differences!) of each entity before making your decision.

The partners pay the taxes!

To understand partnership taxation, you need to understand two concepts:

- ✔ **Distributions:** When a *distribution* occurs, a member is actually handed cash for his share of the company profits.

- ✔ **Allocations:** When a member is *allocated* a percentage of the company's profit (which is stated on his Schedule K-1), he has to state the amount on his personal tax return and pay taxes on that profit on behalf of the company. This has nothing to do with the actual cash he gets from the company (the distribution).

After the members get together and decide what profits and losses are to be allocated to whom and how the cash is to be distributed, a Form 1065 is filed. Form 1065 isn't very extensive — it just asks for the names and addresses of each of the members and the amount of each member's share of the company's taxable income and deductions. Later in the chapter, I give you more information on how to file Form 1065.

At this point, the company notifies the members of the profits and losses that were allocated to them, and each member is responsible for paying the taxes on these profits. The company notifies each member of the percentage of profit they have to pay tax on by issuing the member a Schedule K-1. Unfortunately, paying taxes on behalf of the company sounds easier than it is. Members can't just write in the amount that they are to be taxed on. They have to list things such as their allocated share of the company's income, gains, losses, deductions, and credits as well as the LLC's tax preference.

Tax basis and taxing distributions of profits and losses

When working with your accountant, you'll probably hear a lot about your *tax basis.* Your tax basis is the amount that you have invested in the company over the years. It's adjusted every time an allocation or distribution is made or your LLC takes on debt. Your *adjusted tax basis* determines how much tax you pay when the company makes cash distributions to you. If the amount of your cash distributions exceeds your adjusted tax basis, then you'll normally be required to pay tax on the overage.

Your tax basis starts with the amount that you initially invested in the company. (If you contributed services, then you need to determine the value of those services.) Then, you add the amount of any monies that the company allocated to you but didn't distribute to you (called *phantom income*). After you have that number, you add the amount of your share of the company's debts that you're personally responsible for to determine your adjusted tax basis. Don't throw in the towel yet — I explain this all in detail below.

You usually will be allocated more profit than is actually distributed to you. Your tax basis is increased by the amount of company profits that are allocated to you and decreased by the amount of profits that are distributed to you. So if the company allocates $10,000 in profits to you that you must pay taxes on, but only distributes $5,000 in cash to you, then your tax basis increases by the difference — $5,000.

It doesn't stop there. If your LLC has liabilities such as loans and/or mortgages that you are personally responsible for, you can include the amount of your share of those liabilities in your basis. There are two types of liabilities:

✔ **Recourse:** Debt that you *are* personally responsible for

✔ **Non-recourse:** Debt that you *are not* personally responsible for

Only loans that the member can be held personally responsible for repaying can be included in a member's tax basis. When calculating your percentage of liabilities, you may want to seek the assistance of an accountant because it can get pretty complex.

Now that you know what your tax basis is, you can calculate your taxes. Generally, your distribution amount minus your adjusted tax basis equals your gain. Also, if you decrease the amount of your share of the company's liabilities, then that is treated as a cash distribution. If this amount is over your adjusted tax basis, then you will have to recognize the difference as gain.

Obviously, I'm simplifying this process so you have a basic idea of how it works. I strongly recommend that you have a qualified tax professional work out all of your calculations for you, because they get much more complex when you throw things such as heavily appreciated assets and real estate into the mix.

Deducting LLC losses from your other income

If you have sources of income besides your LLC, you may be able to deduct your LLC's losses from that other income to pay less taxes! In the eyes of the IRS, there are three types of income — passive (rental properties), active (wages and 1099 compensation), and portfolio (dividends from stocks held). For the most part, you can use the losses from your LLC to offset your *passive income.* The IRS defines passive income as income from a business or rental property in which you are not an *active participant* (you don't deal with the business on a regular basis, and you don't work very many hours in the business).

If you aren't an active participant, you can't deduct your LLC losses from any other type of income, such as the income from your job. In other words, under the passive income rule, if your LLC isn't doing so well and passes on $50,000 in losses to you, you can't use it to offset the $50,000 you made when you made a good trade on Wall Street (which is considered portfolio income). So you can sound like a smarty-pants when talking to your accountant, this is called a *passive loss limitation.*

The only way to avoid being subject to the passive loss limitation is to actively participate in the LLC's operations. If the IRS considers you to be an active participant, then you can deduct the LLC's losses from your other income, such as wages and stock dividends, without limitation.

If your LLC holds rental property, you will have to be so actively engaged in the managing of the property that you qualify as an active real estate professional. Otherwise, the rental property will be considered a passive investment, and if the LLC distributes losses to you, they will be subject to the passive loss limitation rules.

Preserving pass-through taxation status

Although pass-through tax status is the default for LLCs, your LLC can lose the right to this partnership tax status if it's not structured correctly. Partnership tax status is reserved only for partnerships; therefore, if you don't look and act like a partnership as far as the IRS is concerned, then it won't allow you to be taxed like one.

The IRS differentiates partnerships from corporations in a couple of ways. Basically, three characteristics make a corporation what it is:

- ✔ Ownership is freely transferable.
- ✔ The entity has a perpetual existence.
- ✔ The owners and officers all have limited-liability protections.

If an LLC has all three characteristics, then in the eyes of the IRS, it's a corporation and will be taxed as such. However, if an LLC only has two of these characteristics, then it's a partnership and will be allowed the partnership pass-through tax status.

Considering that you most likely aren't going to want to give up the limited-liability characteristic, your best choice is to keep your membership shares from being transferred freely. Most LLCs don't allow the free transfer of ownership; they require that the members take a vote, and the new member is admitted upon majority approval. If you stick this provision in your operating agreement (see Chapter 9), and then stick to this provision, you should be A-okay when it comes keeping your pass-through tax status.

Selling your membership interests

To determine the amount of tax you have to pay when you sell your membership interest, you first have to figure out your tax basis. You subtract this adjusted tax basis from the sale price to figure out your profit (which, in IRS terms, is called your *capital gain*). Depending on how long you have held the interest, you'll most likely have to pay short-term or long-term capital gains taxes on this amount.

Operating as a single-member LLC

Many states permit you to form and operate a single-member LLC. However, although the state recognizes the entity as an LLC, the IRS doesn't. In the eyes of the IRS, single-member LLCs are "disregarded entities" and taxed as sole proprietorships. You report and pay the company's taxes on your personal tax returns. If your single-member LLC is operating as a business, then you report all income and expenses on a Schedule C, Profit or Loss from a Business, that you attach to your Form 1040. If your single-member LLC is holding rental real estate properties, then you report all income and expenses on a Schedule E, Supplemental Income and Loss, that you attach to your Form 1040.

Being a "disregarded entity" in the eyes of the IRS can be a good thing! Your LLC can still have the limited-liability protections that the state offers, yet be treated by the IRS as if it were an individual. A perfect example of how this can be beneficial to you is if your LLC were to own real estate. Because the property is owned by a single-member LLC, which is considered a disregarded entity by the IRS, you still can engage the property in a like-kind, tax-free 1031 exchange. If this is something you are doing, speak with a tax-free exchange professional.

Now, just because you're a single-member LLC doesn't mean that you don't have choices. You can still make a tax election — you just can't elect partnership taxation. If you are operating as a single-member LLC and you want to be subject to corporate taxation instead, simply file IRS Form 8832, Entity Classification Election, within 75 days of your formation date. After this form is filed, you will pay taxes as if you were a corporation.

If you are operating as a single-member LLC and are still dead set on having partnership taxation, you have an option. You can elect to be taxed as an S corporation. An S corporation is basically just a corporation but with the pass-through tax status that partnerships enjoy. Though the tax differences between sole proprietorships and S corporations aren't very pronounced, it may help protect your limited-liability status in the courtroom. After all, the IRS won't consider you a disregarded entity any longer. I show you how to file for S corporation tax status later in the chapter.

Choosing corporate taxation

No matter how many members you have, you can always elect to be taxed like a corporation. Corporate taxation is completely different than partnership taxation. First and foremost, nothing gets passed on to the members. For the most part, the only thing a member has to report on his personal tax return is the money that he actually receives from the company as income or profit distributions. There is no such thing as allocations when it comes to corporations.

Corporations are taxed as are separate entities. In the eyes of the IRS, your corporation is completely distinct from its owners. But it gets even better. Although you personally have to pay federal tax on all of your *income,* corporations only have to pay federal tax on all of their *profits.* That's right — corporations only are taxed on the profits that remain in the company at the end of the year. Also, the corporate tax rate is much lower — normally around 15 percent — than it is for partnership or sole proprietorship taxation. (The average tax rates for those entities are between 15 percent and 35 percent, plus an extra 15.3 percent for self-employment taxes.)

When it comes to corporations and taxes, most people worry about something called *double taxation.* Double taxation occurs when the owners of the corporation (called *shareholders*) take the profit out of the company, and the profits are taxed on the shareholder level. This means that the same profits are taxed once at the corporate level, and then taxed again at the shareholder level when they are paid out.

When to choose corporate taxation

Different business structures require different types of taxation. First and foremost, if your LLC is being used to hold real estate, you should probably stay away from corporate taxation. When it comes to holding real estate — or any appreciating asset, for that matter — pass-through taxation is always the way to go. Why? Because the double taxation that comes with a corporate tax status can annihilate your profits. You'll have almost nothing left!

If you are in business, however, you may want to consider corporate taxation. First of all, you most likely won't be making too much in profit in your formative years. Second, even if you plan to pay out profits, the double taxation can actually be *less* of a tax burden than the self-employment taxes that come with pass-through taxation.

Until you are profiting more than $75,000 per year, you may want to look into electing corporate tax status. Generally, until you start profiting more, the corporate tax rates are lower than the individual tax rates of the members who will be paying taxes on the LLC's income.

After you have decided that corporate taxation is right for you, you must file a Form 8832, Entity Classification Election, with the IRS within 75 days of your formation date. Your election will go into effect on the date of your choosing (you just enter this date on line 4), or if you don't select a date, the IRS will use the date on which you filed the form. (Later in the chapter I go into how to prepare your tax returns if you have elected to be taxed as a corporation.)

Believe it or not, when it comes to some businesses, I'm somewhat of a proponent for electing corporate tax status. In a lot of situations, the double taxation can actually amount to less than what a partnership tax entity would pay after self-employment taxes are calculated. Also, you have access to more tax deductions than you would if you were taxed as a partnership. If I were you, I would sit down with your tax specialist or corporate consultant and discuss the merits of both types of taxation and see what works best for you!

When you elect corporate taxation, you are stuck with it for five years. This means that you can't go back to pass-through taxation whenever you choose. There are ways around this, but they involve loopholes that lawmakers can amend or close at any minute. Before filing your Form 8832, just make sure that it won't be detrimental to your business to be taxed at the corporate tax rate for the next five years. Also, make sure to speak with a tax professional who can help you plan.

Ways to minimize corporate taxes

Corporate taxation can be great for small businesses because you have a little more flexibility when it comes to tax planning. For instance, by domiciling your corporation in a tax haven, you can avoid a lot of state taxes that would be imposed on you personally in the state that you live in. I go into this in more detail in Chapter 5.

Unfortunately, the most prominent downfall of the corporation — double taxation — is a hard one to get around. Luckily, if you are operating the business, you can be an employee and take money out of the company by having it pay your salary, pension plan, employee benefits, and even loans. At the end of the day, the company's net income will remain the same; however, it won't all be in the form of company profits. Instead, it will be a deductible expense to the company (your salary, for instance), which reduces the amount of taxes you will have to pay on what you take.

Electing S corporation tax status

Although both the partnership and S corporation tax status allow for pass-through taxation, the two have some pretty big differences. The big benefit is that S corporations don't have to pay self-employment tax on all the profits of the business. As an owner, you only pay the tax on amounts that were paid out as compensation for services. Considering that the self-employment tax is about 15.3 percent, this little benefit of the S corporation can save you a pretty good chunk of change.

However, there are plenty of downsides, some of which may or may not apply to you:

✔ **The ownership is restricted.** The S corporation tax status comes with a lot of restrictions on who can be an owner and how many owners there can be (see Chapter 2 for the list).

✔ **You can't add debt to your tax basis.** Earlier in the chapter, I discussed that LLCs allow you to deduct from your distributions the amount of debt that the company has that you can be held personally responsible for. With S corporation tax status, you receive no tax benefits for being personally responsible for the company's debt.

✔ **There is no step-up in basis on assets after you die.** When your heirs inherit your assets in your S corporation, they'll have to pay capital gains tax on the appreciation from the date you first purchased the asset, instead of just from the date that you passed it on to your heirs. I discuss this in more detail in Chapter 16.

It's normally a terrible idea to hold assets in an LLC that has elected S corporation status — especially real estate. Even though you get around the double-taxation nightmare that comes with a regular corporation, you're still limiting yourself by not being able to personally deduct the mortgage.

On the contrary, because of these specific benefits and drawbacks of S corporation tax status, small businesses are the ones that benefit from this sort of taxation. Why? Because they hold their assets elsewhere, so the last two items on the list don't bother them. Also, they are relatively small entities, so the ownership restrictions normally don't apply to them.

If you want to be taxed as an S corporation, then you need to file Form 8832, Entity Classification Election, and Form 2553, Election by a Small Business Corporation, within 75 days of your formation date or the beginning of your fiscal year. Later in the chapter, I go into detail on how to prepare the exact filings required for the S corporation tax status.

Check to see how your state taxes LLCs that have elected S corporation taxation. Most states conform with the IRS on this, but about half a dozen states will tax S corporations as corporations. If you are holding real estate or are in another form of business where double taxation can kill you, you could be in trouble. Make sure to speak with your local accountant or do some research on local state law.

How to File Your Federal Returns

Although you'll most likely delegate the filing of your federal tax returns to a competent accountant, I still recommend that you have a good, basic knowledge about what your LLC needs to do at tax time. This not only helps you have much more educated conversations with your accountant, but also assists you in double-checking his work. After all, you'll be signing these filings — don't you want to know *exactly* what you are signing?

You don't really file a tax return for your LLC. Instead, you only file an information statement — IRS Form 1065, U.S. Return of Partnership Income. On this statement, you report the company's income, deductions, gains, losses, and the allocations that are being made to the partners. After this statement has been filed, the company will then issue Schedule K-1s to each member that shows what income and deductions have been allocated to them. They then report the income and deductions on a Schedule C attached to their personal tax return. All members will personally pay their share of the company taxes.

For the most part, in this section I stick to discussing the pass-through tax status because that is the most common. Regardless, you should use this section for informative purposes only. There is absolutely no way that in one chapter I could get into every piece of tax law that could apply to your specific situation. Even if I were writing an entire *book* on the subject, would you really want to read it? Probably not. That's why, no matter what, I recommend that you find a qualified professional to assist you in filing your company taxes. After all, you're a smart cookie — you should be spending your time making your fortune, not reading up on boring tax code.

Before you can file your IRS Form 1065, or any return for that matter, you need to obtain a tax identification number for your LLC. You can do that by submitting a Form SS-4, Application for Employer Identification Number, to the Internal Revenue Service or applying online at `https://sa1.www4.irs.gov/sa_vign/newFormSS4.do`. I recommend that you apply online; that way you can get your number immediately.

If you've chosen something other than partnership tax status for your LLC, skip ahead to the "Ponying up when you've chosen a different tax status" section. The next couple of sections most likely don't apply to you.

Preparing Form 1065

All partnerships, including LLCs, are required to file a Form 1065 each year. The 1065 isn't a tax return; it's a summary and information statement that lets the IRS know who is responsible for paying which percentage of the company's tax burden for the year. It is four pages long and contains six different schedules. (About ten other schedules can be filed with the 1065 if your accountant deems it necessary.)

The company also must make some tax decisions — called *elections.* Elections can include decisions concerning the research credit, for example, and also depreciation of assets. These decisions can affect all of the members and can have huge tax consequences. Therefore, whoever is preparing and filing the Form 1065 must look to the operating agreement for guidance on how tax elections are to be decided. If the operating agreement doesn't provide guidance on this, then all members should come together for a vote.

After Form 1065 is completed, only one member needs to review and sign it; however, that member must answer to all of the other members if they have a question or problem with the filing.

If you are operating as a single-member LLC, the IRS treats you as a disregarded entity, and you will be taxed as a sole proprietorship. This means that you don't need to file Form 1065. I go over what filings are required for single-member LLCs in the "Coughing up taxes as a sole proprietorship" section.

Taking your accounting system into account

On Form 1065, you indicate the accounting method that your company uses. If you have a bookkeeping service or an accountant, you can just ask them. If not, you will have to choose one yourself.

Cash-based accounting is the simplest method of accounting and is generally used by smaller companies that do their bookkeeping themselves. With cash-based accounting, you classify income only when you actually receive it, and you classify expenses only when the checks you wrote have posted to your bank account. If your register matches your bank statement, with no other debits or credits showing, then there is a good chance that you're on a cash-based accounting system. If your

income is over $1 million, however, I recommend that you ditch this accounting method and go with *accrual-based accounting* instead.

Accrual-based accounting is a little bit more difficult to track, but it offers the most tax benefits. It is a standard for most professional bookkeepers because it provides a more accurate picture of how the business is actually doing. Essentially, with accrual-based accounting, you record income when the sale occurs, not when you actually receive the money. You also record expenses when the invoice is received, not when your check is cashed by the vendor. With this type of accounting, it's virtually impossible to spend more money than you have. Also, at the end of the year, you'll show less of a profit that you will need to allocate and pay taxes on.

 Form 1065 asks for the tax year of the LLC. It's customary to make this a calendar year. LLCs are required to have the same tax reporting period as their majority members, and normally, majority members are U.S. citizens who pay taxes on a calendar-year schedule.

Distributing K-1s to the members

After she fills in the Form 1065 for your LLC, your accountant will create a Schedule K-1 for each member of the LLC. The K-1 contains the allocation information for each partner (see the "The partners pay the taxes!" section), including how much and what type of company income the member has been allocated and what sort of deductions he can write off. It also provides an updated analysis of each partner's tax basis.

Unfortunately, it isn't always as simple as just writing in the portion of each member's profits and losses. The K-1 calls for different types of income to be reported separately, such as short-term capital gains, long-term capital gains, charitable contributions, royalties, interest income, and rental real estate income, among others. You should be able to find what percentage of profits and losses that each member is allocated in the operating agreement.

Having to calculate percentages of different types of income for a multitude of members can be a *huge* headache. That is why I recommend you leave it to the professionals.

Also, remember that one of the benefits of an LLC is that the company profits and losses don't have to be allocated to the members according to their ownership percentages. LLCs allow for *special allocations,* which means that you can own 10 percent of the company and feasibly receive 100 percent of the profits and losses for a specific year. Granted, you can't make these decisions without having a good reason (that doesn't include tax purposes); however, special allocations are common and easy to do. You just have to prove that you have the LLC's business goals in mind and that you aren't making special allocations to avoid tax liability.

When your accountant creates the Schedule K-1s, she will file the originals, along with Form 1065, with the IRS. At this point, you should get a photocopy of your Schedule K-1 that you can use when filing your individual tax return.

The amount of profit that is reported on your K-1 isn't necessarily the profit that was distributed to you. In other words, you may have to pay taxes at the end of the year on the company's profits when you haven't even seen a penny of a cash distribution. Remember — there is a difference between what the LLC *allocates* to you and what it *distributes* to you. Allocations are the profits and losses that you have to report on your personal tax return and pay taxes on. Distributions are your cash portion of the profit that you actually receive.

Paying the actual taxes

If you are a U.S. citizen, you pay your personal taxes on IRS Form 1040. But your 1040 tax return doesn't include a line that specifies "LLC Income." If you take a look at Form 1040, you'll see that line 17 mentions business income. So here, you list the total income stated on your Schedule E, Supplemental Income and Loss, which you submit with your Form 1040.

You use a Schedule E to report all income and losses from business activities that don't constitute your primary source of income. Now, if you are managing the day-to-day business of the LLC, then you should be on the company payroll, and your regular paycheck should be what is considered your primary source of income. The allocations that the company makes on a yearly basis are considered secondary income. In other words, if all you do is sit at home and collect profits from businesses that you don't actually operate, and you don't have any "job" per se, that income will still be reflected on a Schedule E.

If you are a single-member LLC and you are an operational manager of the company, then this doesn't apply to you. You don't list your business income and deductions on a Schedule E. Later in the chapter, I go into single-member LLCs in more depth.

When you are filling out your Schedule E, you report all of the business income and deductions in Part II of the Schedule E. Figure 13-1 is a snapshot of what this section looks like.

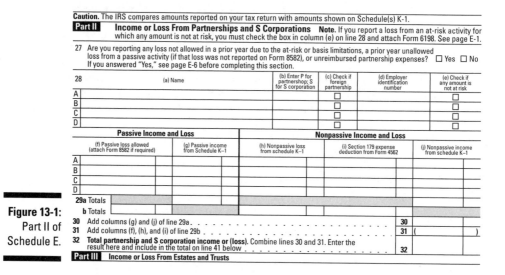

Figure 13-1:
Part II of
Schedule E.

Because the Schedule E isn't as simple as copying and pasting the information from your K-1 (there are a few other schedules involved), I recommend leaving the preparation of this form up to your accountant. I have included the basic how-to in this book so you can familiarize yourself with it. Armed with this information, you can check your accountant's accuracy and have intelligent discussions with your accountant about the documents that she has prepared.

If you are actively engaging in business, you are required to pay self-employment tax on your percentage of the company profit. You must calculate your self-employment tax on the Schedule SE, Self-Employment Tax, that you'll file with your Form 1040.

Ponying up when you've chosen a different tax status

A small portion of limited liability companies choose to be taxed in some way other than the standard partnership tax status. If this is the case for you, you file your taxes just like any other entity with the same tax status you have chosen. For instance, if you have elected to be taxed as a corporation, then you file taxes as if you are a corporation. If you have elected to be taxed as a sole proprietorship, then you file taxes like you are a sole proprietorship.

Coughing up taxes as a sole proprietorship

If you have a single-member LLC, then the IRS will classify it as a disregarded entity by default and will tax it as a sole proprietorship. This means that the company doesn't have to file a Form 1065 information statement and doesn't have to issue you a Schedule K-1. You just report your company's income and expenses on a Schedule C, Profit or Loss from a Business, and attach it to your Form 1040 like you would if you didn't form an LLC in the first place. If you have rental property, the profit and loss information will be listed on a Schedule E, Supplemental Income and Loss, instead.

Keep in mind that as a sole proprietor, you can't pay yourself a salary. Therefore, all of your income is subject to self-employment tax, which you report on a Schedule SE, Self-Employment Tax, that you attach to your Form 1040. You can, however, deduct other employees' salaries as an allowable business expense.

If you have less than $5,000 in expenses for the year, then you may be allowed to file the short form of the Schedule C (the Schedule C-EZ).

Settling your tax bill under corporate tax status

When you decide to be taxed as a corporation, you are subject to the same type of taxation that corporations are — with no exceptions. If you aren't used to corporate taxation, just think of your company in terms of being an official "person" that is separate from yourself. You don't pay taxes on behalf of your company. All taxes are paid *by the corporation* on the profits that are left in the business at the end of the year.

You report all of your business's income and deductions on IRS Form 1120, U.S. Corporation Income Tax Return — a separate tax return. (You should send a signed copy of Form 8832, Entity Classification Election, to the IRS with your corporate tax return.) Your profits will be subject to the federal corporate tax rate, which averages around 15 percent. Then, if you distribute them to the members, those same profits will be taxed again as capital gains income to the members. This is called double taxation.

Shelling out for taxes with an S corporation tax status

If you have elected to be taxed as an S corporation, you no longer file the traditional partnership returns that you filed previously. Instead, you file an IRS Form 1120S, U.S. Income Tax Return for an S Corporation. The 1120S is more of an information statement than anything else. After all, S corporations don't really pay taxes; they just pass the profits on to the owners for them to handle the burden.

When filing a Form 1120S, you prepare a Schedule K-1 for each member, give a copy of the K-1 to each member (so he can use the information when preparing his personal tax returns), and submit one copy to the IRS with your Form 1120S. Keep in mind that when paying taxes as an S corporation, members are referred to as shareholders.

You are required to file Form 1120S by March 15 of the following year, or if you're on a fiscal year, then the 15th day of the third month after the close of the fiscal year. Depending on your state, you may also have to send a copy of Form 1120S and the corresponding K-1s to your state tax board. Or, they may have a similar form that you need to file. Your accountant can assist you in pulling together all of the required filings for your LLC.

Avoiding LLC Tax Traps

Business is business, and often it's easy for the unwary to fall into quagmires. Every entity has its tax traps, and LLCs are no different. You just have to make sure that you plan around them and you'll be fine. Oh, and a great accountant helps too!

Transferring assets into your LLC

For the most part, transferring assets into your LLC in exchange for membership is a *nontaxable event*. This means that, for income tax purposes, no gain or loss is recognized. Problems only arise when debt or liability is involved.

LLCs have a tax pitfall which is known as a *deemed cash distribution*. It only occurs when one of the members reduces the amount of his liability. The IRS considers the reduction in liability to be a cash distribution, and like a cash distribution, the member must pay taxes on any of this amount that goes over his tax basis.

TECHNICAL STUFF

Triggering gains on securities LLCs

Although a securities LLC can be a great way to diversify and protect your investments at the same time, it can also be subject to a pretty serious tax trap. A securities LLC may be subject to the investment company rules that state that the transfer of appreciated securities into the LLC triggers capital gains. This means that after you transfer your securities into your LLC, you'll have to pay taxes on the capital gains that you realized from the date you purchased the securities to the date you transferred them to the LLC.

These rules only apply if

✔ You are classified as an investment company (which means that more than 80 percent of your LLC's assets are in the form of publicly traded securities).

✔ The securities that you have transferred are not already in diversified portfolios, and the transfer results in the diversification of your securities.

If both of these are the case, then the tax basis will be *reset,* which means that all of your appreciation thus far will be subject to capital gains taxes.

A good example is of a member who transfers a piece of property into the LLC. Say that the property has a mortgage on it for $80,000. When the property is transferred into the LLC, the two members decide to refinance the property to include the other member as a personal guarantor. Unfortunately, the partner who was transferring the property didn't realize that by refinancing it he was reducing his debt by $40,000 (one-half) and that the IRS would consider that $40,000 a cash distribution. This means that at the end of the year, the contributing member will have to pay taxes on $40,000 that he never actually received. Had the members talked to a professional before they refinanced the property, the contributing member could have avoided a big tax surprise.

Dealing with phantom income

When a partner is allocated a sizeable company profit that she has to pay tax on, but is not actually distributed any profits, this is called *phantom income.* Phantom income can be dangerous because a partner in the LLC can end up with a pretty hefty tax bill but with no profits to pay it with.

It's common to experience some phantom income — especially in your LLC's beginning stages when you need to keep the profits in the business to help it grow. However, you can feel pinched in the pocket if the business doesn't even distribute enough cash to the members to help cover the tax burden. You'll have to scrounge up the dough on your own. Garage sale anyone?

Now, there's a good and a bad side to phantom income. The bad side is that it can happen to you. The good side is that you can force it upon a creditor who obtains a *charging order* on a member's interest. A charging order is all that a creditor can go after if a member is liable personally, and it only gives a creditor access to the allocations and distributions that a membership interest can receive. Now, if you only allocate profits to the creditor and don't give him any cash to pay the taxes on those profits, how happy do you think the creditor will be? Needless to say, he'll be running for the hills and eager to settle in the member's favor. (Chapter 11 covers charging orders in more depth.)

You can add a provision in your operating agreement that can force the company to distribute enough cash for the members to be able to pay the taxes on their allocations. You can figure out some formula that works for everybody and also includes a percentage for state taxes. However, by doing this, you completely undermine the strategy outlined above that gets rid of creditors who have obtained charging orders.

Minimizing self-employment taxes

Even though LLCs aren't imposed with the same double layer of taxation on profits like corporations are, if you aren't careful, you can still end up paying more in taxes. After all, aren't you're supposed to be saving taxes? Not paying more!

You see, the IRS hits you the hardest with self-employment taxes. Self-employment taxes are Social Security and Medicare taxes, and they are imposed *in addition to* the federal income taxes that you have to pay. These taxes amount to about 15.3 percent of the total income allocated to you. About 12.4 percent goes to Social Security, which will be paid out to you when you reach retirement (I hope), and 2.9 percent goes to Medicare, which is a form of hospital insurance. You figure the self-employment tax that is due on Schedule SE, Self-Employment Taxes, and file it with your personal Form 1040 tax return.

You have to pay self-employment taxes if

- Your LLC offers licensed services to the public, including accounting, actuarial science, architecture, consulting, engineering, health, and law.

- You work more than 501 hours during the LLC's tax year. That is, on average, nine hours per week.

- You have the authority to execute contracts on behalf of your LLC.

If you are an investor or partner in the business, you aren't required to pay self-employment tax on the money you earn.

Luckily, there is a maximum amount of earnings that are subject to self-employment taxes per year. Unluckily, that amount is $94,200, which is way over the national average — and that only applies to Social Security. Anything over that amount is still subject to the 2.9 percent Medicare tax.

Currently, you can only deduct half of what you paid in self-employment tax when calculating your *adjusted gross income* — the amount that you have to pay income tax on.

You are only required to pay self-employment taxes on profits if your LLC is actively engaged in business. If your LLC only engages in passive activities, such as real estate, then you don't have to pay self-employment taxes on what you earn. For instance, if your LLC only holds rental properties and the rent is the only profit distributed to the members, then it's passive income and not subject to self-employment taxes.

Becoming a silent partner

Not everyone is required to pay self-employment tax. SE tax is for wage earners, not necessarily big fish. So if you are a silent partner who doesn't deal with the day-to-day matters of the business, you may be able to find a way around the mandatory self-employment tax.

First, I would make sure that your LLC is manager-managed. If it's member-managed, it's hard to attest that the members aren't doing any managing of the day-to-day affairs! Then, find someone trustworthy who can act as manager and will be able to enter into contracts with your and the company's best interests in mind. Finally, make sure that you work no more than 500 hours per year on that particular company.

Obviously, this will never work if you are one of the operating partners. But if you are a simple investor, it's very possible to eliminate the required self-employment taxes and keep a hefty chunk of change in return.

Choosing to be taxed as an S corporation

Unlike partnerships, the owners of S corporations can hire themselves. In fact, they are expected to hire themselves — an S corporation without any owners on the payroll is a sure path to an audit. The main benefit of hiring yourself is that you are paid as a regular employee, as you would be if you had any regular job. This means that the income you receive isn't subject to self-employment taxes. You'll still have to pay regular payroll taxes, but this is often much less.

Of course, you must hire yourself for a wage that is standard in your industry. If your company hits a windfall, you can't necessarily take all of the cash out as a bonus, because you are limited to having a salary that is believable for an executive of your rank, in a company your size, in your industry. For instance, if everyone else in similar positions is pulling around $100k per year, you can't take home a million bucks and not expect to get audited.

After you've taken your maximum salary, the rest must be taken as a distribution. You'll have to pay tax on this (including self-employment tax!) as you would if you were a regular partner and not an employee of the company.

Keep in mind that if you are an owner who is active in the business's day-to-day operations, the IRS considers you to be an employee. Therefore, you need to include yourself on the company payroll and pay payroll taxes on that income. You don't have to take too much — just enough so that it's standard for your position in your industry. The rest you can classify as company profit.

Chapter 14

Using Your LLC to Protect Your Assets

*T*his very well may be the most important chapter that you read. After all, why would you want to work so hard to build your future only to have someone else take away all the assets you've accumulated? If you think that because you observe good business practices you won't be sued, think again. There's a reason for the term *frivolous lawsuits* — because lawsuits don't need to be soundly based or even well-intentioned.

A lot of people out there are looking to get something for nothing. Unfortunately, that means that hardworking folks like yourself, who have built up a sizeable nest egg, are a target. Aside from expensive insurance policies that may or may not cover everything, the only thing that you can really do to protect yourself is to plan ahead and structure your assets so they're safe. It's important to do this now because once you're in a lawsuit, it's too late. And if you've ever been sued, you know — lawsuits can come out of nowhere when you least expect them!

You need to keep asset protection in mind from the beginning. From here on out, you must take asset protection into consideration every time you save money, start a new company, register intellectual property, or make any big purchases. LLCs are such a big facet of asset protection that normally, when an attorney sees that you're protecting your assets in an LLC, she'll advise her client not to sue you in the first place. In this chapter, I show you how you can protect your assets for the rest of your life by forming an LLC, and how you can safely own high-risk assets (assets that are very likely to be sued) while protecting everything else that you have worked for.

Worst-Case Scenarios: What Can Happen Without Asset Protection

More than 50,000 lawsuits are filed in the United States every day and the numbers keep growing. Litigation has become a way of life for Americans, and we are suffering because of it. Our collective mindset is shifting to that of "get somethin' for nothin'," and our small businesses — the lifeblood of the American dream — are suffering. Although it may be relatively easy for a large corporation to cover the costs of an everyday lawsuit, to a small business these legal fees may be debilitating.

You may think you're exempt, but chances are, if you haven't been sued yet, it won't be long. Although businesses tend to get sued most often, it's still very likely that you'll be sued personally. Actually, statistics say that within your lifetime you'll be sued twice. And that's at today's numbers — can you imagine tomorrow's? Just think — as hard as it can be for a small business to pay the $75,000 legal bill on a frivolous lawsuit, it can be even harder for an individual. Even if you win, you may have nothing left! This is why it's just as important for individuals to use LLCs to protect their assets and deter lawsuits as it is for businesses.

Often, attorneys tie in asset protection with estate planning. Although it's imperative to protect your estate — making sure that it actually makes it to your kids and not into the hands of some Joe Schmo who tripped over a sprinkler in your front lawn — estate planning doesn't really have much bearing on protecting your assets from litigators. In other words, just because you have an estate plan, does *not* mean that your assets are protected while you're alive. See Chapter 16 for more on using an LLC with your estate planning.

When lawyers and creditors come calling

The saddest thing about lawsuits is that even if you win, you lose. A lot of these lawyers who take on frivolous cases work on a *contingency basis.* This means that they don't charge the client unless they win the case. So, ultimately, you may be the victor, but you are the only one paying the legal fees — and they can be debilitating. The only way to protect against having to pay outrageous sums of money for seemingly petty arguments is to stay out of court in the first place. I'm not saying that you should settle a lawsuit brought against you. I'm saying that you should make your assets either unapparent or unattractive to the wolves who are scoping them out. LLCs can do just that.

The birth of the frivolous lawsuit

Back in the old days, business was done on a word and a handshake. Should a person not live up to his agreement, he would face the shame and disappointment of the people around him. That disgrace was enough to keep people in their place. Money was only associated with hard work, not simple accidents. If you slipped in the supermarket, you would simply be embarrassed. That's all. You wouldn't be thinking about all of the free cash you could get from the local family business.

Nowadays, things have changed. Lawyers patrol hospitals, and commercials run on TV for class-action lawsuits. If you've ever been in a car accident, however minor, you have most likely received a flood of letters from personal-injury attorneys looking to make a buck.

If you backed out of a parking spot too fast and got into a fender bender, there's a good chance that an attorney will be looking to sue you. If you don't have deep enough pockets, or they can't get to your assets, they will sue the insurance company, the car maker, your Aunt Margaret who purchased the car and loaned it to you to drive — basically, they will sue anyone and everyone who has money. Often, it doesn't matter whether you injured someone — all that matters is whether someone with deep pockets can be targeted. Lawyers play on jurors' emotions — they make them sympathize with the plaintiff, who may work a dead-end job and can barely support her kids — and chastise you for being one of the lucky few who has struck it rich. The game is called Robin Hood — and it's one you needn't play.

According to the *Wall Street Journal,* frivolous lawsuits cost the average family approximately $3,520 per year. Don't be a statistic. Using LLCs to protect your investments and your assets is normally enough of a deterrent to keep you out of the courtroom in the first place!

Those people and businesses who loan you money — your creditors — also have their eye on your hard-earned assets. Had a bad month and didn't keep up with your debt? Your creditors will no doubt be looking at how they can capitalize on their loss — and rightfully so. They lent you the money, and they need to get it back. If you let an angry creditor have his way with your assets, you'll be in a huge hole with no way to climb out. To prevent this, make sure that you have an LLC in place that protects your assets. When you are in control of your assets, attractive settlements are pretty easy to come by.

When it comes to suing a member of an LLC (where the person's assets are held), a judgment creditor only has one remedy — a *charging order.* This means that the creditor can only receive the same distributions and allocations that the member previously received. He can't take the actual asset, liquidate it, and spend the money. Because of this charging order remedy, creditors can spend a long time holding their hand out without receiving a penny if the other members don't want them to (see Chapter 11 for more details). This isn't a good scenario for them and is rarely worth the time. Therefore, an attorney will offer to settle for a lower amount or even avoid the lawsuit altogether when she sees that an LLC is involved.

Now, if you aren't at enough risk from lawsuits and creditors, remember that you still have to worry about the IRS. You probably think that the IRS is part of the all-powerful government and can just seize bank accounts, no matter the reason. Nope! The IRS is subject to the same laws and restrictions as most creditors; it just has a little bit more knowledge and disclosure.

Hiding your assets from the IRS can be difficult because you are most likely reporting them and/or depreciating them on your tax returns. You don't want to hide from the IRS (that's tax evasion), and you shouldn't have to. Your asset protection plan should be so solid that the IRS doesn't have the ability or, better yet, the justification for going after your assets to settle an IRS debt.

Liens can kill your business

Some of these lawyers are really good, and the worst thing that can happen is to get sued by one of them without having any sort of asset protection plan in place. Imagine . . . you get taken to court over a contract dispute and the attorney talks the judge into placing a *prejudgment lien* on your assets — this means that you can't move, touch, or transfer your assets or even conduct business with them until the lawsuit has been decided.

Say the amount of the lien covers the entire amount due on a ten-year contract. It's pretty hefty, and your assets don't quite cover it. Your home and your bank account are attached to the lien, and you aren't even able to write checks. If this happens, you may have a hard time buying necessities, such as gas and food, but the worst thing of all is that you most likely won't be able to afford to pay your attorney to defend the case. Eek! You're trapped! If this happens, unless you have some good friends to keep you going in the meantime, you may have to settle immediately and for unfavorable terms.

What about when this happens to your business? What if you're unable to move money, write checks, pay bills, pay your rent, pay on your business loans, or make payroll for two months or longer? Where would your business be then? The damage could be so great that you would possibly lose everything you've worked so long to build. Unless you have significant savings, this could be debilitating.

Even if you get through the lawsuit without a prejudgment lien, you aren't necessarily in the clear. If you win the lawsuit, you're okay, but what if you lose? Say someone gets a judgment on you for more than you can afford to pay at the moment? Unless you can immediately write a check for a big chunk of change, the judgment creditor can request to have a *judgment lien* placed on your assets. This means that your bank account is completely frozen. Your home, rental property, savings account, mutual funds, CDs, kid's college fund, *everything* is frozen and can be liquidated to pay the lien. Have equity in your house that you want to use to pay for the lawsuit? You can't refinance or sell! Instead, your home will be put on the auction block, right before your eyes. You can't even collect income from your investment properties or invoice your clients in your business. Liens are the worst thing that can happen to you in business. Unless you have an LLC, that is.

You don't have to lose a lawsuit to have a judge impose a lien. Anyone can request a lien on your assets, including creditors or the IRS.

Why LLCs Are the Best Choice for Asset Protection

Some asset protection plans just try to hide your assets from prying creditors and potential plaintiffs. Although that should be the first line of defense, it isn't nearly enough. You see, if you do get dragged into court, you probably will be subpoenaed for the information or asked about it while on the stand. In either case, you shouldn't lie. If you do, you'll have a lot more to lose than your assets — you can lose your freedom.

If these predators see that you have hordes of cash and real estate sitting in an LLC, there's a good chance they won't go after the assets in the first place. Why? Because LLCs are very tough nuts to crack, and they know this. They also know that if you are smart enough, you can trap them in a situation where they are paying out money for *you!* And because most credit agencies work on commission and attorneys work on a contingency basis, they don't want to waste their time on you if they know they aren't going to get paid.

When you choose to protect your assets with an LLC rather than another entity, you win on multiple fronts.

✔ Because LLCs are *pass-through entities* (the business's income and expenses are reported to the IRS on the owners' tax returns), you don't face as many tax consequences as you would if you held your assets in a corporation. With a corporation, the profits are taxed at the end of the year and when the profits are distributed to members, the distribution is taxed again (see Chapter 2 for details).

✔ Although it's advisable to do so, you aren't legally required to hold an annual meeting and keep the minutes on file. With a corporation, you have a lot more paperwork to complete and hoops to jump through to maintain your liability protection. (See Chapter 11 for more on meetings and minutes.)

LLCs versus corporations: An example

Josh took over his father's business, J.R. Marine Inc., when he was only 23. He was smart and good with numbers, and the business grew steadily over the years. Ten years in, J.R. Marine had taken over the market. It was good timing too, because Josh had just met the love of his life and was eager to start a family.

One day, he was in the parking lot of the local supermarket, and he accidentally backed into a woman's car. The woman seemed all right to him. They traded insurance information, and he helped her on her way. Two months later, Josh was served with a lawsuit. The woman claimed that she was severely injured in the accident and was unable to work her waitress job and support her four kids (she was a single mom). She was suing Josh for wages and emotional trauma.

Josh's attorney referred him to a partner who handled litigation. After slapping down a $10,000 retainer to defend the case, Josh wiped the sweat off of his brow and left the attorney to do his work. Four months later, the case went to trial. Josh couldn't believe how the woman's attorney made him seem like the big, wealthy, bad guy who thinks he can drive however he wants to just because he has money, or how the attorney portrayed the woman as a struggling cocktail waitress who can't afford to feed her kids and now will never get ahead in life. The woman, wearing a neck brace, cried on the stand. Her attorney asked the jury to "do the right thing." Of course, their idea of the "right thing" was to award the woman more than $2 million of Josh's money.

At first Josh thought he was okay — after all, he didn't have too much money in his bank account. However, what he did have was the ownership of the family business, which is considered a personal asset. Before long, his business was seized. They liquidated the inventory, the building, everything — just to pay off his judgment. Josh was destroyed. He thought because he had a corporation he was protected. The reality is that the business — his livelihood — was never protected from him. Had he formed an LLC, this would never have happened.

If J.R. Marine Inc. had been J.R. Marine LLC, Josh may not have been sued in the first place. When the personal-injury lawyer did an asset search to determine whether Josh had any assets that could be taken away, he would have seen that Josh's business (or his share of the business) was held in an LLC. Attorneys know that LLCs are notoriously hard to get to, and the smart ones will avoid them at any cost.

But if the plaintiff's attorney was a rookie and had never been bitten by an LLC before, he may have tried to seize the LLC interests anyway. In that case, he would have hit a brick wall called a charging order. After the attorney obtained the charging order, he would only have received the distributions that the LLC's manager (in this case, Josh's dad) decided to give to him. Josh's dad — being the smart guy that he is — would have decided that instead of distributing the profits, he would just keep them in the company. Therefore, the unknowing lawyer would have just indebted his client, the waitress, into paying the taxes on Josh's business. The lawyer would have been rushing to settle the case for $2,000 to pay the medical expenses, and Josh's business would be safe.

What's the deal with trusts?

A couple of years ago, trusts were the hot thing for asset protection, especially *spendthrift trusts* where your assets couldn't be touched by creditors. You just named yourself as the beneficiary and you were good to go! Unfortunately, thanks to a *New York Times* article, which blasted these trusts for allowing the wealthy to avoid creditors, and Jim Talent, a Missouri senator, spendthrift trusts aren't what they used to be.

Here's the deal: Senator Talent slipped an act into a bankruptcy bill, right before it was about to pass, that allows creditors to get to any assets that were put into trusts within the ten years previous to the claim. Therefore, you can still create a spendthrift trust, but it doesn't do much good if anything happens within the next ten years. Not a good idea!

Unless you're looking to add a trust to your arsenal for estate-planning purposes, I'd just stick with an LLC.

✔ LLCs protect your personal assets from lawsuits against the business. This is called the *veil of limited liability*. With corporations, CEOs, shareholders, directors, and even employees can be attached to lawsuits against the business. LLCs don't allow the owners or employees to be personally attacked for the actions of the business as a whole. (Chapter 11 contains more information on the veil of limited liability.)

✔ If you are sued personally, a *charging order* prevents a creditor from seizing your membership shares, and thus the LLC's assets as payment. The creditor gets no rights to the business and no say in the business. He just waits for payment. If this happened to you and you had shares in a corporation, the creditor could sell your shares of stock for payment. (See Chapter 11 for more information on charging orders.)

✔ Contributions and distributions are tax-free. This means that, for the most part, when you transfer assets in and out of the LLC, there's no taxable event. (For more information, see Chapter 13.)

Protecting Your Assets with Some Simple Strategies

Protecting your assets is so simple that I challenge you to give me one good reason why you shouldn't do it. Not later in the year, not in a couple of months, but *now*. You see, asset protection strategies only work if you do them *before* you ever get into trouble. After you are sued by a creditor (or if the IRS is after you), you can't transfer your assets into an LLC to protect them. Otherwise, it looks like you did what is called a *fraudulent conveyance of assets*. This means that you set up your asset protection plan to defraud your creditors and prevent a specific claim. In this case, your assets will not only be handed over to the creditor on a silver platter, but you may also face some pretty steep fines and maybe even some jail time.

So you need to set up your asset protection plan when you don't have any lawsuits pending or creditors looming. After all, you never know what tomorrow may bring. That's why you need to set up your defenses early and make sure that as you accumulate more and more in life, no one can take it away.

In the following sections, I go over a few simple strategies that you can use:

- ✔ Using a nominee to make it harder for others to find your assets

- ✔ Using the charging order law to your advantage to trap a creditor in a bad position so he'll have more incentive to settle in your favor

- ✔ Using multiple LLCs to segregate your assets from one another, so that if one asset, such as a piece of property, is engaged in a lawsuit, the others will be safe from seizure

- ✔ Forming two companies in different states to separate your business's assets from the actual operations of the company

- ✔ Transferring all of your personal assets into a family LLC that keeps financial instruments, such as stocks, bonds, cash, and mutual funds, safe

Privacy as the first step: Electing a nominee

Privacy is the first line of defense when it comes to asset protection. If people don't think you have anything, then they won't bother suing you in the first place. You know how the saying goes: "Own nothing, control everything." But that doesn't mean that you shouldn't own and enjoy the finer things in life because people may take those things. You've worked hard; you deserve to enjoy the fruits of your labor. The world can see that you have money; that's fine — they just don't need to know where it is. That's where privacy comes in handy.

Some states, like Nevada, protect the privacy of the LLC's members. This means that the members don't need to be publicly listed in the articles of organization or the annual reports your company must file with the Secretary of State; only the managers have to be listed. If the members don't need to be listed in your state, then you can just hire a nominee to serve as your LLC's manager. A *nominee* is a person who can truthfully state on the stand that she is unrelated and unknown to you. You can hire a nominee from a nominee company, usually for under $500 per year. Keep in mind, though, this only works if your LLC is manager-managed.

If you're in a state that doesn't allow privacy protection for members, consider forming your LLC in another state, such as Nevada, that does allow it.

After you have a nominee manager in place, unless you broadcast to the world that you own the LLC, people won't even think to look into the issue further. Your name won't be on public record, and unless they ask you directly, creditors will have no way of knowing that you are even associated with the LLC.

If your LLC is currently member-managed, then you need to amend your articles of organization to make it manager-managed. Otherwise, you have to list your members (namely, you) on your annual report — which is public record.

Here's the thing: Privacy won't fully protect you. It's not a strategy in and of itself, per se, but more like an add-on. It's icing on the cake. If you solely use a manager-nominee and think that you are completely protected, you'll get the shock of your life when you get dragged into court. The lawyers will ask you about your assets, and at that point, you have two choices: Give up the goods, or perjure yourself. Considering that perjury is a pretty serious criminal offense, I would take door No. 1 — and that leads to you revealing the location of your assets so they can be taken.

Setting up a booby trap

LLCs have two types of liability protection — they protect the individual from the LLC's liability and the LLC from the individual's liability (called *charging order protection*). Charging order protection is a powerful tool that you can use to protect your LLC and its assets from any lawsuits or creditors that you may acquire personally. Corporations don't have this type of protection. If your business is structured as a corporation with you as the sole or majority owner, your personal creditors can seize your ownership of the corporation and easily liquidate its assets and dissolve it to pay your debts. However, because you own an LLC, the creditor can't seize your ownership of the LLC; he can only obtain a charging order against it.

You see, when a creditor obtains a charging order on your membership shares, he doesn't have the same powers that you do. Actually, he has zero powers or say when it comes to your LLC; he can only receive the profit and loss distributions that you receive as a member. So, assuming you have a different manager (preferably a corporation that you own, a nominee, or a close family member), the manager can determine how the distributions are made. (See Chapter 11 for lots of other facts about charging orders.)

Say, for instance, that your buddy manages the company; do you think that he will hang you out to dry if a creditor obtains a charging order? Not likely. Instead, he will do the following: He will make sure to report a profit at the end of the year, but not distribute any of the profits. That way, the members will have to pay taxes on the profits but won't actually receive any money to pay them. This is called *phantom income.* Now, when I say "members," this includes the creditor. Can you imagine?! A naïve creditor, instead of receiving his check in the mail, gets a notice that he has to pay thousands of dollars in taxes? (If the other members complain about having to pay taxes and not receiving any income for a while, they can just borrow money from the LLC and it can all be sorted out at a later date.)

To ensure the creditor (also known as the unwelcome member) knows what's going on, here's what you do:

1. **Send a letter to the creditor making them aware of the tax debt that he owes and is obligated to pay.**

2. **Send a letter to the IRS letting them know how much the creditor owes.**

   Include in the letter a point stating that you want to keep your LLC current on its tax debt, and you suggest that, should the IRS not receive payment, an audit on the creditor may be required.

3. **Make sure to send a copy of this IRS letter to the creditor.**

I guarantee you that it won't be long before the creditor is approaching you with a settlement amount that is definitely in your favor.

LLCs get special charging order protections because they are considered to be partnerships. If you are operating as a single-member LLC, the judge in your case may not grant you charging order protections and may allow the creditor to foreclose on your membership. If you insist on flying solo, then I recommend that you issue a small percentage of shares to a trusted friend or to a corporation that you control.

Using charging order protections is a really powerful strategy for LLCs; however, it's a common mistake for people to rely on this strategy when they have member-managed LLCs. The manager has to be the one to determine the profit and loss allocations. If the LLC is member-managed, then a creditor stepping in as a member may be able to actually determine these allocations on his own. This depends on the operating agreement and the judge's decision. To avoid this risk entirely, do not make your LLC member-managed. Even if all of the current members are managing, you should still designate your LLC as manager-managed; then name all of the current members as individual managers.

What happens if your charging order protection fails you?

Lawsuits are still open to interpretation; thus, a judge can decide your case however she wants, depending on how she sees the evidence. Although uncommon, if a judge finds good cause, she can circumvent the charging order protections that LLCs offer and instead allow a creditor to foreclose on a member's interest. In this case, you and your partners can do a couple of things to minimize the damage:

✔ **You can draft a provision in the operating agreement that requires a debtor member to sell his membership shares back to the LLC or to the other members.** You will have to give a formula that determines the value of those shares, or the buy-back can be done for the exact amount of the member's original investment in the LLC. This way, you and your partners are assured that you won't have to deal with any unscrupulous, transplanted members who don't have your company's best interests in mind.

✔ **If a member is already in the process of having his membership shares seized, creating a huge problem for the other members, the remaining members can vote to dissolve the LLC and purchase all of the assets upon liquidation.** They can also choose to form a new LLC without the indebted member and transfer the assets to the new entity. Any monies that would be given to the indebted member instead go to the creditor who holds those membership shares.

The more LLCs, the merrier!

So, your business is protected from you, and you are protected from your business — but what protects your business from itself? When your business is sued, the creditors may not be able to go after your personal assets, but they can still go after the business's assets! We need to fix that.

Any business or property that operates directly with the public is at risk of being sued. If you have all of your business assets in your operating company and you get sued, all of your business assets can be seized. The same goes for personal assets. If you own ten properties and put them all in the same LLC, then someone slips and falls on your first property and sues you, everything in that LLC is up for grabs, namely all ten properties.

The best and easiest way to protect what's yours is by insulating each of your major assets in its own LLC. This can be somewhat costly, but on large assets, it's a small price to pay. For instance, New York taxi cab companies often place each taxi into a separate LLC. That way, if one driver gets into an accident and the cab company gets sued, only that one cab can be seized and liquidated to pay off the claim. That LLC can then be dissolved, and the taxi company is still standing. You don't have to worry about million-dollar judgments now!

Make sure you aren't already facing a lawsuit when setting up a structure like this. If you have been sued and start transferring entities to different LLCs to protect them from the creditor, then you are engaging in *fraudulent conveyance.* Not only will it not hold up in court, but it's also illegal. Make sure to set up your asset protection now. After you are sued, it's too late.

You may have heard about a new version of the LLC that is popping up in some states and gaining popularity called a *series LLC.* A series LLC is like having lots of smaller entities under one umbrella LLC. I go into more detail on the series LLC in Chapter 2. They are great entities and may save you some dough in state fees; however, they are newer entities and don't have much case law to back them up. Therefore, I would speak with your corporate consultant at length before setting one up.

You don't need to spend a lot of money in legal fees to jump on the asset protection boat. Although some attorneys may charge you thousands of dollars for fancy-sounding trusts or family limited partnerships (read Chapter 2 for more info on FLPs), when it comes to asset protection, all you normally need is a simple LLC. More than one LLC is ideal for many people, but if you only want to dole out the cash for one — that's a lot better than nothing.

Following the dual-company strategy

An easy way to protect your business's assets is to simply not keep them in the LLC that operates with the public. You can do this by creating a separate LLC that holds your primary LLC's assets (making this a *dual-company* strategy). This is my favorite strategy by far, and in addition to keeping your assets safe, you also save on some of your state and local taxes. This can work no matter the LLC's tax structure and whether it's manager-managed or member-managed.

Here's how it works: Say you decide to start a local pizza delivery company. You live in a high-tax state such as California. In this case, I would advise you to form your LLC in the state of California (not much you can do about this — if you're located there, you have to register and pay taxes there, no matter what). Then, place all of your assets, such as your pizza ovens, cash registers, and so on, into a Nevada LLC that has elected corporate taxation (see Chapter 13 to find out how to make tax elections). For extra protection, I would have you make this Nevada LLC a completely private entity by hiring a nominee (see the "Privacy as the first step: Electing a nominee" section earlier in the chapter).

Your Nevada LLC that owns the assets then leases those to your California LLC (your *operating company* — the one that deals with the customers, vendors, and so on). This way, your company's assets are 100 percent protected. Why? Because they are in a completely separate entity. Your California LLC controls the assets, but doesn't own them, which is the most powerful position to be in. If your company gets into a legal predicament, such as a customer gets injured, the inquiring attorney will see that your company is completely devoid of assets. Even if he finds out that you own the Nevada LLC, he can't do anything.

If you choose to use this strategy, make sure the lease between the California LLC and the Nevada LLC is legitimate. You need to pay a reasonable leasing fee to the Nevada LLC every month or every quarter. This may seem like a pain in the butt, but believe me, this is a good thing because if you ever go to court, your strategy will be legitimate.

One of the main reasons you should form your LLC in Nevada is because Nevada has absolutely zero taxes. Zero business taxes, zero franchise taxes, zero personal income taxes — zilch. And you have to elect corporate taxation on that Nevada LLC because if you were to try this plan with an LLC with pass-through taxation, although your assets would still be protected, the profits would flow through to you personally, and you would be required to pay taxes in whatever state you live in.

So, here's how the tax reduction goes. If you have $100,000 in profit at the end of the year that you want to keep in the company, instead of having the profit flow through to you and your partners and paying state and federal taxes on it, you can have it go to your Nevada LLC as a lease payment for the use of the assets. This $100,000 payment is a legitimate tax deduction, so it eliminates the profit in your LLC. After the money is in your Nevada LLC, it's only taxed at the federal corporate tax rate (which is usually just above 15 percent), as opposed to the personal income tax rate (which can be 35 percent or more!). If you want to save money for assets or other business-related items, this is a great strategy to use.

Keep in mind that you can also use Wyoming as a tax haven; however, Wyoming doesn't allow single-member LLCs, so you would have to find some partners.

Depending on your state laws, your Nevada LLC may have to register in the state that you are doing business in. This won't affect the strategy as a whole, but you'll lose some of your privacy. Speak with your corporate consultant about this so she can plan accordingly.

When family comes first: The family LLC

Although a family LLC sounds really official, it's really just an LLC like any other — you don't have to do anything different when you file your articles of organization. It just serves a different purpose. The family LLC protects the assets you and your family will need in the future. If you are like the majority of folks, you have a savings or money-market account that is coupled with your checking account. Maybe you have some mutual funds. Regardless, everything is in your name. That's not good. Remember: *Own nothing, control everything.* Instead, your assets should grow under the protection of an LLC.

The usual arrangement for a family LLC is that you and your spouse both own 50 percent of the membership. If you can throw a couple of shares to a non-family member for good measure, that helps protect your assets even further. After the LLC is set up, all savings accounts, insurance policies, brokerage accounts, mutual funds, CDs, bonds, and so on are transferred into the LLC. Don't worry — this isn't a taxable event.

Do not place your home in your family LLC. Your home can be the source of many lawsuits. For example, if a neighborhood kid sneaks onto your property and accidentally drowns in the pool, all of the assets in the LLC can be taken. Instead, form a separate LLC for your home or get a homestead exemption.

Now, if you or your spouse is sued, the assets will be safe in the entity, and the creditor can only obtain a charging order. In this case, you use the booby-trap method that I outlined in the "Setting up a booby trap" section earlier in the chapter to resolve the situation.

Also, if your LLC acquires any debts or obligations, you (and your spouse) aren't liable for them. For instance, say you are extended a margin on your brokerage account and you make a few bad trades; unless you personally guaranteed the loan, you aren't responsible for it — although all of your other assets in the LLC may be at risk of being liquidated to repay the debt.

The more that your family LLC is legally separated from you, the better it is. You can do this by using nominees and finding a way to make your personal assets seem like a normal course of business. Create a paper trail that separates you from the assets in the LLC. For instance, if your vehicles are in the LLC, make sure to lease them to your family. This is also a good way to have a legitimate purpose for transferring savings into the LLC on a regular basis. Make sure to document everything — have legitimate contracts and keep your records in order as if it were a real business. The less obvious it is that the LLC only serves to protect your assets, the more certain you can be that the LLC will be rock solid in the courtroom.

Chapter 15

Real Estate and LLCs

....

In This Chapter

▶ Using an LLC to protect your real estate holdings

▶ Working with land trusts

▶ Transferring the title and dealing with mortgage companies

▶ Harnessing the power of series LLCs

....

*R*eal estate offers the easiest path to success . . . and the easiest path to lawsuits. If someone is living in a rental property that you own and is injured, he will most likely sue, especially because he doesn't even have to do an asset search to know that you have at least one valuable asset — the property he's living in.

Even if you just own vacant land, you are still open to multitudes of liabilities. It seems as though no matter how clear the signs are, trespassers will always end up on your property. If an accident happens, you will most likely be held responsible. Not to mention all of the environmental liabilities that can occur with vacant land. Although you should be wary, all of these potential liabilities aren't the end of the world. With some good advice (starting with this chapter!), and an LLC or two, you'll be fine!

LLCs: The Entity of Choice for Real Estate Assets

There is absolutely no doubt that LLCs are the best entities for holding real estate. They offer the most liability protection of any entity type out there (Chapter 2 goes into detail about the other entities), and when you're looking to protect valuable assets this peace of mind is priceless.

Different people need different strategies. I'm writing in generalities, so keep in mind that you may be one of the few cases where a corporation or S corporation is your best bet. For instance, if you are flipping properties so often that it's considered an operating business, a corporation may not be such a bad thing.

Before you create your plan for protecting your real estate investments, make sure to speak with a qualified professional. You need to get everything right in the beginning because you normally only find out that you have made a mistake after it's too late to fix it.

In the following sections, I go over some of the best reasons for using LLCs for holding your real estate (or land trusts). Before you proceed, though, here are some other goodies to keep in mind about the benefits of an LLC:

✔ LLCs are the most flexible entities around. You decide how the property is managed — you make your own rules. You can put whatever you want in your operating agreement, including what rights, powers, and limitations the company's manager is subject to.

✔ LLCs don't require the same intensive formalities that corporations require. For LLCs, minutes, resolutions, and so on are optional (but recommended!). For instance, if you don't do your annual meeting minutes, you won't have to worry about such dire consequences as your entity being disregarded in court and your personal assets seized.

✔ Everyone involved in the LLC — all members, managers, and employees — is protected from being held liable for the actions of the company itself. This is a stark contrast to the limited partnership, where only the limited partners, and not the general partners, are protected.

Corporations: The worst choice

When it comes to real estate, corporations are by far an inferior choice. Don't get me wrong — I don't dislike corporations at all. Actually, I recommend them to a lot of clients who are starting up small businesses. But when it comes to real estate, corporations are the worst! Corporations are to real estate like kryptonite is to Superman . . . they are poisonous. Don't do it.

I wish that were enough to convince you, but regardless of what I say, there is always a skeptic out there who needs more information. Well, here you go — two important things to keep in mind:

✔ Corporations don't offer the same level of liability protection that LLCs do. They only offer one layer instead of two. Your personal assets are protected in the event that the corporation gets sued; but if you get sued personally, your corporation is toast — in other words, it's liquidated to

> pay off your judgment. Considering that real estate is normally pretty expensive and not something that you want to lose, this may sway you to use an LLC instead.
>
> ✔ Double taxation. The term "double taxation" alone should make you want to run far, far away. This is the main reason why you should never use a corporation to hold your real estate assets, especially if they are rental properties. You see, all income that the property receives is first taxed at the corporate tax level and then taxed at the high capital gains tax rate after you take the cash out of the company.

Here's an example of how double taxation can hurt you. Say you purchased an investment property -*in an LLC* - at $500,000 during the California real estate boom, then held it for four years until it appreciated to $1 million (only in California!). You now want to sell it at this price before the market turns. This means that you will realize a $500,000 profit which is passed on to you. This profit will be taxed at a long-term capital gains rate, which is only 15 percent — a pretty good deal!

Let's say, instead, you chose to hold that same investment property in a corporation. First, the profit is taxed at the corporate rate, which means your corporation will pay about $170,000 in taxes (15 percent on the first $50,000, then 34 to 37 percent on the remaining). Then, after you take the remaining $330,000 personally, you'll need to pay *personal* tax on the dividend income. That means you'll be paying an additional $129,030 in federal taxes (assuming you are in the 39.1 percent tax bracket) for a grand total of $299,030 in taxes. Yikes — and you haven't even figured in state taxes yet!

At this point, clients often bring up the value of the S corporation. After all, S corporations can elect to have the similar pass-through taxation as the LLC and therefore are not subject to double taxation, so there is very little difference. Although the differences appear slight on the surface, you'll actually still dish out more cash for taxes with an S corporation than an LLC. Say you want to transfer the property out of the S corporation without selling it (maybe to convert it to a personal residence for the added tax benefits, for instance); then you'll be taxed. LLCs, on the other hand, allow you to transfer property in and out of the entity without being taxed.

If your business is operating as a corporation and wants to purchase some property for its operations, you should put the building into a separate LLC. Not only will the building then be insulated from any lawsuits filed against the business, but holding the building in an LLC can also save you from the whole double taxation debacle. The corporation can be a member of that LLC and contribute the money for the purchase (which is a tax-free event). The corporation can then lease the office space, which is a deductible cost. As far as the LLC goes, the rental income it receives from the business is offset by the operating expenses of the property and its depreciation. You only pay taxes on what is left over.

Land trusts are just icing on the cake

If you are currently in real estate, or have been heavily researching it, then you've probably heard of *land trusts*. (For those of you who don't know what a land trust is, it's trust where one person, "the trustee," agrees to hold the title of the property for the benefit of another person, "the beneficiary".) Although they seem like a newer thing and are gaining popularity, land trusts have been around for a while — a long while. They go back as far as the Roman Empire. In Western history, they were heavily used during the Tudor period in England, when owning land came with many more burdens than just kooky tenants, such as serving in the military. Because land trusts offer such a thick veil of privacy, citizens of England hid their land ownership to get out of fighting the war of the week.

Today, land trusts are used to avoid a different type of war — that which exists in the courtroom. Land trusts not only allow you to keep your real estate out of your name, but you can also use them to avoid probate and have the property immediately pass on to your heirs upon death. Because of a trust's privacy protection, large corporations often use them to secretly buy up large plots of land in little chunks without anyone being the wiser.

How land trusts are set up

Like all trusts, land trusts have a trustee and a beneficiary. The *trustee* is the one that is on public record and can be a person, LLC, corporation, or other type of entity. Although the trustee is on public record, they don't own the trust; the beneficiary does. You are the *beneficiary*. Therefore, you indirectly own and ultimately control the trust; however, your name is kept private and can't be accessed by the roving eye of a litigation attorney looking to sue you.

Sounds great, right? Well, it is! Sort of. You see, land trusts sound really official, but the reality is that they are no more separate from yourself than a sole proprietorship is. They aren't separate entities with separate identities. What does this mean for you? You guessed it — it means *zero* liability protection. If one of your tenants burns himself while messing around with the water heater and decides to sue, you can kiss your house, your car, and the property in your land trust goodbye. Also, if your neighbor sues you personally for running over her cat (accidentally, of course!), your land trust is considered personal property and it and everything in it, including your real estate holdings, can be taken away. Your attorney may have you place your assets in a land trust for estate planning purposes, but considering the lawsuit statistics nowadays, there is a good chance that your assets won't even make it past your retirement without being taken away by some snarling personal injury attorney.

A good question that all of my clients ask me is, if the attorney doesn't know I own it, how can they take it away? Well, that's easy. They get you on the stand and ask you point blank if you own any real estate properties. You can't lie. After all, you are the land trust's beneficiary, also known as a beneficial *owner.* You have to tell the court that you own the real estate and also disclose any other assets you have, whether in land trusts or not. So as soon as you get dragged into court, the little protection that your land trust offered you disintegrates.

Pluses and minuses of land trusts

Land trusts do have their benefits. Privacy is *huge* nowadays, and if you don't want to use a *nominee* (a person who allows you to maintain your privacy as the LLC's owner) for your LLC (see Chapter 14), then a land trust will be perfect for you, as long as it's paired with a good ole LLC that can deliver on its shortcomings. Put an LLC and land trust together, and it's double trouble for anyone who wants to steal your hard-earned assets. The LLC has the liability protection, and the land trust offers the privacy and estate planning advantages.

The best way to maximize the benefits of both the land trust and the LLC is to make the LLC the beneficiary of the land trust. That way, if you need to take the stand, you can easily say that you don't own the land trust, your LLC does. If the plaintiff wants to continue to sue you, great! Then you can just snag him in the awesome LLC booby trap that I outline in Chapter 14. But that will rarely come to pass. If the attorney is smart, he'll know you're as smart as you look and won't want to mess with you any further. He'll most likely drop the case or offer a reasonable settlement.

Now, holding your real estate in a land trust with an LLC as the beneficiary has some other pluses and minuses. Because it would take pages and pages to go over them all, I'm just going to give you a brief overview.

Here are some advantages:

- ✔ The property's sales price can be kept off public record. This can help keep property taxes lower than they would be at the property's fair-market value.

- ✔ When you sell or gift the property, it can be done quickly and efficiently. You don't have to record a new deed; you just name a new beneficiary.

- ✔ You can easily continue the project in the event that a partner dies.

Here are the disadvantages:

✔ You cannot do a tax-free, like-kind (IRS Section 1031) exchange with property in a land trust. You must transfer the land out of the trust for the like-kind exchange to be possible. This may involve sizeable fees and taxes and also removes the veil of privacy during the transfer.

✔ Often, trustees are unwilling to take certain necessary actions on your behalf, such as signing mortgage documents. The mortgage may need to be placed in your name, and this eliminates all privacy protection.

Looking at the LLC Property Logistics

Like many things, putting property into a newly formed LLC sounds easier than it actually is. Instead of just figuring it out as you go, you'll need some real-world advice to guide you. The reality is that mortgage companies are skittish about loaning money to newly formed LLCs. I mean, wouldn't you be? The LLC has no financial history, no assets, no credit score to go by . . . the bank would probably be better off lending money to a 4-year-old. If you already own the property and want to transfer the title — this can also quickly become a sticky situation. You need to prepare for these situations, among others, when setting up your asset protection plan.

Deciding which state to form in

Unfortunately, in the case of rental properties, you don't gain too many tax benefits by forming the LLC that holds the property in a tax haven, such as Nevada or Wyoming, unless, of course, the property is actually located in Nevada or Wyoming — in that case, good thinkin'! Renting a property to someone is considered "doing business," and therefore, you are required to register in that state and also pay *franchise fees* (a common term for state business taxes or fees). Also, for the most part, the lawsuits against your property will be handled in the state that the property is in and where the incident occurred. So, if another state has better laws than yours does, you may not be able to take advantage of them, even if your LLC is domiciled there.

You may get around having to register to transact business in a particular state if all you're doing is holding vacant land. Holding onto land is not considered "conducting business" as long as you haven't started the development process and aren't receiving any rent payments. In this case, you can probably form your LLC in Nevada or Wyoming and not have to worry about foreign filing or paying taxes in the state that the property is actually located in.

Protecting your home

I know that with all of the benefits of LLCs that I have laid out, you're going to be tempted to put your personal residence into an LLC. After all, you know that LLCs can protect your assets from creditors and lawsuits — and what more important asset do you have than the home you have built your life in? Well, as tempting as it may be, don't do it.

Owning a home comes with a lot of amazing tax benefits that you could lose if you transfer it out of your name. For instance, when you sell the property, you won't have the tax-free benefit that you are currently getting. You will also lose your mortgage interest deduction.

Most states have laws that automatically protect your home in the event of a lawsuit or lien. This is called a homestead exemption and only applies to your personal residence — investment properties don't count. You should check with your state laws to see whether this exemption is automatic or whether you have to file a claim to acquire it. With the exception of a possible small filing fee, homestead exemptions are free.

Depending on your state, your homestead exemption may cover all or part of the equity you have in your home. Some states, like Florida, Texas, and Oklahoma, cover your home 100 percent, while other states only cover it up to a certain dollar amount.

If your rental property is going to make a lot of profit and your state imposes some pretty hefty taxes, then I would use the dual-company strategy that I outlined in Chapter 14 to reduce the amount of state taxes you pay. In this case, you just form an LLC in the state your property is located in, and then transfer the property to that LLC. You then form a Nevada or Wyoming corporation and set this up as a management company that you pay to manage the property. You then pay a reasonable percentage of the LLC's profits to the management company. These profits are now safe and secure in a tax-free entity and away from the potential creditors and lawsuits of the property.

Getting lenders to loan to an LLC

If you just formed your LLC yesterday, you may have a hard time getting your banker to loan it money. After all, when banks loan money, they have certain criteria that they use to evaluate credit-worthiness. For instance, with businesses, they look at cash flow and assets. With individuals, they look at income and credit scores. Your LLC has none of these. From the bank's perspective, your LLC has no credit history, no track record, and no assets. Therefore, you'll most likely be required to personally guarantee the loan.

Now that you understand this fact, you have to try to persuade the bank to allow the LLC to hold the property's title (the legal document which shows the ownership of the property). Banks obviously don't like this. They want the person guaranteeing the loan to hold the title. However, the bank usually relents in certain instances.

I guarantee you that the worst way to get the bank to let the LLC hold the title is to tell your banker that you want to transfer the property into the LLC for asset protection purposes. Banks hate that phrase. After all, they are some of the biggest creditors around. However, bankers do understand (and respect!) estate planning issues. Let your banker know that you want to transfer the property into the newly formed LLC for estate planning purposes. If your banker isn't savvy enough to understand what you're doing, then shop around. I'm sure you can find a bank that is more than willing to accommodate you.

After you get a banker on board, you'll get the loan personally. Then, when the title is in your name, you can transfer it into the LLC's name. The whole process shouldn't take more than a few days to complete. You'll still be personally guaranteeing the loan; however, the title will be in the name of your LLC and protected from creditors.

If you are currently financed and want to transfer the title into your LLC, check with your mortgage company first. Transferring the title may trigger a due-on-sale clause in your contract, which means that you'll have to pay your mortgage back in full. That will force you to refinance. Mortgage companies will often enforce this when you have locked in a really low fixed rate and they want you to refinance at a higher rate.

If your mortgage company won't allow you to transfer your property into an LLC, you may want to see if it will allow you to transfer the property into a living trust for "estate planning purposes." Most mortgage companies have policies that accommodate this sort of thing. If so, have an attorney form a *living trust* (a trust that a grantor creates while he is still alive), then make your LLC the trust's beneficiary. Now you'll still get the protection that an LLC offers, and you won't trigger a due-on-sale clause when you transfer your property.

Transferring the title

After the LLC has been formed and you are in the clear to transfer the title of the property to the LLC, you are ready to prepare a deed (a document which transfers the ownership of a property). You can choose from a lot of different types of deeds. Some make the original owner responsible for all current defects or liabilities of the property, while others waive the previous owner from all responsibility — the property is just transferred as is. If you are transferring the property from your own name to an LLC that you control, I'd use the latter. After all, it is a much easier deed to draft. The deed you will want to use is called a *quit-claim deed.* You can download a copy of a sample quit-claim deed at `www.myllc.com/dummies`.

Making the 1031 exchange work when you have partners

If you have property that you want to eventually do a 1031 exchange on, and you have multiple owners, the best way to structure the deal is to have each partner form his own single-member LLC, like Jack and Mary in the figure. Then, all of the members' LLCs will own their portion of the property as tenants-in-common. This way, you still have liability protection (through your LLC), and you can still execute a like-kind 1031 exchange.

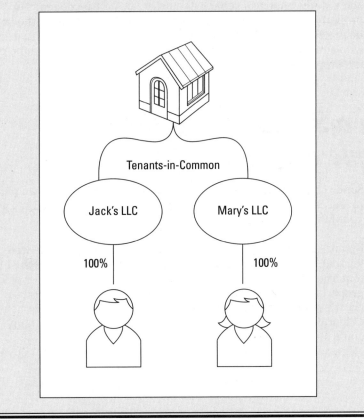

The deed should be in the LLC's name and be signed by you and anyone else who will be authorizing the transfer of the property. The deed will most likely have to be notarized. Now you're ready to file! The deed must be filed in the county that the property is located in. As to exactly where you file it, I can't tell you specifically. The exact office differs from county to county, so you need to do a little bit of research to get the office's name and address. I'd start with the county recorder's office or the county clerk's office and go from there.

Your property should be held in the name of your LLC. For instance, your county recorder should show that your parcel number is titled to your LLC. If this isn't recorded properly, your assets could be in jeopardy.

Make sure to check with your title insurance company before transferring the title. Some insurance companies will cancel coverage if the title has been transferred to a new entity.

You have to be careful, because although contributions to an LLC are tax-free, some states impose a separate transfer tax. It often depends on why the property is being transferred, and in some circumstances, the tax burden can be pretty hefty. This is why I recommend you do a quick phone consultation with a real estate attorney or tax advisor who specializes in the county that the property is located in.

Using a Series LLC to Hold Multiple Properties

Series LLCs are the newest, coolest things around. If you own multiple pieces of real estate (or other assets), you're going to love them! They will make your life so much easier.

Up until a couple of years ago, advisors and attorneys alike were recommending that business owners and real estate investors place each of their important assets (be it a vehicle, a trademark, some equipment, or piece of property) into a separate LLC. Although this was the safest thing you could do, the paperwork could get a little ridiculous. Not to mention, in states like California where the annual franchise fee is over $700 *per entity*, this strategy could also get really expensive, really fast.

Well, the folks in Delaware — always itching to provide the latest and greatest in asset protection vehicles — saw an opportunity. They decided to eliminate all headaches associated with forming and managing multiple LLCs and thus created what's now referred to as a *series LLC.* A series LLC is like a lot of little LLCs all put together under one big umbrella. These little LLCs are referred to as *cells.* Each cell is a separate and distinct entity and can have different members and managers than its brother cells.

Series LLCs have recently caught on and are available in more and more states every year. Even if your state does not yet allow you to form a series LLC, you can still create one in another state. You'll just have to work with a consulting company to analyze your business strategy and set up the structure for you.

Unfortunately, the Series LLC is so new that there is no guidance from most federal or state taxing authorities as to how Series LLC's will be treated. However, in 2006 the California Franchise Tax Board issued a ruling that it would treat each series or cell as a separate LLC that requires a separate franchise tax return. This is on top of the usual state law requirement that each series or cell needs to have a separate checking account and accounting.

Although the series LLC adds extra flexibility and saves you some dough in filing fees, these features don't compare to the added benefit of liability protection. With a regular LLC, if your LLC gets sued, your personal assets are protected — we've already established that. However, everything inside the LLC is fair game. If you have a prosperous business or a lot of real estate holdings, creditors don't need to worry about going after your personal assets — the business assets alone will keep them happy and fed for years to come! Well, the series LLC takes away this incentive.

If someone sues a series LLC, she's limited to taking the assets that were actually involved in the lawsuit. For instance, if you have five rental properties held by one regular LLC, and the tenant of one rental property gets injured and sues the LLC for damages, then all five rental properties can be seized to settle the debt. With a series LLC, though, things are a lot different! If you place each of the five properties into different cells of the series LLC, then when the tenant sues you, only the property that she lives in and is suing about can be seized to settle the judgment. All of the other properties are safe. Think of each cell of a series LLC as a veil of protection that keeps that particular asset from being seized for the actions of another asset in a different cell (see Figure 15-1).

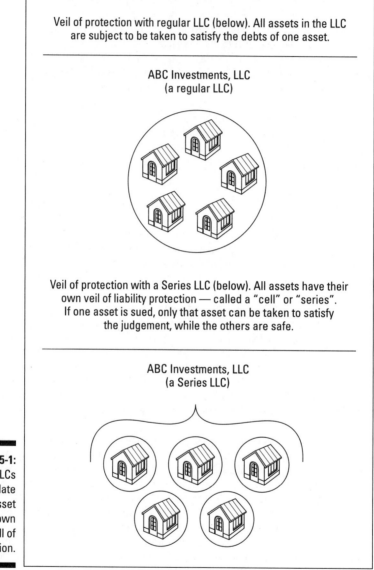

Veil of protection with regular LLC (below). All assets in the LLC are subject to be taken to satisfy the debts of one asset.

ABC Investments, LLC
(a regular LLC)

Veil of protection with a Series LLC (below). All assets have their own veil of liability protection — called a "cell" or "series". If one asset is sued, only that asset can be taken to satisfy the judgement, while the others are safe.

ABC Investments, LLC
(a Series LLC)

Figure 15-1:
Series LLCs
insulate
each asset
in its own
cell of
protection.

Chapter 16

Estate Planning: Avoiding Death Taxes

. . . .

In This Chapter

▶ Understanding estate taxes

▶ Dodging the gift tax

▶ Using LLCs to protect your estate

. . . .

*Y*ou know what they say: "Nothing is as certain as death and taxes." Well, if you leave it to me (and a qualified estate planning attorney), those two don't have to go hand in hand.

I know, I know. Death isn't an easy thing to talk about. Almost everyone seems to think that it won't happen to them. Unfortunately, it's pretty inevitable. It will happen to you, and sometimes sooner than you think. If you were to die tomorrow, where would that leave your loved ones financially? You have worked very hard over the course of your lifetime, and upon your death, you'll most likely want to keep the rewards in the family or give them to charity. You surely won't want to give them to the IRS.

Estate taxes were meant to be taxes on the super-rich, but under the new tax law, it has been proved that individuals with estates from $1 million to $5 million end up paying the most tax. I think this happens for two reasons:

  ✔ The new tax law plays around with the tax basis of the assets (which I cover later in this chapter).

  ✔ The super-rich are generally more prudent about structuring their estates to take advantage of as many tax breaks as possible. This is what I'm going to show *you* how to do in this chapter.

In this chapter, I introduce you to estate planning and gift taxes, and then show you how LLCs give you better control over what happens to your assets and taxes after you pass away. I also give you a couple of pointers on using gifts and trusts in your estate planning strategy.

It would be impossible to cover all of the facets of estate planning in a single chapter. In this chapter, I only cover the federal estate tax structure and the role of LLCs in estate planning. For a more in-depth analysis of the topic, get the book *Estate Planning For Dummies* (Wiley) by Jordan Simon and Brian Caverly. I also encourage you to work with a qualified attorney who specializes in estate planning and family law.

Getting Acquainted with Estate Planning and Gift Taxes

Clients often ask me how much they need to be worth to make estate planning necessary. My answer: If you have $1 million or more in assets, then you need an estate plan. Also, if you own property that has appreciated a sizeable amount (even if you have refinanced and taken the equity out of it), then you must plan your estate. And with estates come estate taxes.

Even if you are young, you shouldn't ignore estate planning. Life is a fragile gift that can be taken away at any moment. If you are successful and have accumulated any measure of wealth, you need to plan now to protect your money from falling into the wrong hands upon your death.

You need estate planning not only to reduce the tax burdens of your heirs, but also to dictate who your heirs are. Your offspring may be warm and wonderful now, but you'd be surprised. Upon your death, all bets are off, and it isn't uncommon for large estates to end up divvied out in court because of outraged children. Wills can normally do the trick when it comes to doling out inheritances, but a well-crafted estate plan using LLCs can be pretty bulletproof should anyone decide to contest your last dying wish.

In the next few sections, I go over the tax regulations in more detail so you can use the information to better plan your approach to your estate planning.

Understanding the basics of estate taxes

Estate taxes, often called *death taxes,* can be an astronomical burden to your children or grandchildren if you aren't careful. The government wants you to think that with the new tax breaks, estate taxes have been nearly eliminated. Unfortunately, that isn't the case.

Let me explain how the IRS figures estate taxes. Upon your death, everything you own is added up — business interests, real estate, securities, insurance, cash, annuities, and so on — and this amounts to what the IRS calls your *gross estate.* Normally, these assets are calculated based on their current fair market value, not what you originally paid for them. After your gross estate is calculated, the IRS allows certain deductions, such as mortgages, certain charitable expenses, and any costs associated with administering the estate. With these deductions in place, you now have what the IRS calls your *taxable estate.*

From here, you add all of your *lifetime taxable gifts* (the amount of money you gift in your lifetime that goes over your $12,000 per year limit), and the estate tax is computed. You then subtract the available credit (courtesy of Uncle Sam) — which varies from $1 million to $3.5 million, depending on the year you pass away — and your children are taxed on the remaining amount. The tax rate ranges from 45 percent to 55 percent, depending on the year (with the exception of 2010, which I discuss later in the chapter). The kids generally have to pay the estate taxes within nine months of the date of their parent's death.

Because many estates consist of property, it is not uncommon for the total amount of the estate to go over the $1 million exemption. When this occurs, the kids can face pretty astronomical tax burdens. Unless the heirs are independently wealthy and have a lot of liquid cash to pay the tax outright, they'll need to sell the property or qualify for a loan to use the equity to cover the tax debt. This is why it's even more imperative to have an estate plan if you intend to pass on assets that aren't liquid.

Knowing when your estate won't be taxed

If you pass away while you're still married, then to the extent you leave assets to your spouse, your estate won't be subject to federal gift or estate taxes, no matter the amount. The U.S. has what is called an *unlimited marital deduction.* This means that whatever you pass on to your spouse is tax free and doesn't eat up any of your $1 million gift tax exemption or your estate tax exemption (which I discuss in further detail in the next section).

Estates under $1 million are never required to pay any estate tax. The heirs aren't even required to file a return. The only exception occurs when you have been gifting more than $1 million per year to the heir who receives the estate. In that case, you should speak with an attorney who specializes in estate planning so she can add up all of your gifting overages from the past years and give you an exact amount of tax that your heir will be required to pay.

Understanding the Tax Reconciliation Relief Act

In 2001, Congress passed the Economic Growth and Tax Reconciliation Relief Act, which implemented a reduction of federal estate taxes on a sliding scale. This means that your children could feasibly be paying a lot less in estate taxes — as long as you die before December 31, 2010, when the act expires. Now, unless you plan on taking your own life so your kids can receive some extra dough, you'd be much wiser to implement an estate plan instead of relying on the government to cut you a break.

Here's how the act works: From 2002 to 2010, the estate tax credit will go up (from $1 million to $3.5 million), and the tax rate will simultaneously go down (from 55 percent to 45 percent). In 2010, there will be no estate taxes, per se (although you could end up paying more taxes, which I discuss later in the chapter).

Table 16-1 shows a breakdown of the estate tax credit, the gift tax credit, and the estate tax level on a per year basis. In 2011, the taxes revert to their 2002 levels. If you are a high-worth individual, you can see from the chart that the act probably doesn't apply to you.

For instance, if you are passing on a $10 million estate in 2008, then $8 million will be subject to taxes (after you deduct the $2 million estate tax credit). That $8 million will be taxed at an astronomical 45 percent tax rate! Your kids will pay at least $3.6 million in taxes. And if you were to pass away in 2013, then your kids will pay 55 percent on $9 million!

Table 16-1	Estate and Gift Tax Credits and Estate Tax Levels on a Per-Year Basis		
Year	**Estate Tax Credit**	**Gift Tax Credit**	**Estate Tax Rate**
2007	$2 million	$1 million	45%
2008	$2 million	$1 million	45%
2009	$3.5 million	$1 million	45%
2010	Tax repeal	Tax repeal	0%
2011	$1 million	$1 million	55%
2012	$1 million	$1 million	55%
2013	$1 million	$1 million	55%

If you have just inherited an estate that contains simple assets such as cash, securities, and so on, that is under the exemption amount (refer to Table 16-1), then you don't have to file an estate tax return.

It's possible that when 2011 rolls around Congress will renew the act. If lawmakers decide to implement some of the changes on a more permanent basis, it will probably be only random bits and pieces and entail a tax structure that doesn't fluctuate from year to year. This is a huge unknown that makes it very difficult for the elderly and the sick to plan accordingly.

2010: The year of capital gains

Although the 2001 act was a good thing, it's still a devil in disguise — especially when 2010 rolls around. The act wrongly leads folks to believe that they don't need an estate plan. Believe it or not, if you pass away in 2010 when it appears that there is no estate tax, your children may pay a lot more in taxes than you anticipated.

You see, if you inherit property, stocks, or other appreciating assets in 2010, your offspring may be forced to pay the capital gains tax on all of the appreciation that occurred from the date you first purchased the asset. The IRS allows a $1.3 million *step-up in basis* (where you add $1.3 million to the original purchase price before calculating the appreciation), but for kids whose parents were good investors, this still could amount to huge chunk of change.

For instance, say John purchased $1 million in real estate and stocks in 1990. Having invested wisely, those assets are worth $10 million upon his death in 2010. Because he had cancer and knew that he would be passing away in 2010, he assumed that he wouldn't need an estate plan because no estate taxes would be imposed for that year. Unfortunately, he wasn't aware of the little provision in the act that states that there is no step-up in basis on the assets that his children receive. This means his kids have to pay capital gains tax on the $9 million in appreciation from when he purchased the assets.

What does this amount to? Well, the IRS allows a $1.3 million step-up in basis, so that means that you would subtract the $2.3 million (instead of just the $1 million purchase price) from $10 million. That leaves the kids with $7.7 million in capital gains, which are subject to the 15 percent long-term capital gains rate. This means that as soon as John's heirs sell the assets, they will have to pay about $1.15 million to the IRS — ouch! In other years, there would be what is called a *full step-up in basis,* and John's children wouldn't have to pay any capital gains taxes when they sell the assets. In other words, they wouldn't be penalized for their parent's savvy business decisions. LLCs can help you with this, which I explain later in the chapter.

Skipping a generation can kill your estate

Way back in the day, the wealthiest families in America avoided paying estate taxes by using a loophole that allowed them to use repetitive life estates to freely pass assets on to their grandchildren. In 1976, Congress decided to close this loophole once and for all and created what we now know as the *generation-skipping transfer tax,* or GST tax for short.

This means that if you decide to transfer assets directly to your grandchildren, the same taxes will be imposed as if you were to transfer your assets to your child and then your child passed the assets to her children. In short, you'll be taxed twice. And unless you pass away in 2010 when this tax is temporarily suspended, your grandchildren most likely won't receive much more than the $1 million to $2 million exclusion amount.

For the most part, the GST tax rate matches the estate tax rate for that year. So, if you pass away in 2011 — when the estate tax rate is 55 percent — then your grandchildren will owe approximately $7.2 million in taxes on a $10 million estate. Here's how the math would look:

Total Estate	**$10,000,000**	
Minus Exclusion	-$1,000,000	
Total	**$9,000,000**	
55% Estate Tax	-$4,950,000	
Total	**$4,050,000**	
55% GST Tax	-$2,227,500	
Total	**$1,822,500**	
Plus Exclusion	+$1,000,000	
After-Tax Total	**$2,822,500**	*This is the amount your grandchildren will receive.*

The GST tax only applies when you pass money to your grandchildren while their parents (your children) are still alive, thereby skipping a generation. It also applies if you pass money to someone who is more than 37.5 years younger than you.

The GST tax applies to gifts also, so if you're planning on giving pieces of your estate to your grandchildren or to someone who is significantly younger than you while you are still alive, then you need to sit down with a qualified estate planning attorney to discuss your specific needs. The sooner the better.

Deciphering the gift tax

One strategy that I discuss later in the chapter is minimizing your estate tax burden by gifting assets to your heirs while you're still alive. Individuals often use this strategy to avoid estate taxes. Unfortunately, the IRS has caught on and has imposed a *gift tax,* which is very similar to the estate tax. Gifting can still be a good strategy though, because when all is said and done, your heirs will still pay less to Uncle Sam.

While alive, you can gift up to $12,000 per year to each person, tax free (this amount is adjusted each year for inflation). If you have a spouse, you and your spouse can collectively gift $24,000 per year to each person, tax free (this is known as a *joint gift*). Anything over that amount will be added up and taxed upon your death at the current gift tax rates.

Table 16-2 shows the current gifts tax rates (with estate tax rates included) for each year.

Table 16-2	Estate and Gift Tax Rates	
Year	*Estate Tax Rate*	*Gift Tax Rate*
2007	45%	45%
2008	45%	45%
2009	45%	45%
2010	0%	35%
2011	55%	50%
2012	55%	50%
2013	55%	50%

If you gift more than $12,000 in one year to a particular recipient, don't worry. As long as your collective *overages* don't amount to too much, your estate won't be burdened with any gift taxes upon your passing. You see, you get a $1 million *lifetime gift tax exclusion.* This means that as long as your overages don't amount to more than $1 million, your gifts won't be taxed.

Unfortunately, if you're gifting assets and/or cash to your heirs, you still have to pay income tax on that money. Gifts to heirs aren't deductible expenses — unless your heirs are 501(c)3 charities, that is.

As long as you're alive, you can gift as much as you want to educational institutions (such as for your grandchild's college education) or to pay for medical services. This money doesn't count toward your $12,000 allowance. However, the money must go directly to the educational institution or the medical service provider, not to the person using those services. Keep in mind though, that if you're paying for college expenses, the money for room, board, books, entertainment, and so on doesn't count — only tuition. The money you spend on these ancillary items goes toward the $12,000 tax-free allowance.

As long as your gifts remain under the excluded amounts — $12,000 per year per recipient and under $1 million in overages — then the gifts won't be subject to generation-skipping taxes. This means that you can gift a pretty sizeable amount to your grandchildren — as long as you have some forethought and act quickly!

How LLCs Help with Estate Planning

Planning your estate is sort of like shooting at a moving target — you can't plan for a future that you are unsure of. Nothing is certain in estate taxes, and you can pretty much bet that Congress will pass another tax act in the coming years that changes the estate tax structure. Who knows what the tax rates will be when you pass on!

You need to take control of your estate and not leave everything up to the fickle whims of the U.S. government. LLCs are the perfect tool for this. With LLCs, you maintain control of your assets as the ownership passes on to your heirs, all the while avoiding probate. You can also rest assured that your estate is protected from the roving eye of creditors and lawyers who want to take it away.

LLCs avoid probate

One of the greatest benefits of using LLCs in your estate planning is that no probate process is required. *Probate* is a lengthy and expensive process where the court settles your estate for you. The court resolves all creditors' claims and distributes your assets according to law or according to your will (if you recorded one). Probate is managed by someone whom you designate in your will, called an *executor*.

Probate often undermines all of the tax-saving steps that you take (such as gifting) because the legal fees and court costs can become so astronomical that the taxes are nominal in comparison. And if someone contests the will or the executor, the courts can take many years to execute the will, and there may not be too much of an estate left to divvy up after it's all over.

When you set up your estate in an LLC, the LLC just transfers to your heirs, and all is said and done. This way, you can rest assured that your loved ones won't be hit with any huge legal fees that eat up your estate before it's ever delivered into their hands.

If you are married and live in a community property state (Arizona, California, Idaho, Louisiana, New Mexico, Texas, Washington, and Wisconsin), all of your assets will be transferred to your spouse upon your death. In this case, no probate is necessary. If your spouse is no longer alive, then your estate will enter into probate.

LLCs provide asset protection

The biggest problem with most estate planning techniques is that as you collect assets to pass on to your heirs, the assets aren't protected from creditors and lawsuits. Without this protection while you're alive, you are a walking target. Although most trusts help ease the transfer of your assets upon your death, they don't protect your assets from creditors like an LLC does.

When you work with your attorney on an asset protection plan, he will probably suggest using a trust. (A *trust* is a legal situation where someone gives financial control over certain assets to a person or institution for the benefit of another person [the *beneficiary*].) In my opinion, LLCs, when structured properly, offer the same benefits as trusts when it comes to avoiding probate and reallocating income, but many attorneys hold other positions. After all, LLCs are newer entities, and trusts are the standard, age-old way of estate planning.

When you meet with your attorney to draw up an estate plan, make sure that your attorney incorporates asset protection strategies into the plan. There is no use in preventing your assets from being taxed after your death if your assets get seized by a creditor before your heirs can even get to them. An LLC, if used by itself, should do the trick because it offers many layers of asset protection. You can read Chapter 14 for more information on how to protect your assets using an LLC.

If you want to use a special trust in your estate planning endeavors, then I recommend that you use an LLC (or two or three) to hold the assets, thereby protecting them from creditors. The trust will be the majority owner of the LLC to help avoid probate and reduce estate taxes. This way, if you get sued personally, the estate is protected by the charging order.

When you work with your estate planning attorney, he may not look at the situation from an asset protection perspective. Or, he may look at it *only* from an asset protection perspective and ignore the tax implications. Make sure that you have all of your bases covered and that whoever you work with looks at both of these important aspects when planning your estate.

LLCs give you control

If you've ever delved into asset protection before, you've probably heard of *family limited partnerships* (or FLPs, for short). FLPs gave some of the partners full managerial control (the general partners), while others had none whatsoever (the limited partners). In return for having no say in business matters, the limited partners had limited liability protection, while the general partners had no liability protection. The LLC is the next generation of the limited partnership. Although the LLC offers limited liability for all partners, it offers even more flexibility in how the entity is controlled.

An LLC can be either member-managed, where all partners share equal control of the day-to-day affairs, or manager-managed, where one or a few people (who don't make up 100 percent of the partners) make managerial decisions. In estate planning, it is common to use manager-managed LLCs, where the managing partners are the parents and the non-managing (the "silent") partners are the kids. This way, as the LLC is transferred to the children, the parents can still manage the assets even if they no longer own the LLC.

Also, with the LLC's operating agreement, you can set it up so that basically anything goes. You can have different types (*classes*) of membership, where some partners have more voting rights than the others. You can restrict the transfer of ownership so your kids can't sell their shares in the family estate. You can describe in detail how you want the succession to go after you pass away, and you can name the successor managers. You can even distribute the profits and losses however you want, meaning they don't have to be distributed according to the membership percentages.

Looking At Some Easy Planning Strategies

You can plan your estate in so many ways; you can't possibly discover them all in a book. It's really important for you to sit down and work with a qualified attorney. But before you do, you should understand some important concepts that will no doubt be brought up in the meeting.

For larger estates, gifting away your assets while you are alive is a common strategy. LLCs are especially good for this because only a limited amount of your assets can be gifted each year (see the "Deciphering the gift tax" section earlier in the chapter), and when it comes to noncash assets, such as real estate, it's much easier to gift shares of the LLC than it is to retitle the property each year. Not to mention that LLCs offer a bulletproof layer of asset protection.

Because LLCs are such flexible entities, they are perfect for transferring expensive assets, such as real estate and business interests. Think of these as the gifts that keep on giving. Say that you have a family business that is set up as a corporation. Being the smart cookie that you are, you place the stock (the ownership) of that corporation into a manager-managed LLC. You set it up so the LLC is managed by a second corporation (that you and your spouse both own).

Now that the LLC contains an asset, you have to determine the value of the LLC membership shares. You start by having the asset appraised by a qualified business appraiser. Then, the IRS allows you certain deductions from the fair market value by making the membership shares less appealing — namely, by limiting the control of the members. This is where it's good to have a corporation as the member.

Your entire goal here is to continually reduce the value of your taxable estates. And no, that doesn't mean you want the real estate market to tank and your properties to go down in value! It means you want to slowly "leak" the assets to your children in such a way that it doesn't raise any red flags with Uncle Sam. Currently, the best way to do this is to make sure that you and your spouse give a maximum combined amount of $24,000 to each recipient every year.

So, given the previous example, how is this done? Well, say that the business that you transferred into your LLC is worth $4 million. Because you restrict the control of the members, the IRS will allow you to knock 30 percent off of that valuation. That leaves your total estate valued at $2.8 million. If you have 100,000 shares, that means each share is worth $28. If you have five kids who will equally own and manage the family business upon your death, then you and your spouse can transfer 857 shares ($24,000 ÷ $28 = 857) to each of your children every year, tax free. This means that every year, you can lower the value of your estate by $120,000 ($24,000 × 5 = $120,000) by slowly gifting it away under the radar and without having to pay gift tax. Without factoring in inflation, after approximately 11 years, your estate will be under the $1 million exclusion amount, and upon your death, your heirs won't be required to pay any estate taxes.

You have to be careful when you transfer noncash assets that have appreciated a lot. When your heirs decide to sell the assets after you pass away, they will have to pay long-term capital gains tax on the appreciation from the date you purchased the asset. If you have ever gone through a real estate boom, you can understand what sort of money I'm talking about here. LLCs have the unique ability to force a step-up in the tax basis by having certain provisions in their buy-sell agreements. If you have a lot of heavily appreciated assets, then you should definitely work with an accountant to assist you in minimizing your heirs' capital gains tax burdens.

Part V
The Part of Tens

In this part . . .

Now for the easy stuff. The Part of Tens was made for you type-A personalities who need to cram worlds of information into a few paragraphs. Here, you get the need-to-know information on such topics as keeping your LLC intact and impenetrable from outside forces, popular uses for LLCs (you'll definitely get some ideas in this chapter!), and those common mistakes that some LLC owners make that you must avoid.

Chapter 17

Ten Good Reasons to Form an LLC

*B*y now, you've probably figured out that I think LLCs are the best entity structure around. And for good reason! LLCs are flexible — you can use them for practically any purpose — and they offer more benefits than any other entity type. They have a favorable pass-through tax status, and with the dual liability protection that LLCs offer, corporations and limited partnerships can't compare.

What I love the most about LLCs is that they are completely customizable. You can pretty much draft whatever rules you want in the operating agreement. Most people don't realize that many state laws can be overwritten by a simple paragraph. This is incredibly powerful. You can also choose whatever tax structure you want. LLCs can elect to be taxed like corporations. So much can be done with LLCs that most people don't realize their power. They are stuck in their comfort zone dealing with older entity types that they are more familiar with. Wake up — LLCs are the future, and they're a good thing!

Small-Business Owners Can Customize an LLC

LLCs are great for small businesses because they are adaptable to all situations. No matter if you have 100 silent investors or are a two-person small-business operation, the LLC is so flexible that you can pretty much write the operating agreement to suit your needs; you can make your own rules, pave your own path, and tailor your entity to suit the intricacies of your business. With corporations, you are limited to the stiff corporate formalities and weighty infrastructure of shareholders, directors, and officers.

If you're operating as a sole proprietorship (which is how most small businesses are structured), you would be crazy not to drop this book (after you have finished reading it, of course!) and form an LLC today. A sole proprietorship is the most dangerous form of doing business. It offers zero protection against creditors and lawsuits, and therefore, leaves your personal assets on the table for pretty much anyone to grab. Not to mention that you can't raise capital as a sole proprietorship (and you won't go very far when it comes to impressing people).

By combining a lot of the advantages of C and S corporations (see Chapter 2) with their own special attributes, LLCs have become exceptionally attractive to small-business owners. They offer the same liability protection that corporations offer, but with an added layer of protection from the charging order (see Chapter 11). They have the pass-through tax structure (see Chapter 13) but with *zero restrictions*. This means that any person or entity can be an owner. You can also have an unlimited number of members.

Real Estate Moguls Can Protect Their Assets

LLCs are awesome for real estate — you just can't beat 'em! First, LLCs have dual liability protection that shields your investments from the frivolous lawsuits filed against people like you every day. This means that if someone sues you personally (say you rear end someone in the parking lot, for instance), they can't seize and liquidate your investment properties to settle the claim. If that's not reason enough to form an LLC, I don't know what is! (Chapter 15 has more information about LLCs and real estate holdings.)

Plus, you can easily transfer your property in and out of the entity because LLCs don't impose taxes on contributions or withdrawals of the assets. As long as no money is changing hands, you're good to go. Of course, make sure you talk to your accountant about any hidden tax issues or your attorney if there are any mortgages on the property.

LLCs are so great at holding real estate that I advise each of my clients to form one LLC per property that they own. This way, each property is isolated from the others. If one property gets sued, the others are safe from being seized. With the ease of operation and the limited record-keeping requirements, having multiple LLCs isn't as difficult as you may think.

If you own multiple properties, you can form a series LLC. A *series LLC* is one LLC that is composed of multiple cells — each with its own layer of liability protection. Think of it like this: You put all of your properties into one LLC — which minimizes the paperwork — then you separate each of your properties into a different cell in that LLC. This way, while all of the properties are in one entity, if one property gets sued, the others are still safe from being seized and liquidated to settle the judgment.

Series LLCs aren't available in all states because they're a relatively new entity. Because they are so new, some old-fashioned accountants and attorneys may not want to work with them. If you run into this situation, I recommend finding a professional who has educated herself on series LLCs.

Einstein Types Can Shield Their Intellectual Property

I am a firm believer in keeping your intellectual property as far away from your operating business as possible. Think about it. What is more valuable than your brand which you have worked so hard to build? Or the patents that you have centered your business around? Nothing. Therefore, you need to protect those things with your life. Or with an LLC. Your choice.

Unless you have a bunch of important patents, it is overkill to place all of your intellectual property in separate LLCs. Your intellectual property shouldn't be operating with the public — only your operating company should be dealing with the public. So how do you link your intellectual property in your LLC to your operating company? The LLC that holds your intellectual property should *lease* the patents, trademarks, or copyrights to the operating company for its use. You need to sign paperwork and transfer money to make the arrangement official. After all, if it doesn't look legit, then there's no point in doing it in the first place.

Now, who owns the LLC? Because of the charging order protections, it doesn't really matter too much. But, investors generally like to have the intellectual property of the business be owned by the business; therefore, the operating company should own the LLC. To be on the safe side, a common holding company can be the owner of both the operating company *and* the LLC with the intellectual property. The investors invest in the holding company and voila! They are happy, and the property is safe from lawsuits and angry creditors.

Only LLCs should be used for holding intellectual property — not corporations. You see, if the LLC is owned by the operating business, and the business is sued, then the corporation that owns the intellectual property will be considered an asset of the business and subject to liquidation. Corporations don't have the same charging order protections that LLCs have (see Chapter 11 for more on charging orders). Therefore, if the intellectual property is in a corporation and the owner (in this case, the business) gets sued, then the intellectual property is toast.

You Want to Ask Donald Trump to Invest in Your Company

LLCs are quickly becoming the entity of choice for raising capital. First of all, investors *love* the pass-through tax status. Why? If your little upstart doesn't turn a profit, they can use the losses to offset other income they may have. That is *huge* to an investor. If the business fails, they may not get their investment back, but they'll still get a nice little deduction.

Yes, S corporations offer the same type of pass-through tax status as LLCs do; however, S corporations are an inferior choice because they restrict who can and can't be an investor. Why limit yourself like that? LLCs can have as many investors as you choose — even hundreds of thousands! — and anyone can invest. One investor can be a small business in Wichita, while your other can be a newly formed hedge fund based out of London.

One of the LLC's features is that the membership shares can't be transferred freely. Your investors can't go around selling or transferring your shares to random people. If they do transfer them, the new owner has no voting rights until the rest of the members take a vote and grant them to him. Although this can work in your favor — you don't end up with some crazy, not-so-silent silent partners — it can also be a drawback for potential investors. You can handle this by clearly explaining your membership transfer policies in the marketing materials for your investment. If some people are turned off by it, so what. I guarantee you that more people will appreciate the pass-through taxation than they will dislike the restrictions on the transference of membership.

With an LLC, you can have different *classes* of membership. For instance, you can give members with Class A membership full voting rights, whereas members with Class B membership have absolutely no voting rights. Or, you can allow one class of membership shares to be transferable, whereas the other class of membership shares can't be transferred without the approval of all members.

You're Planning Your Estate

You shouldn't overlook the value of LLCs when you plan your estate. While a simple entity, in comparison with some of the uber-complex trusts that your attorney may recommend, LLCs are powerful in the way of asset protection. They not only protect you from creditors, but also from probate lawyers and court costs. LLCs allow you to avoid probate altogether, which means that your estate isn't subject to the nickel-and-diming (I wish they were just nickels and dimes!) that the probate attorneys will deduct from your estate as the courts divvy up your assets.

With LLCs, you can structure the management however you like. This is useful if you are minimizing your estate (to reduce or eliminate estate taxes) while you're alive by gifting a little bit of your assets to your heirs each year. An LLC is especially convenient for gifting property — you can just gift some membership interests. It beats having to re-title the property each year! In the meantime, you can be the LLC's sole manager as the membership interests are transferred. This way, you control the property, but the kids get to own it. Upon your death, you can assign the kids as managers, or you can name someone else a temporary manager until your children reach a certain age. (Flip to Chapter 16 for more details.)

LLCs are commonly used with different types of trusts. Don't get me wrong — trusts are great and definitely have their place in most estate plans. However, don't make the mistake of only looking at your estate from a tax-saving perspective. Trusts don't offer anything in the way of liability protection, and if you don't use an LLC to cover your assets, then you may not have anything to leave your heirs. Those assets may go to the dogs (errr . . . I mean, creditors)!

A Short-Term Project Is in the Works

LLCs were made for short-term projects. When these entities were first introduced, they were never supposed to live forever like corporations do. That's why when you create your articles of incorporation, you state a specific dissolution date or term. The *term* is the number of years that the LLC is to be in existence. Although most states allow you to extend the LLC beyond this term with a simple vote of the members, this scheduled termination of the company is convenient for short-term projects, such as real estate development and film financing.

With their pass-through taxation for investors, LLCs are especially great for those flash-in-the-pan projects that you have to raise money for. Normally how it works is the investors come together, pool their money, do the project, and make the profit; and then they dissolve the company. Upon dissolution, all assets are liquidated, the creditors are paid off, and the remaining profit gets split among the members according to their ownership percentages. All profits flow through to the investors' personal tax returns, so they don't have to worry about double taxation. (Chapter 12 covers the dissolution process in more detail.)

When you are doing a short-term project, all members must be on the same page from the get-go. When bringing on members, make sure that you give plenty of information about the project and be sure to specify that the LLC will be liquidated and dissolved, and tell them when this is expected to take place. Remember that you will need a vote of the members to dissolve on a date other than the dissolution date specified in the articles of organization. If all members aren't in agreement, you'll have trouble moving forward with your plans.

You Need to Segregate Assets

Segregating assets is vital in business because segregation puts your assets out of reach of your company's creditors or someone who wants to sue you.

A lot of people incorrectly think that if they're operating as a corporation or LLC, then their assets are safe, but that's not necessarily true. If you're like most entrepreneurs, your business is your biggest asset. If you lose the ability to operate, you're doomed. Your business may be protected from your personal creditors, and you may be protected from your business's creditors; however, what protects your business from its own creditors? If your LLC gets sued, everything inside of it can be seized and liquidated. Even worse, the courts can put a lien on your company and then do an *asset freeze*. This means that you have zero access to the cash — you can't write checks or invoice clients. Tell me — how stable will your business be after three months or more of an asset freeze?

The best way to fully protect against this is to make sure that there are no assets in the operating company. Instead, the company uses leased assets. Now, this doesn't mean that you have to start looking for furniture- and equipment-leasing companies — the assets are leased from their respective LLCs. You see, each asset is put into a different LLC. The LLC then leases these assets back to the operating company. When the operating company is sued, it has no assets with which to settle the claim. So, in the worst case, you dissolve the operating company and form a new one. You once again set up the lease agreements with the various LLCs, and you're back in business!

Entrepreneurs Can Minimize Their Tax Burden

When you first go into business, chances are your company won't be profitable right away. It takes time for businesses to build up, and in the first year or two, you probably will incur thousands of dollars in losses. A lot of entrepreneurs, eager to soften the financial blow of the startup phase, decide to form an LLC. With an LLC, the losses of the business flow through to the members so they can use them as deductions for other income.

Say, for instance, your business incurs $40,000 in losses in the first year of operation. If you and your partner each own 50 percent of the company, then you each get a $20,000 business deduction on your personal tax returns. That could save each of you as much as $6,000 in federal income taxes alone!

Don't try to implement these strategies yourself. When it comes to tax law, don't try to figure it out as you go. Speak with a qualified attorney or a corporate consultant.

Members Can Change the Profit Distributions

An LLC's profits can be paid out disproportionately to the actual ownership percentages. So you and your partners can set up the company so that you receive all of the profits and losses — even if you only own 10 percent of the company. Why would you want to do that? Well, a common reason for changing the distribution is to provide an extra incentive for investors. For instance, if an investor invests all of the capital, he will get 50 percent of the company. However, the profit distributions will be varied so that he receives 100 percent of the profits until his investment has been paid back (plus 10 percent in some cases). Then the profit distributions will return to normal, and the profit will be split equitably among members.

The only contingency that the IRS places on altering the distributions is that it delivers *substantial economic effect.* This is just a fancy way of saying that you gotta have a decent reason for changing up the distributions. For instance, in the above example, you have proven substantial economic effect; that is, you aren't just varying the distributions to avoid taxes.

If you want to vary your profit distributions, you should work with your accountant, who knows all of the IRS rules surrounding this. I don't recommend doing this on your own, because you could get yourself into some serious tax trouble if you don't do all of the due diligence that the IRS requires.

You Need to Protect Your Personal Assets

Although I don't recommend putting your home into an LLC (you'll lose all of the great tax breaks that you get as an individual), I do recommend putting all of your other personal assets into one. When you spend your entire life saving for retirement, your children's education, or even that second home you've long dreamed about, nothing can be more crippling than losing it all in a lawsuit.

Almost 50 years ago, an incredibly smart man by the name of Rockefeller gave the world a sound piece of advice: "Own nothing but control everything." You don't have to be a billionaire to walk in his footsteps. If you're like most people, you currently hold all of your personal assets in your own name. Your savings account is in your name; your cars are in your name; your mutual funds, stocks, and bonds are probably in your name. This means that the reverse of Rockefeller's advice is true — you own everything, yet control nothing. It can all be taken away from you.

If you really want to follow in the footsteps of giants, I would start with forming an LLC. Better yet, form a series LLC. Then, contribute all of your personal assets to the LLC and make sure that they are all isolated from each other. That way, if a creditor arises with one of your assets — for instance, you get a margin call that you can't quite pay for — then all of your other assets are safe. LLCs are cheap — I form them for clients every day for under $200. You don't have to be a millionaire to take advantage of strategies of the rich. After all, whatever your net worth is at the moment, you worked hard for it and deserve to keep it safe.

Chapter 18

Ten Ways to Keep Your Limited Liability Intact

*N*ow, really — what is the point of a limited liability company without the "limited liability" part? Without limited liability, it's just a company really — no special protections, no special tax treatment, no ability to issue shares of ownership. If you don't do the simple things necessary to keep your limited liability intact, you might as well not even file your LLC. Instead, you can save yourself the filing fee and kiss all your hard-earned personal assets goodbye.

Before you even think about taking extra steps to protect your limited liability, you gotta do one thing for me: Be on your best behavior. No, I don't mean keeping your elbows off of the dinner table and saying "please" and "thank you." I mean don't lie, cheat, and steal in the name of your LLC. Wrongful misconduct on the part of a member is the easiest way for your LLC's veil of limited liability to be pierced. Don't think that your company will protect you from purposeful fraud that you initiated. So, *be good!* Now, with that said, I can go on.

Filing the LLC Properly

The first step to obtaining liability protection is filing the LLC. I know this may sound sort of elementary, and trust me — I don't want to insult your intelligence. But plenty of extremely intelligent and accomplished individuals have failed at this first step and ended up being taken to the cleaners. Often, entrepreneurs get too busy and distracted — after all they're running a business! They start their LLC paperwork and then leave it to sit on their desk, collecting dust, until they find the time to get around to filing it.

If this description makes you think I've been spying on you (I haven't), you should hire an incorporating company to file the documents for you. You don't even have to sign anything (except maybe the check to pay the company!). Your incorporating company can list itself as the *organizer* — a temporary position that only lasts until the company is filed. The fee is normally small, and it can get this task off your plate.

Regardless of the situation, just file the paperwork. Use the forms I provide on the accompanying CD and the provisions I include in Chapter 6, do some research at your Secretary of State's office or Web site, fill the forms out, and then drop them in the mailbox. You'll still have to take care of other filings, but at least the company is filed — your first step to protecting your assets.

Often, situations will come up when you don't have any time for preparation and want to file quickly. Keep in mind that when you rush to file, you run the risk of getting your articles of organization rejected because you didn't do the requisite research and preparation. Also, you need to attach to your articles certain provisions, such as the limited liability provision and the charging order provision that are never included on the state's generic articles of organization.

Finding a Partner

One of the easiest ways to have your LLC disregarded and thrown out by the courts is to have a single-member LLC. LLCs were created to be *partnerships,* which means they are meant to have partners. So little separates a single-member LLC from a *sole proprietorship* (which is just one person operating a business without any liability protection) that many states don't even allow them.

If you live in a state that does allow single-member LLCs, don't blur the line between what is *allowed* and what is *advised.* You may be able to form and operate a single-member LLC without a problem; however, when a business lawsuit comes up, the courts often won't even recognize your LLC as being a real entity with real liability protections. This means that all of your personal assets are at risk of being taken away. In fact, the IRS already requires single-member LLCs to file as "disregarded entities."

If you plan to go it alone and are totally intent on having a single-member LLC, then you must follow all the tips in this section — especially the ones about having meeting minutes and a good, solid operating agreement. I also recommend that you elect corporate tax treatment. Treat your LLC as a corporation — you may have to jump through more hoops, but the peace of mind will be worth it.

Keep in mind that if you are operating as a single-member LLC, you will get no charging order protections (see Chapter 11). Charging orders protect the other partners in the business from a personal lawsuit filed against another member, and judges have decided that if there are no partners to protect, then a charging order can't be issued. Although this isn't completely set in stone, case law sets a powerful precedent, and you must know this before going in.

If you aren't dead set on having a single-member LLC and are willing to fight for your liability protection, then I recommend that you do one of two things:

- ✔ Find a friend or family member (not a spouse, for IRS purposes) whom you can trust, and issue them a small membership percentage. Make sure that you have a contract or your operating agreement states that they can't sell or transfer the shares without your approval. Because they aren't contributing anything to the business, you can also state in your operating agreement that they get a very small percentage of the distributions or none at all.

- ✔ Form a corporation that you can control — preferably in a tax-free state — and make the corporation your second partner in the business. Remember — LLCs can have anyone as a member, and they don't even need to live in the same country.

If you want to completely protect your LLC, you should have more than ten members. Historically, any organization that has more than ten members has never been pierced (or "disregarded"). If you have more than ten members, you should be in the clear, no matter what.

Creating an Operating Agreement

If you have read any part of this book, I'm sure that you have a pretty good idea of how absolutely necessary I feel an operating agreement is to have. Your operating agreement is the backbone of your company. It creates the infrastructure and acts as an operations manual that you and your partners will fall back on time and time again to sort out the gray areas and disputes that occur during the normal course of business.

The operating agreement should be tailored to your own company, but if you can't do this, keep in mind that something is better than nothing. Even just filling out the operating agreement on the accompanying CD is better than walking into court empty-handed. Just make sure that the template you use is tailored to the type of management that you have. If your LLC is member-managed, then you can't want to use the agreement on the CD because it's for manager-managed LLCs.

However, you really should take the time to create your own operating agreement. It will be a good experience for you to build your business from the ground up and decide how you want your enterprise to be structured. LLCs are very flexible entities — you can tailor your LLC to whatever your needs are. Whether you are raising capital, building a business, or flipping a real estate property, you'll want different people in your organization to have different authority, and you'll want to create a system for keeping everyone on the same page. You can create a customized agreement in less than a day — see Chapter 9 for instructions on how to put it together.

Capitalizing the Company

The term *capitalizing the company* means investing money into your business. A business without even a little bit of money is not really a business at all. Although I don't like to trot out the old adage that it takes money to make money, it's often true that you need to invest *some* capital to get your business going. I'm not the only one who thinks this — the courts agree.

The easiest way for the court to determine whether your company is a separate operating business or an *alter ego* (a company put into place to protect its owners) is to see whether you've invested in the business. After all, most small businesses aren't profitable when they're starting out, so the courts can't base their decision on profitability. They must go on capitalization.

What if you're starting small and didn't invest any money into your LLC? In this case, if you can show substantial cash flow and prove that your business is operational and deals regularly with the public, then you have a good chance of being in the clear. Make sure that you have a reason for your shares being issued to you, though — whether for services rendered, assets given, or money invested. You must put this in your meeting minutes.

Filing Your Annual Reports

You must file your annual reports on time each year. If you fail to file your reports, you will go out of good standing with the Secretary of State. If you remain out of good standing for a certain amount of time (usually a year), then your LLC will automatically be revoked, and you'll have no limited liability protections at all. Not good!

Often, the filings are one page and require minimal information such as the names and addresses of the LLC's members and/or managers, the name and address of the LLC's registered agent, and the corporate office address (Chapter 8 has more details about annual reports). You file your annual report with the same state office that you filed your articles of organization with — in most states, this is the Secretary of State. See Appendix A for the address and phone number of your state's office that handles LLC filings.

Holding Member Meetings Regularly

Although annual meetings are only required for corporations and not LLCs, you must hold them anyway. If a creditor of your LLC wants to attach your personal assets to a lawsuit, he will attempt to prove one of two things

- ✔ Your LLC is an "alter ego."
- ✔ Your LLC appears to be a sole proprietorship or general partnership and should be treated as one.

The best defense against this is to choose to go through the same formalities that corporations are required to go through. I know what you're thinking. You're a busy entrepreneur! How on earth can you find the time to draft meeting minutes and issue financial reports? Rest assured, though, that it won't take as much time as you think. Not only does all this documentation help designate the LLC as a separate entity (so as to disprove it's an "alter ego"), but it helps prevent your LLC from being classified as a sole proprietorship or general partnership, which have no meeting minutes at all.

You must have annual meetings, but you also must hold a meeting whenever a major action affecting the company is to take place. Whenever you have meetings, you must keep a record of everything that takes place in the meeting — these are called the meeting *minutes* and *resolutions*. Meeting minutes show that important business decisions were made after a successful vote of the members — these decisions are called resolutions. They prove that an action of the company wasn't done by some rogue member deciding things himself (in which case, there is a good chance he would be personally liable), but instead by the company as a whole, with all in agreement as to the course of action.

The IRS also will look to your meeting minutes to show that certain loans and financial transactions were approved. In other words, if you issue yourself a loan from the company, the IRS may not allow it if they don't see it properly documented in the company's minutes or some other form of agreement. Minutes are also good to have when requesting a ruling from the IRS, such as a 1031 exchange (for all of you real estate investors out there!), or defending a position to the IRS or Department of Revenue during an audit of the company or an LLC member. The minutes must also authorize any major salaries and pension contributions, contractual relationships, and the election of managers.

In addition to all of these things, minutes also can be used to explain any mistakes or company oversights that may have occurred. You can state what actions the company has taken to remedy the situation. Minutes are also good for justifying why the company took a certain questionable action. A good example of this is changing the income distributions to be disproportionate to the ownership percentages. (For more information about meetings, minutes, and resolutions, see Chapter 11.)

Obtaining Your Licenses and Permits

Before opening your doors and taking orders from customers, you need to make sure that you are squared away in the eyes of the law. Many state governments require businesses to have licenses and permits in an effort to control various industries and obtain tax revenue. Most companies only need to file a state and city (or county) business license. However, if you're in a heavily regulated industry, such as gambling, alcohol, or land development, you need to inquire as to which licenses and permits you must obtain. (Chapter 8 covers licenses and permits in more detail.)

When you aren't in good standing with the state and its departments, you won't be held in high favor with the judge when he is determining whether to disqualify your LLC. If you find the ordeal of determining which business licenses you must file a bit overwhelming, contact your registered agent — she can either file the business licenses for you or point you in the right direction.

While you are applying for your state licenses and permits, don't forget the ever important federal *employer identification number* (also called an EIN or a tax ID number). Think of it as a Social Security number for your LLC. Until you obtain an EIN, you can't do much business without it. It is incredibly easy to apply for a number online at the IRS's Web site (www.irs.gov). The direct link is https://sa1.www4.irs.gov/sa_vign/newFormSS4.do.

Avoiding Commingling Funds and Assets

If you're treating your company account as your personal piggy bank, stop. When you treat your business's money as your own, it's called *commingling of funds*. Not only do you run the risk of being heavily penalized by the IRS, but you also run the risk of jeopardizing your LLC's liability protections.

This goes back to that "alter ego" thing again. If the courts decide you're treating your money and the company's money as one in the same, they could easily disregard your entity as being separate from you — hence the term "alter *ego*." Freud, anyone? No? Okay, moving on . . .

Here are a few examples of commingling:

- You use the funds from your business for obvious personal expenses without documentation. For example, unless you're a model or newscaster, getting your teeth bleached is *not* a business expense. Good try though!

- Your personal bank account and your business bank account are one and the same.

- You endorse checks to yourself that are made payable to your business.

- You often move money between your business and personal accounts without keeping proper records.

The best way to stay on the safe side and avoid mixing your personal and business funds is by taking the following advice:

- Make sure your LLC has its own bank account.

- Do not use the business money to pay for personal items. (If you absolutely must, then carefully document it on the company's books.)

- Do not pay yourself indiscriminately. The money you receive from the company should be in the form of a loan, salary, or distributions.

Signing Your Documents Properly

In the course of business, you'll have to sign stuff. Lots of stuff. When you are doing business under your company name, you must sign as a representative of the company. What this means is that under your signature, you must include your title and the company name, or you must write "on behalf of" and your company name. Also, always use "LLC" or "Limited Liability Company" after your company name.

Your signature should look something like this:

By: Your signature

Name: Your name

Title: Manager (or Member)

Your LLC Name, LLC

 The *Wurzburg Bros. Inc v. James Coleman* case shows how important it is for you to sign documents correctly. In this case, James Coleman was the president of Coleman American Moving Services, Inc. When the company was behind on its payments to Wurzburg Bros. Inc., one of its vendors, Mr. Coleman decided to send over a promissory note to ease the tensions. When Mr. Coleman signed the promissory note, he failed to put his title and the company name under his signature. Wurzburg Bros. successfully sued James Coleman, the person, and succeeded in taking his personal assets to cover the judgment.

Giving Up Some Control

To avoid having the courts determine that your company is an "alter ego," you need to limit your control somewhat. If you have 100 percent control over all of the company's decisions and finances, and your company does something wrong, the courts could easily hold you personally liable. This is one of the most common ways to lose your liability. It happens most often in civil cases; however, the IRS has been known to force members to pay for their company's debts on this basis.

If you're a very small company, you often won't have too many people making decisions on a day-to-day basis. It is common that small companies are controlled by a small handful of people. In this case, just make sure that you don't have any nonfunctioning managers — that is, anyone who can be viewed as your puppet — and that you observe all formalities.

Chapter 19

Ten Things to Absolutely Avoid Doing with an LLC

In This Chapter

▶ Keeping your hands clean and steering clear of trouble

▶ Dotting your *i*'s and crossing your *t*'s

▶ Staying out of the courtroom

*L*LCs are pretty powerful entities that you can do some pretty amazing things with. But you know how the old saying goes: "With great power comes great responsibility." In other words, if you don't watch out, you can get yourself into trouble.

Business doesn't have to be time consuming or difficult to navigate. Although you may encounter pitfalls along the way, with some prudent record keeping, good intentions, and an eye for details, you'll be fine. Just make sure that, above all, you love what you do. If you don't love what you do, none of it is worth the hassle.

Fraudulent Conveyance of Assets

If you picked up this book because you just got sued and want to protect your assets, I'm sorry to say that it's too late. If you were to transfer your assets into an LLC, you would be *fraudulently conveying* them. According to the law, you are fraudulently conveying assets when you do one of two things:

✔ Sell or transfer the assets at less than fair-market value, which results in a creditor being defrauded

✔ Transfer the assets so a creditor can't seize them to recoup his claim

Fraudulent conveyance is a civil offense and can cost you a lot more money in the long run than if you were to just hand over your possessions. If you formed an LLC with the intent to defraud a creditor (as opposed to forming an LLC not knowing that your assets were immediately at risk), you're even worse off. Not only will the creditor still be able to get your assets, in some states, you may be subject to penalties and even imprisonment. Futhermore, federal laws say knowingly committing fraudulent conveyance can be a criminal offense.

You can even unknowingly fraudulently convey assets. This can happen when you're setting up your asset protection strategy and transferring your assets into an LLC or two, and little to your knowledge, a lawsuit is already pending against you. Even though you don't know about the pending lawsuit, the assets still have been fraudulently conveyed. You probably won't get criminal charges in this instance, but you still may be required to turn over the assets that you thought were protected.

Evading Taxes

Although it's prudent for you to take every action within the law to reduce your tax burden, actually *evading* taxes is a huge no-no. *Tax evasion* is when you dodge paying taxes by illegal means. *Tax avoidance,* on the other hand, is perfectly acceptable and legal. This just means that you legally reduce the amount of tax that you owe. For instance, putting your retirement savings in a Roth IRA, which allows you to defer taxes, is considered tax avoidance. It's a perfectly legal way to reduce your tax burden. All the strategies that I outline in this book legally allow you to avoid taxes.

To determine whether you are *avoiding* taxes or *evading* them, remember this: Tax avoidance occurs when you avoid the creation of tax liability in the first place. However, you're guilty of tax evasion when you have done something to owe taxes and you don't pay them. Then you'll probably end up in jail.

The scariest thing about tax evasion is that it's a criminal offense — a felony — which has no regard for how much tax you even evaded. Evading $500 in taxes is the same as evading $5 million in taxes in the eyes of the law (although, I hope the judge will be more lenient in the former case).

Choosing a Bad Partner

Partnerships are like marriages — you should jump into them with your eyes open. Fifty percent of marriages end in divorce, and the numbers are much worse for business partnerships. This shouldn't be a deterrent — after all, when you have a partner whom you work well with, your efforts are compounded tenfold. You just need to make sure that

- ✔ You know the person whom you're going into business with.
- ✔ You have policies and procedures to go by when disagreements come up — and they *will* come up, I promise you.

When you're first getting into business, you'll sit down with your partner and agree on where you both want the company to go and what you want your ownership percentage and different roles to be in the company. The problems usually occur many years after inception, when your or your partner's life goes in different directions. For instance, you may want to expand into a new market, but your partner is happy with the income he has and just wants to let the business coast along. Or your partner needs cash and wants to sell out, but you don't have the money to buy out his share at the moment. In these moments, you need to have a plan to follow.

You need to have a partnership agreement, which can be a part of your operating agreement. You must take the time to sit down with your partner and plan your partnership all the way to the end. In Chapter 4, I offer tips on selecting your members.

Ignoring the Bureaucratic Paperwork

I know, I know. State filings, tax returns, permits, and so on — they're all time consuming, bureaucratic, and you hate doing them. Trust me, you're not alone. But unfortunately, it's imperative that you don't drop the ball and that you stay on top of these things.

This especially goes for state filings. Here's the thing: Your LLC is registered under the laws of the state, and that which giveth can taketh away. Yep, that's right. If you don't keep up with your filings, the state will revoke your LLC, and you'll (often unknowingly) be operating as if you were a sole proprietorship. You'll have zero liability protections if you get taken to court.

Trademark Infringement

Infringing on another company's trademark is one of the easiest pitfalls in business and can end up costing you a fortune. I urge you to be cautious about trademark infringement because not only can you fall into this trap without any knowledge of it, but a lot of Fortune 500 companies hold hundreds of trademarks each. They have attorneys and paralegals who spend their days scouring the Internet and local communities for small businesses that may be infringing on a trademark they own. The company is then nice enough to send a cease-and-desist letter.

When you receive one of these letters, you have two options.

- If you're an upstart and don't have a lot of money wrapped up in the name that the company is disputing, stop using the name and choose another one.

- If you have spent a lot of time and money marketing the name and feel as though you have the right to use it and that it doesn't confuse consumers in any way, then I would spring for a good trademark attorney. Your trademark attorney can point you in the right direction. Just keep in mind that if you end up going to court, you'll be shelling out lots of dough, especially if your opponent has much deeper pockets.

  If you don't have a trademark attorney, you can find one at www. lawyerdex.com. (Also, see Chapter 3 for information on how to find a great attorney).

Not Creating an Operating Agreement

Even though operating agreements aren't legally required, you'd be absolutely crazy not to have one! LLCs can make up a lot of their own rules — you just have to put them in the operating agreement. If no operating agreement exists, then the state laws automatically apply by default. Letting your state government tell you how to run and structure your business isn't a smart practice. You not only miss out on one of the LLC's most major benefits — flexibility — but you also aren't in control of your business.

Now, please take my advice and create a real operating agreement that is unique to your company. I go into very specific details on how to do this in Chapter 9. All you have to do is copy the provisions that you want into your own document, and voilà! You have a customized, detailed operating agreement that will serve your business for years to come.

After you have your operating agreement, use it! You should read it over on occasion so you know your company's policies when it comes to certain issues. If you decide to change your policies, that's fine. Just make sure that you have a meeting with the other members and vote in the changes. Meeting procedures can be found in none other than your LLC's operating agreement.

Not Documenting Company Activities

LLC law is pretty lenient when it comes to keeping records, but don't let it fool you. Documenting your company activities is still incredibly important. At some point in time, your business decisions will be questioned, and you'll be relieved when you have your company minutes there to defend your reasoning. Not only this, but your company records prove that you do things by the book. So, if an angry member sues because he didn't get his way at the last meeting of members, you can show that the proper vote was taken and that correct formalities were practiced.

Here are a few good reasons to keep your company records in order:

- ✔ When applying for loans or creating other banking relationships, your record-keeping practices allude to your reliability as a business owner.

- ✔ The most common lawsuits among partners in an LLC happen when one or more members disagrees with a course of action that another member has taken. By properly documenting your actions, you can prove that you went through the proper channels and made and acted upon decisions according to your powers as described in the operating agreement.

- ✔ Should you ever wish to sell your company, take it public, or enter into a joint venture, you need to have all of your previous company actions properly recorded.

- ✔ If you're ever audited, the IRS will look at your corporate records to see your intentions behind various transactions.

Treating Your LLC like a Personal Piggy-Bank

This is really simple and really important: Only use your company's money for company-related expenses. I know this sounds elementary, but it's a common mistake and can cost you a lot in the long run — not only in penalties to the

IRS, but it could also cost you your liability protection. I know that it's often tempting to write checks or use a debit card from whichever account has the most money in it — but don't do it. Personal expenses that you'll especially want to avoid are things such as your mortgage or groceries. Restaurant bills are okay, as long as the dining experience was business-related.

If you really need to pay for a personal item out of your company bank account, then do it. Just make sure that this doesn't occur very often and that you properly document the transaction and classify it as a loan or officer income. If the transaction was a large one, then you'll also want to document it in the company minutes.

Neglecting to Foreign File

Transacting interstate business has gotten easier as the world has gotten smaller. To make matters worse, each state has a different idea of what "transacting business" actually means. Regardless, you're still required to register to transact business (*foreign file*) in every state that you operate in. In Chapter 5, I show you how to go through the foreign-filing process in detail.

Here are some questions to ask yourself to help you determine whether you're transacting business in a certain state:

- Does your LLC have a physical location in the state, such as a corporate office or manufacturing facilities?
- Do you accept orders in, or originating from, the state?
- Do you have employees (not independent contractors) in the state?
- Do you have a bank account in the state?

Refusing to Delegate

Some people trust no one to help them and do everything themselves. This is because, in their mind, no one can handle the job as well as they can. I call this the disease of the self-employed, and it can weaken you substantially. Why? Because you can only do so much, and until you start to delegate, your organization will never grow — not to mention that you'll most likely get burned out before you know it.

You have to delegate some things in business, or else you can get into some pretty big trouble. For instance, tax laws are incredibly complex, and unless you studied to be an accountant, there's a good chance that if you handle your own taxes, what you don't know will destroy you, especially if your business is on the larger side, has employees, and is somewhat complex.

The same goes for attorneys. Don't try to represent yourself in court. I haven't heard of one self-represented case that actually won. Lawyers, although they can be expensive, are incredibly necessary to a small business. Don't operate on assumptions — seek the knowledge of a competent lawyer when legal matters come up.

When handling your corporate filings, especially if you are registered in multiple states, have your registered agent assist you. Not only is a registered agent required by law, but he also has more knowledge and resources in corporate matters than you do. Use a registered agent who is part of a competent incorporating company. That way, you can save legal fees when seeking information about simple, non-complex corporate matters or getting answers about your filings.

Don't be a jack of all trades. Master one thing, and then delegate the rest. For instance, if you aren't so hot at sales, don't worry! Hire a great sales manager and empower her to take the reins and build a phenomenal sales floor. Even if you are decent at something, find someone who is better than you and recruit him. When you find these people, take a leap of faith and don't undermine them. After all, your business is only as good as the people in it.

Appendix A

LLC Formation Information by State

• •

*H*ere, I provide you with the contact information for the secretary of state's office (or equivalent), LLC statutes, and filing information for all 50 states (plus the District of Columbia). Use this information as a starting point for organizing your LLC. Then you should seek competent advice from a corporate consultant or an attorney. I also suggest that do your own research so you're aware of any changes that your state has made after this book was published. You may also go to www.myllc.com/dummies for an updated and current listing.

Alabama

Business formation department:
Alabama Secretary of State
Corporations Division
Physical location:
11 S. Union St., Suite 207
Montgomery, AL 36104
Mailing address:
P.O. Box 5616
Montgomery, AL 36103-5616

Phone: 334-242-5324   **Fax:** 334-240-3138
Web site: www.sos.state.al.us

State statute: The Alabama LLC Act, Ala. Code §§ 10-12-1 through 10-12-61

Filing your articles: Articles must be filed with the probate judge in the county where the LLC's registered office is located. The filing fee is $40 (made payable to the Secretary of State) plus any additional local fees that the county or probate judge may impose (normally $35 and up). Single-member LLCs are allowed.

State business/franchise tax: LLCs operating in Alabama are subject to a privilege tax, which ranges from 0.25% to 1.75%, with a maximum of $15,000.

Alaska

Business formation department:
Alaska Department of Community and Economic Development
Corporations Section
Physical location:
333 W. Willoughby Ave., ninth floor
Juneau, AK
Mailing address:
P.O. Box 110808
Juneau, AK 99811-0808

Phone: 907-465-2530   **Fax:** 907-465-3257

Web site: www.commerce.state.ak.us/occ/home.htm
E-mail: corporations@commerce.state.ak.us

State statute: Alaska Code §§ 10.50.010 through 10.50.995

Filing your articles: Articles must contain a statement that says the LLC is being filed under the provisions of the Alaska Limited Liability Company Act. The filing fee is $250 — a $150 filing fee plus the $100 biennial license fee. Single-member LLCs are allowed.

State business/franchise tax: The only tax imposed is the biennial fee of $100.

Arizona

Business formation department:
Arizona Corporation Commission
Corporations Division
Phoenix office:
1300 W. Washington, first floor
Phoenix, AZ 85007-2929
Tucson office:
400 W. Congress, Suite 221
Tucson, AZ 85701-1347

Phone: Phoenix: 602-542-3026 or 800-345-5819;
Tucson: 520-628-6560   **Fax:** Phoenix: 602-542-4100;
Tucson: 520-628-6614

Web site: www.cc.state.az.us
E-mail: filings.corp@azcc.gov

State statute: Arizona Code §§ 29-601 through 29-857

Filing your articles: Articles must be filed with the Arizona Corporation Commission with a filing fee of $50. Within 60 days after the filing date, the LLC must publish a public notice with the company's address and resident agent information in a publication of general circulation in the county that the LLC is headquartered. After the publication, the LLC must file an Affidavit of Publication with the Arizona Corporation Commission. Single-member LLCs are allowed.

State business/franchise tax: LLCs are not required to file periodic reports. LLCs with pass-through taxation are not taxed.

Arkansas

Business formation department:
Corporations Division
Arkansas Secretary of State
Address:
State Capitol, Room 256
Little Rock, AR 72201

Phone: 888-233-0325 or 501-682-1010

Web site: www.sos.arkansas.gov/corp_ucc_business.html
E-mail: corporations@sos.arkansas.gov

State statute: Arkansas code §§ 4-32-101 through 4-32-1401

Filing your articles: The filing fee is $50, and you can file online. When filing your articles, you must also file a Franchise Tax Registration Form. Single-member LLCs are allowed.

State business/franchise tax: You must file an LLC Franchise Tax Report with the Secretary of State by June 1 of each year.

California

Business formation department:
LLC Unit
California Secretary of State
Physical location:
1500 11th St., third floor
Sacramento, CA 95814
Mailing address:
P.O. Box 944228
Sacramento, CA 94244-2280

Phone: 916-657-5448   **Web site:** www.ss.ca.gov

State statute: California Corporations Code §§ 17000 through 17655

(continued)

California (continued)

Filing your articles: File an original plus two copies of the articles with a $100 filing fee. Single-member LLCs are *not* allowed.

State business/franchise tax: LLCs registered in California must pay an $800 annual franchise fee, which is due within three months of the close of the LLC's accounting year.

Colorado

Business formation department:
Business Division
Colorado Secretary of State
Address:
1700 Broadway, Suite 200
Denver, CO 80290

Phone: 303-894-2200, press 2   **Fax:** 303-869-4864

Web site: www.sos.state.co.us/pubs/business
E-mail: sos.business@sos.state.co.us

State statute: CRS §§ 7-80-101 through 7-80-1101

Filing your articles: The filing fee for the articles of organization is $50. The statutory life span of an LLC is 30 years, unless specified otherwise. Single-member LLCs are allowed.

State business/franchise tax: You must file a report every other year. The biennial fee is $25, unless you file online, in which case the fee is $10.

Connecticut

Business formation department:
Commercial Recording Division
Secretary of State
Physical location:
30 Trinity St.
Hartford, CT 06106
Mailing address:
P.O. Box 150470
Hartford, CT 06115-0470

Phone: 860-509-6002   **Fax:** 860-509-6068

Web site: www.sots.ct.gov/CommercialRecording/Crdindex.html
E-mail: crd@po.state.ct.us

State statute: Connecticut General Statutes §§ 34-101 through 34-242

Filing your articles: The filing fee is $60. Single-member LLCs are allowed.

State business/franchise tax: Annual reports are due by the end of the anniversary month of the LLC's organization. The fee for the annual report is $10.

Delaware

Business formation department:
Division of Corporations
Delaware Secretary of State
Physical location:
John G. Townsend Building
401 Federal St., Suite 4
Dover, DE 19901
Mailing address:
PO Box 898
Dover, DE 19903

Phone: 302-739-3073, press 2
Fax: 302-739-3812 or 302-739-3813

Web site: www.corp.delaware.gov
E-mail: DOSDOC_WEB@state.de.us

State statute: The Delaware Limited Liability Company Act; Delaware General Code §§ 6-18-101 through 6-18-1109

Filing your articles: The filing fee is $50, with a $20 additional fee for each certified copy of the certificate of formation. Single-member LLCs are allowed.

State business/franchise tax: The annual report is due every March. The current filing fee is $25. All Delaware LLCs are required to pay a minimum franchise tax of $200, which is due June 1 of each year.

District of Columbia

Business formation department:
Corporations Division
Department of Consumer and Regulatory Affairs
Physical location:
John A. Wilson Building
1350 Pennsylvania Ave., NW
Washington, DC 20004
Mailing address:
P.O. Box 92300
Washington, D.C. 20090

Phone: 202-442-4432
Web site: http://mblr.dc.gov/corp/index.shtm

(continued)

District of Columbia *(continued)*

State statute: The District of Columbia Limited Liability Company Act; D.C. Code §§ 29-1001 through 29-1075

Filing your articles: The filing fee is $100. You must submit a Written Consent to Act as Registered Agent Form that is signed by your registered agent with your articles. You must also file a Form F500, a Combined Business Tax Registration Application, along with the articles.

State business/franchise tax: Every two years, you must file a Two-Year Report for Foreign and Domestic Limited Liability Companies. Your first report is due on the first June 16 after your formation and every second June 16 after that. If your franchise tax liability potentially exceeds $1,000, then you must file a Declaration of Estimated Franchise Tax Voucher. If your company's gross receipts exceed $12,000 for the year, then you must file an Unincorporated Business Franchise Tax Return.

Florida

Business formation department:
Division of Corporations
Florida Department of State
Physical location:
Clifton Building
2661 Executive Center Circle
Tallahassee, FL 32301
Mailing address:
Corporate Filings
P.O. Box 6327
Tallahassee, FL 32314

Phone: 850-245-6051
Web site: www.sunbiz.org/corp_dir.html
E-mail: corphelp@dos.state.fl.us

State statute: The Florida Limited Liability Company Act, Florida Code §§ 608.401 through 608.703

Filing your articles: The filing fee is $100. A Designation of Resident Agent Form must accompany the articles of organization with an additional fee of $25. Single-member LLCs are allowed.

State business/franchise tax: A Uniform Business Report (UBR) must be filed before May 1 of each year. The fee for this filing is $50. If your LLC is classified as a partnership for tax purposes, then it must file Form F-1065, an information statement, with the Florida tax board.

Georgia

Business formation department:
Corporations Division
Secretary of State
Address:
315 West Tower
2 Martin Luther King Jr. Dr.
Atlanta, GA 30334-1530

Phone: 404-656-2817   **Fax:** 404-657-2248
Web site: http://sos.georgia.gov/corporations

State statute: Georgia Code §§ 14-11-100 through 14-11-1109

Filing your articles: The filing fee is $75. Single-member LLCs are allowed.

State business/franchise tax: Each LLC must file an annual report before April 1 of each year. You can file your annual reports online at the Web site listed above. All LLCs that are taxed as partnerships and are operating in Georgia must file Form 700, a Georgia Partnership Income Tax Return.

Hawaii

Business formation department:
Business Registration Division
Department of Commerce and Consumer Affairs
Physical location:
King Kalakaua Building
335 Merchant St., Room 201
Honolulu, HI 96813
Mailing address:
P.O. Box 40
Honolulu, HI 96810

Phone: 808-586-2744   **Fax:** 808-586-2733

Web site: www.hawaii.gov/dcca/areas/breg
E-mail: breg@dcca.hawaii.gov

State statute: Hawaii Code §§ 428-101 through 428-1302

Filing your articles: The filing fee is $100. Single-member LLCs are allowed.

State business/franchise tax: Annual reports are due each year. LLCs must pay Hawaii's general excise tax at a 0.4% to 0.5% tax rate.

Idaho

Business formation department:
Business Entities
Idaho Secretary of State
Physical location:
700 E. Jefferson, Room 203
Boise, ID 83720-0080
Mailing address:
P.O. Box 83720
Boise, ID 83720-0080

Phone: 208-334-2301   **Fax:** 208-334-2080

Web site: www.idsos.state.id.us/corp/corindex.htm
E-mail: sosinfo@sos.idaho.gov

State statute: Idaho Code §§ 53-601 through 53-672

Filing your articles: The filing fee is $100. Single-member LLCs are allowed.

State business/franchise tax: An annual report is due on the anniversary month of your LLC's formation date. The fee for the annual report is $30. The state tax rate on LLCs is 7.6% (the minimum payment is $20). If you have elected partnership taxation, you must also file Form 65, an Idaho Partnership Return of Income.

Illinois

Business formation department:
Business Services
Secretary of State
Springfield office:
Michael J. Howlett Building
501 S. Second St., Room 328
Springfield, IL 62756
Chicago office:
69 W. Washington, Suite 1240
Chicago, IL 60602

Phone: Springfield: 217-782-6961; Chicago 312-793-3380

Web site: www.cyberdriveillinois.com/departments/
business_services/home.html

State statute: ILCS §§ 805.180/1-1 through 805.180/60-1

Filing your articles: The filing fee is $400. Single-member LLCs are allowed.

State business/franchise tax: An annual report is due each year on the anniversary month of your LLC's formation along with the filing fee of $200. LLCs are imposed a replacement tax of 1.5% of your company's net income. You must file a Form IL-1065, an Illinois Partnership Replacement Return.

Indiana

Business formation department:
Business Services Division
Indiana Secretary of State
Address:
302 W. Washington St., Room E018
Indianapolis, IN 46204

Phone: 317-232-6581   **Web site:** www.in.gov/sos/business
E-mail: Liz Keele: lkeele@sos.IN.gov

State statute: The Indiana Business Flexibility Act; Indiana Code §§ 23-18-1-1
through 23-18-13-1

Filing your articles: The filing fee is $90. Single-member LLCs are allowed.

State business/franchise tax: On the anniversary month of the LLC's formation
each year, the LLC must file an Indiana Business Entity Report along with a filing
fee of $30. You must also file Form IT-65 if you have elected partnership taxation.
This is an information return, and no fee is due.

Iowa

Business formation department:
Business Services Division
Iowa Secretary of State
Address:
First Floor, Lucas Building
321 E. 12th St.
Des Moines, IA 50319

Phone: 515-281-5204   **Fax:** 515-242-5953

Web site: www.sos.state.ia.us/business/index.html
E-mail: sos@sos.state.ia.us

State statute: Iowa Code §§ 490A.100 through 490A.1601

Filing your articles: The filing fee is $50. Single-member LLCs are allowed.

State business/franchise tax: No periodic reports are required. LLCs that have
elected partnership taxation must file Form IA-1065, an Iowa Partnership Return.
This is a purely informational return, and no tax is due.

Kansas

Business formation department:
Business Services Department
Secretary of State
Address:
Memorial Hall, first floor
120 SW 10th Ave.
Topeka, KS 66612-1594

Phone: 785-296-4564
Web site: www.kssos.org/business/business.html
E-mail: corp@kssos.org

State statute: Kansas Statutes §§ 17-7601 through 17-7709

Filing your articles: The filing fee is $150. Single-member LLCs are allowed.

State business/franchise tax: Annual reports are due by the 15th day of the fourth month after the close of your tax year. If you have elected to be taxed on a calendar year, this means that your annual report is due every April 15. You must also submit, along with your report, your franchise taxes, which is $1 for every $1,000 of net capital accounts that are located in Kansas (with the minimum being $20).

Kentucky

Business formation department:
Business Services
Kentucky Secretary of State
Address:
700 Capital Ave., Suite 154
Frankfort, KY 40601

Phone: 502-564-2848   **Web site:** www.sos.ky.gov/business

State statute: KRS §§ 275.001 through 275.455

Filing your articles: The filing fee is $40. Single-member LLCs are allowed.

State business/franchise tax: You must file an annual report by June 30 of each year, along with a $15 filing fee.

Louisiana

Business formation department:
Corporations Section
Secretary of State
Mailing address:
P.O. Box 94125
Baton Rouge, LA 70804-9125

Phone: 225-925-4704   **Fax:** 225-925-4726

Web site: www.sos.louisiana.gov/comm/corp/corp-index.htm
E-mail: commercial@sos.louisiana.gov

State statute: Louisiana Revised Statutes §§ 12.1301 through 12.1369

Filing your articles: The filing fee is $60. Single-member LLCs are allowed.

State business/franchise tax: Annual reports are due on or before the anniversary date of your LLC's formation, along with the $10 filing fee. If your LLC has elected partnership taxation, then you must file Form IT-565, a Partnership Return of Income. No tax will be assessed; this is for informational purposes only.

Maine

Business formation department:
Bureau of Corporations, Elections & Commissions
Maine State Department
Address:
101 State House Station
Augusta, ME 04333

Phone: 207-624-7736   **Fax:** 207-287-5874

Web site: www.maine.gov/sos/cec/corp/index.html
E-mail: cec.corporations@maine.gov

State statute: Maine Code 31 § 601 through 31 § 762

Filing your articles: The filing fee is $125. Single-member LLCs are allowed.

State business/franchise tax: An annual report is due by June 1 of each year. along with the $60 filing fee. You can obtain an annual report form by calling 207-624-7752. If you have elected partnership taxation, you must file Form 1065ME. No tax will be assessed; this is for informational purposes only.

Maryland

Business formation department:
Corporate Charter Division
Department of Assessments and Taxation
Address:
301 W. Preston St., eighth floor
Baltimore, MD 21201-2395

Phone: 888-246-5941   **Fax:** 410-333-7097

Web site: www.dat.state.md.us/sdatweb/charter.html
E-mail: charterhelp@dat.state.md.us

(continued)

Maryland (continued)

State statute: Maryland Code §§ 4A-101 through 4A-1103

Filing your articles: The filing fee is $50. Single-member LLCs are allowed.

State business/franchise tax: You must file an annual Form 1, Personal Property Report, by April 15 of each year, along with the filing fee of $300. If you have elected partnership taxation, you must file Form 510, Pass-Through Entity Income Tax Return. This is an informational return, and no tax is due, unless you have members who don't live in Maryland. In this case, the LLC must pay a 4.8% personal income tax.

Massachusetts

Business formation department:
Corporations Division
Secretary of the Commonwealth
Address:
One Ashburton Place, 17th floor
Boston, MA 02108

Phone: 617-727-9640   **Fax:** 617-742-4538

Web site: www.sec.state.ma.us/cor/coridx.htm
E-mail: corpinfo@sec.state.ma.us

State statute: MGL 156C § 1 through 156C § 68

Filing your articles: The filing fee is $500. Single-member LLCs are *not* allowed.

State business/franchise tax: An annual report is due on or before your LLC's anniversary date each year, along with the filing fee of $500. If you have elected partnership taxation, you are required to file Form 3, a partnership return, each year. This form is for informational purposes only; no tax is required.

Michigan

Business formation department:
Corporation Division
Department of Labor and Economic Growth
Physical location:
2501 Woodlake Circle, first floor
Okemos, MI 48864
Mailing address:
P.O. Box 30054
Lansing, MI 48909-7554

Phone: 517-373-1820   **Fax:** 517-373-2129

Web site: www.michigan.gov/cis
E-mail: corpsmail@michigan.gov

State statute: MCL § 21,187(4101) through § 21.958(5200)

Filing your articles: The filing fee is $50. Single-member LLCs are allowed.

State business/franchise tax: You must file an annual statement by February 15 each year. If you were formed after September 30, then you can skip a year. Unless you have elected corporate taxation and your gross receipts are more than $250,000 each year, then you are not required to pay business tax.

Minnesota

Business formation department:
Business Services
Secretary of State
Address:
Retirement Systems of Minnesota Building
60 Empire Dr., Suite 100
Saint Paul, MN 55103

Phone: 877-551-6767 or 651-296-2803
Web site: www.sos.state.mn.us
E-mail: business.services@state.mn.us

State statute: Minnesota Statutes §§ 322B.01 through 322B.960

Filing your articles: The filing fee is $135. Single-member LLCs are allowed.

State business/franchise tax: You must file an annual report by the end of each year. You can file online using the link above. If you have elected partnership taxation, then you must file Form M3, a partnership return. You may be imposed franchise fees up to $5,000.

Mississippi

Business formation department:
Business Services
Secretary of State
Physical location:
700 North St.
Jackson, MS 39202
Mailing address:
P.O. Box 136
Jackson, MS 39205-0136

Phone: 601-359-1350   **Fax:** 601-359-1499
Web site: www.sos.state.ms.us/busserv/index.asp

(continued)

Mississippi (*continued*)

State statute: Mississippi Code §§ 79.29.101 through 79.29.1204

Filing your articles: The filing fee is $50. Single-member LLCs are allowed.

State business/franchise tax: Each year by April 15, you must file Form 86-105, a partnership tax return. This is purely an information statement; no tax is actually imposed.

Missouri

Business formation department:
Business Services
Secretary of State
Physical location:
600 W Main St.
Missouri State Information Center, Room 322
Jefferson City, MO 65101-0778
Mailing address:
James C. Kirkpatrick State Information Center
P.O. Box 778
Jefferson City, MO 65102

Phone: 866-223-6535 **Web site:** www.sos.mo.gov/business
E-mail: SOSmain@sos.mo.gov

State statute: RSMo §§ 347.010 through 347.740

Filing your articles: The filing fee is $105. Single-member LLCs are allowed.

State business/franchise tax: No periodic reports are required; however, you must file Form MO-1065, Partnership Return of Income, each year. This is for informational purposes only; no tax is imposed.

Montana

Business formation department:
Business Services Division
Secretary of State
Mailing address:
P.O. Box 202801
Helena, MT 59620-2801

Phone: 406-444-3665 **Fax:** 406-444-3976

Web site: http://sos.mt.gov/BSB/index.asp
E-mail: sosbusiness@mt.gov

State statute: MCA §§ 35-8-101 through 35-8-1307

Filing your articles: The filing fee is $70. Single-member LLCs are allowed.

State business/franchise tax: You must file an annual report before April 15 of each year. The fee for this report is $10. You must also file Form PR-1, a Partnership Return of Income, for each year. There are no taxes due, and this is an informational return only.

Nebraska

Business formation department:
Business and Licensing Division
Secretary of State
Address:
Room 1301
State Capitol
P.O. Box 94608
Lincoln, NE 68509-4608

Phone: 402-471-4079   **Fax:** 402-471-3666

Web site: www.sos.state.ne.us/business/corp_serv
E-mail: Corporate_Inquiries@sos.ne.gov

State statute: Nebraska Code §§ 21-2601 through 21.2653

Filing your articles: The filing fee is $100, plus an additional $10 fee for the certificate of organization that you receive from the state after your articles have been filed. Single-member LLCs are allowed.

State business/franchise tax: There are no annual reports due in Nebraska. Unless you have only Nebraska residents as members and your income is only derived from Nebraska, then you must file a Partnership Return of Income with the tax board by the 15th day of the fourth month of your company's fiscal year. If your company operates on a calendar year, this means that the return is due by April 15.

Nevada

Business formation department:
Commercial Recordings Division
Secretary of State   **Address:**
202 N. Carson St.
Carson City, NV 89701-4201

Phone: 775-684-5708   **Fax:** 775-684-5725

Web site: http://sos.state.nv.us/business
E-mail: sosmail@sos.nv.gov

State statute: Nevada Revised Statutes §§ 86.011 through 86.590

(continued)

Nevada (continued)

Filing your articles: The filing fee is $75. Also, before the second month of your formation date, you must file an Initial List of Managers or Members and Resident Agent Form with a fee of $165. Single-member LLCs are allowed.

State business/franchise tax: An annual report is due each year with a filing fee of $125. There are no business or franchise taxes in Nevada, and no tax returns need to be filed.

New Hampshire

Business formation department:
Corporation Division
Department of State
Physical location:
State House Annex, Room 341
25 Capitol St., third floor
Concord, NH 03301
Mailing address:
107 N. Main St.
Concord, NH 03301-4989

Phone: 603-271-3246
Web site: www.sos.nh.gov/corporate/index.html
E-mail: corporate@sos.state.nh.us

State statute: The New Hampshire Business Flexibility Act, New Hampshire Revised Statutes §§ 304-C:1 through 304-C:85

Filing your articles: The filing fee is $35. Single-member LLCs are allowed.

State business/franchise tax: All New Hampshire LLCs must file an annual report every year by April 1, along with the filing fee of $100. If you gross more than $50,000 in one year, then you must file a Business Profits Tax Return and pay an 8.5% tax. If you gross more than $150,000 in one year, then you must file a Business Enterprise Tax Return and pay the tax rate of 0.75% of the total value of your company. All gross amounts only count income that is derived within the state of New Hampshire.

New Jersey

Business formation department:
Business Services
Division of Revenue
Mailing address:
P.O. Box 308
Trenton, NJ 08625

Phone: 866-534-7789   **Fax:** 609-984-6851
Web site: www.nj.gov/njbusiness

State statute: New Jersey Code §§ 42:2B-1 through 42:2B-70

Filing your articles: The filing fee is $125. Single-member LLCs are allowed.

State business/franchise tax: You must file an annual report each year, along with a filing fee of $50. If you have elected partnership taxation, you must also file Form NJ-1065, which is an information return only and requires no accompanying tax payment.

New Mexico

Business formation department:
Public Regulation Commission
Corporations Bureau
Physical location:
1120 Paseo de Peralta
PERA Building, Room 413
Santa Fe, NM 87501
Mailing address:
P.O. Box 1269
Santa Fe, NM 87504-1269

Phone: 505-827-4508   **Fax:** 505-827-4387
Web site: www.nmprc.state.nm.us/cb.htm

State statute: NMSA §§ 53-19-1 through 53-19-67

Filing your articles: The filing fee is $50. Single-member LLCs are allowed.

State business/franchise tax: LLCs are not required to file periodic reports; however, if your LLC has elected partnership taxation, it must file Form PTE, a New Mexico Income and Information Return for Pass-Through Entities. As long as you have pass-through taxation, no tax is due. If you have elected corporate taxation, then you are required to pay a $50 annual franchise tax.

New York

Business formation department:
Division of Corporations
New York Department of State
Address:
41 State St.
Albany, NY 12231-0001

Phone: 518-474-4752   **Fax:** 518-474-4597

(continued)

New York *(continued)*

Web site: www.dos.state.ny.us
E-mail: corporations@dos.state.ny.us

State statute: The New York Limited Liability Company Law § 101 through 1403

Filing your articles: The filing fee is $200. Single-member LLCs are allowed.

State business/franchise tax: You must file a biennial statement every two years with a filing fee of $9. You must also pay an annual filing fee to the Department of Revenue. This fee ranges from $325 to $10,000, depending on the number of members your LLC has.

North Carolina

Business formation department:
Department of the Secretary of State
Physical location:
2 S. Salisbury St.
Raleigh, NC 27601-2903
Mailing address:
P.O. Box 29622
Raleigh, NC 27626-0622

Phone: 919-807-2225   **Fax:** 919-807-2039
Web site: www.secretary.state.nc.us/corporations

State statute: North Carolina Code § 57C-10-01 through 57C-10-07

Filing your articles: The filing fee is $125. Single-member LLCs are allowed.

State business/franchise tax: All LLCs are required to file an annual report by the 15th day of the fourth month of the close of the fiscal year (April 15 for all LLCs operating on a calendar year). The filing fee for this is $200. There are no other franchise fees or taxes that are imposed on North Carolina LLCs.

North Dakota

Business formation department:
Business Services
Secretary of State   **Address:**
600 E Boulevard Ave., Dept 108, first floor
Bismarck, ND 58505-0500

Phone: 800-352-0867, ext. 8-4284, or 701-328-4284   **Fax:** 701-328-2992

Web site: www.nd.gov/sos/businessserv
E-mail: sosbir@nd.gov

State statute: North Dakota Cent. Code §§ 10-32-01 through 10-32-156

Filing your articles: The filing fee is $135. Single-member LLCs are *not* allowed.

State business/franchise tax: Annual reports are due each year on November 15, unless your business engages in farming or ranching, in which case they are due on April 15. The fee for the annual report is $50. You must also file Form 1065, North Dakota Return of Income, which, like the IRS version, is an informational return only.

Ohio

Business formation department:
Office of Business Services
Ohio Secretary of State
Mailing address:
P.O. Box 670
Columbus, OH 43216

Phone: 877-767-3453 or 614-466-3910   **Fax:** 614-466-3899
Web site: www.state.oh.us/sos

State statute: Ohio Revised Code § 1705.01 through 1705.58

Filing your articles: The filing fee is $125. Single-member LLCs are allowed.

State business/franchise tax: Ohio doesn't subject LLCs to any periodic reports or franchise tax reports. Pretty cool!

Oklahoma

Business formation department:
Business Filing Department
Secretary of State
Address:
2300 N. Lincoln Blvd., Room 101
Oklahoma City, OK 73105-4897

Phone: 405-521-3912   **Fax:** 405-521-3771
Web site: www.sos.state.ok.us/business/business_filing.htm

State statute: Oklahoma Statutes § 18.2000 through 18.2060

Filing your articles: The filing fee is $100. Single-member LLCs are allowed.

State business/franchise tax: An annual report is due by July 1 of every year along with a filing fee of $25. Oklahoma doesn't impose any tax or franchise fees on LLCs, and you don't need to file any returns.

Oregon

Business formation department:
Corporation Division
Secretary of State
Address:
255 Capitol St., NE, Suite 151
Salem, OR 97310-1327

Phone: 503-986-2200   **Fax:** 503-378-4381

Web site: www.filinginoregon.com
E-mail: BusinessRegistry.sos@state.or.us

State statute: Oregon Revised Statutes § 63.001 through 63.990

Filing your articles: The filing fee is $20. Single-member LLCs are allowed.

State business/franchise tax: You must file an annual report by the anniversary of your formation date each year. The report must be accompanied by a $20 fee. The filing for the subsequent years after the first is called a *renewal coupon* — not an annual report. If you have elected partnership taxation, you are required to file Form 65, Partnership Return, each year. This form is for informational purposes only, and no tax is imposed.

Pennsylvania

Business formation department:
Corporations Bureau
Department of State
Address:
206 North Office Building
Harrisburg, PA 17120

Phone: 888-659-9962 or 717-787-1057

Web site: www.dos.state.pa.us/corps/site/default.asp
E-mail: RA-CORPS@state.pa.us

State statute: Pennsylvania Consolidated Statutes § 15.8901 through 15.8998

Filing your articles: The filing fee is $100. You must also file a docketing statement along with the articles, which you can obtain from the Department of State's Web site. Single-member LLCs are allowed.

State business/franchise tax: You are not required to file any annual reports, however if you change your resident agent, you must submit a Statement of Change of Registered Agent to the Department of State. If you have elected pass-through taxation, you must file Form PA-20s/PA-65, PA S Corporation/Partnership Information Return, each year. This is an informational return only, and no tax is imposed.

Rhode Island

Business formation department:
Corporations Division
Secretary of State
Address:
148 W. River St.
Providence, RI 02904-2615

Phone: 401-222-3040

Web site: www.sec.state.ri.us/corps
E-mail: corporations@sec.state.ri.us

State statute: Rhode Island Code § 7-16-1 through 7-16-75

Filing your articles: The filing fee is $150. Single-member LLCs are allowed.

State business/franchise tax: You must file your annual report by November 1 of each year, along with a $50 filing fee. You must also pay a franchise tax of $250 each year.

South Carolina

Business formation department:
Secretary of State
Physical location:
Edgar Brown Building
1205 Pendleton St., Suite 525
Columbia, SC 29201
Mailing address:
P.O. Box 11350
Columbia, SC 29211

Phone: 803-734-2158   **Web site:** www.scsos.com

State statute: South Carolina Code § 33-44-101 through 33-44-1207

Filing your articles: The filing fee is $110. Single-member LLCs are allowed.

State business/franchise tax: You have approximately one month after the anniversary date of your LLC's formation to file your annual report. For instance, if your LLC's anniversary is July 10, you must file your annual report by the end of August. You must also file Form SC-1065, which is an informational return only and doesn't require any accompanying tax payment.

South Dakota

Business formation department:
Secretary of State
Address:
Capitol Building
500 E. Capitol Ave., Suite 204
Pierre, SD 57501-5070

Phone: 605-773-4845   **Fax:** 605-773-4550

Web site: www.sdsos.gov/busineservices/corporations.shtm
E-mail: corporations@state.sd.us

State statute: South Dakota Code §§ 47-34-1 through 47-34-59

Filing your articles: The fee for organizing a South Dakota LLC is based on the amount of member contributions the LLC receives. LLCs with contributions of $50,000 or less must pay $90. LLCs with contributions of $50,001 to $100,000 must pay $150, and LLCs with contributions over $100,000 must bay $150 for the first $100,000 and $0.50 for every $10,000 in contributions over that. With your articles, you must file your first annual report. Single-member LLCs are *not* allowed.

State business/franchise tax: You have approximately one month after the anniversary date of your LLC's formation to file your annual report. For instance, if your LLC's anniversary is July 10, you must file your annual report by the end of August. No franchise or business taxes are imposed on South Dakota LLCs.

Tennessee

Business formation department:
Business Services
Department of State
Address:
312 Eighth Ave. North
Sixth floor, Snodgrass Tower
Nashville, TN 37243

Phone: 615-741-2286

Web site: http://state.tn.us/sos/bus_svc/index.htm
E-mail: business.services@state.tn.us

State statute: Tennessee Statutes § 48-201-101 through 48-248-606

Filing your articles: The filing fee depends on the number of members your LLC has upon formation. The filing fee is $50 per member with a minimum fee of $300 and a maximum of $3,000. There is also a $20 fee for the certificate of formation, which is issued by the Department of State. Single-member LLCs are allowed.

State business/franchise tax: You must file an annual report by the end of the third month after the close of the accounting year. If you operate on a calendar year, then your annual report is due by April 1. The filing fees will be $50 per active member, with the minimum fee being $300 and the maximum being $3,000. You must also file Form FAE 170, Franchise and Excise Tax Return, along with a tax payment of 0.25% of the LLC's entire value, with a minimum payment of $100. Additionally, LLCs must pay an excise tax of 6% on all income derived from business transactions in Tennessee.

Texas

Business formation department: Corporations Section
Secretary of State
Mailing address:
P.O. Box 13697
Austin, TX 78711-3697

Phone: 512-463-5555   **Fax:** 562-463-5709
Web site: www.sos.state.tx.us

State statute: Texas Civil Statutes § 32.1528n.1.01 through 32.1528n.11.07

Filing your articles: The filing fee is $200. Single-member LLCs are allowed.

State business/franchise tax: You aren't required to file any annual reports with the Secretary of State; however you must still file Form 05-143 and pay a franchise tax of 0.25% of the LLC's net taxable capital.

Utah

Business formation department: Division of Corporations and Commercial Code
Utah Department of Commerce
Physical location:
160 E. 300 South
Salt Lake City, UT 84114
Mailing address:
P.O. Box 146705
Salt Lake City, UT 84114-6705

Phone: 801-530-4849   **Fax:** 801-530-6438
Web site: http://business.utah.gov/business/#

State statute: Utah Code § 48-2b-101 through 48-2b-158

Filing your articles: The filing fee is $52. Single-member LLCs are allowed.

State business/franchise tax: Annual reports are due each year on the anniversary date of your LLC's formation. If you have elected partnership taxation, you must also file Form TC-65, Partnership Limited Liability Company Return of Income. This is an informational return only, and you won't be subject to taxation.

Vermont

Business formation department:
Secretary of State
Address:
81 River St.
Montpelier, VT 05609-1104

Phone: 802-828-2386   **Fax:** 802-828-2853
Web site: www.sec.state.vt.us/corps/corpindex.htm

State statute: Vermont Statutes § 11-3001 through 11-3162

Filing your articles: The filing fee is $75. Single-member LLCs are allowed.

State business/franchise tax: You must file an annual report within 75 days of the end of your fiscal year. If you are operating on a calendar year, then your annual report is due March 15. The filing fee for the annual report is $20. You must also file a Business Income Tax Return, even if you are a pass-through entity. LLCs with pass-through taxation must pay only the minimum tax of $250.

Virginia

Business formation department:
Department of Business Assistance
Physical location:
707 E. Main St., Suite 300
Richmond, VA 23219
Mailing address:
P.O. Box 446
Richmond, VA 23218

Phone: 804-371-9733   **Web site:** www.dba.virginia.gov

State statute: Virginia Code § 13.1-1000 through 13.1-1073

Filing your articles: The filing fee is $100. Single-member LLCs are allowed.

State business/franchise tax: You must pay a $50 annual registration fee by September 1 of each year to the State Corporation Commission. You aren't required to file any tax returns with the Department of Taxation, however.

Washington

Business formation department:
Secretary of State
Physical location:
Dolliver Building
801 Capitol Way South
Olympia, WA
Mailing address:
P.O. Box 40234
Olympia, WA 98504-0234

Phone: 360-753-7115
Web site: http://www.secstate.wa.gov/corps/
E-mail: corps@secstate.wa.gov

State statute: RCW § 25.15.005 through 25.15.902

Filing your articles: The filing fee is $175. You must also file your first annual report within 120 days of your formation date. Single-member LLCs are allowed.

State business/franchise tax: You must file an annual report, which can be done online, with the Secretary of State's Office. You must also pay the business and occupation tax each year. The amount of this tax depends on a variety of things, such as your gross income or the total value of your products.

West Virginia

Business formation department:
Secretary of State
Address:
Building 1, Suite 157-K
1900 Kanawha Blvd., E.
Charleston, WV 25305-0770

Phone: 304-558-8000   **Fax:** 304-558-8381

Web site: http://www.wvsos.com/business/main.htm
E-mail: business@wvsos.com

State statute: West Virginia Code § 31B-1-101 through 31B-13-1306

Filing your articles: The filing fee is $100. Single-member LLCs are allowed.

State business/franchise tax: You must file an annual report by April 1 of every year, along with a fee of $10. You must also file a Business Franchise Tax Return each year at a tax rate of 0.75% of your LLC's taxable income, with the minimum tax payment being $50.

Wisconsin

Business formation department:
Department of Financial Institutions
Physical location:
345 W. Washington Ave.
Madison, WI 53703
Mailing address:
P.O. Box 7846
Madison, WI 53707-7846

Phone: 608-261-7577   **Fax:** 608-267-6813   **Web site:** www.wdfi.org

State statute: Wisconsin Statutes § 183.0102 through 183.1305

Filing your articles: The fee for filing your articles is $170; however, you can reduce that fee to $130 by filing online using the Department's QuickStart program. Single-member LLCs are allowed.

State business/franchise tax: Each LLC must file an annual report along with a fee of $25. The filing date of the report varies upon which quarter of the year your formation date falls in. If you have elected pass-through taxation, you must also file Form 3, Partnership Return of Income. This is an informational return only, and no tax will be due.

Wyoming

Business formation department:
Secretary of State
Address:
The Capitol Building, Room 110
200 W. 24th St.
Cheyenne, WY 82002-0020

Phone: 307-777-7311   **Fax:** 307-777-5339

Web site: http://soswy.state.wy.us/corporat/corporat.htm
E-mail: corporations@state.wy.us

State statute: Wyoming Statutes § 17-15-101 through 17-15-144

Filing your articles: The filing fee is $100. Single-member LLCs are *not* allowed.

State business/franchise tax: Annual reports are due each year and can be filed online. If you are transacting business in Wyoming, you must pay an Annual Report License Tax, which is 0.02% of all assets located and employed in Wyoming, with the minimum fee being $50.

Appendix B

On the CD-ROM

● ●

*T*he CD-ROM accompanying this book contains a sample Operating Agreement document, in Microsoft Word form, that you can fill in and print out for your own use (see Chapter 9). It also contains current applicable IRS forms, and also state documents, on a state-specific basis, to help you with your LLC.

All state-specific documents are in Adobe Acrobat PDF (Portable Document Format) form, so you need to install Adobe Acrobat Reader on your computer to use them. A copy of Adobe Acrobat Reader is included on the CD-ROM. You can also download the most recent version of Adobe Reader from the following Web site, free of charge: www.adobe.com/products/acrobat/readstep2.html

Because the documents are in PDF format, you can't change them, but you can print them when you're ready to fill out the forms you need. Included are the articles, amendments, dissolutions, Change of Agent forms, and Name Reservation documents for each state in the USA.

On the CD-ROM, the state documents are arranged in file folders named for each state. The table in this appendix summarizes all the documents included on the CD. The X's indicate documents required for that state; N/A indicates where a particular document isn't necessary. Some states now have online systems and resources in place of printable documents, so in those cases I've supplied you with a Web address where you can find more information. If you have further questions about a specific state's processes or requirements, please refer to Appendix A.

State	Articles	Amendment	Dissolution	Change of Agent	Name Reservation
Alabama	X	X	X	X	X
Alaska	X	X	X	X	X
Arizona	X	X	X	X	X
Arkansas	X	X	X	X	X
California	X	X	X	X	X
Colorado	*Everything is now done online, via their automated system:* www.sos.state.co.us/pubs/business				
Connecticut	X	X	X	X	X
District of Columbia	X	X	X	X	X
Delaware	X	X	X	X	X
Florida	X	X	X	X	*N/A*
Georgia	*Visit online for more information:* http://sos.georgia.gov/corporations. *No forms are available; you have to create your own*				
Hawaii	*Everything is now done online, via their automated system:* www.hawaii.gov/dcca/areas/breg				
Iowa	*N/A*	*N/A*	*N/A*	X	X
Idaho	X	X	X	X	X
Illinois	X	X	X	X	X
Indiana	X	X	X	X	X
Kansas	*Everything is now done online, via their automated system:* www.kssos.org/business/business.html				
Kentucky	X	*N/A*	*N/A*	X	X

State	Articles	Amendment	Dissolution	Change of Agent	Name Reservation
Louisiana	X	X	X	X	X
Massachusetts	*Visit online for more information:* www.sec.state.ma.us/cor/coridx.htm. *No forms are available; you have to create your own.*				
Maryland	X	X	X	X	N/A
Maine	X	X	X	X	X
Michigan	X	N/A	N/A	X	X
Minnesota	X	X	X	X	X
Missouri	X	X	X	X	X
Mississippi	X	X	X	X	X
Montana	X	X	X	X	X
North Carolina	X	X	X	X	X
North Dakota	X	N/A	N/A	X	X
Nebraska	X	X	X	X	X
New Hampshire	X	X	X	X	X
New Jersey	*Visit online for more information:* www.nj.gov/njbusiness				
New Mexico	X	X	X	X	X
Nevada	X	X	X	X	X
New York	X	X	X	X	X
Ohio	X	X	X	X	X
Oklahoma	X	X	X	X	X

(continued)

State	Articles	Amendment	Dissolution	Change of Agent	Name Reservation
Oregon	X	X	X	X	X
Pennsylvania	X	X	X	X	N/A
Rhode Island	X	X	X	X	X
South Carolina	X	X	X	X	X
South Dakota	X	X	X	X	X
Tennessee	X	X	X	X	X
Texas	X	X	X	X	X
Utah	X	X	X	X	X
Virginia	X	X	X	X	X
Vermont	*Visit online for more information:* www.sec.state.vt.us/corps/corpindex.htm				
Washington	X	X	X	X	X
Wisconsin	X	X	X	X	N/A
West Virginia	X	X	X	X	X
Wyoming	X	X	X	X	X

If you have trouble with the CD-ROM, please call the Wiley Product Technical Support phone number at 800-762-2974. Outside the United States, call 317-572-3994. You can also contact Wiley Product Technical Support at http://www.wiley.com/techsupport. John Wiley & Sons will provide technical support only for installation and other general quality-control items. For technical support on the applications themselves, consult the program's vendor or author.

To place additional orders or to request information about other Wiley products, please call 877-762-2974.

Glossary

allocation (noun): The amount of company income and deductible expenses that are assigned to each member and reported to them on their Schedule K-1.

alter ego (noun): When the courts determine that an entity is fully controlled by an individual and its only function is to provide a legal shield for a person. Although it's hard to prove an entity is an alter ego, the liability protection that the entity provides could be disregarded.

amendment (noun): An approved and ratified change to the articles of organization or the operating agreement.

articles of organization (noun): The document that is created and ratified by the LLC's organizers. The articles define the name of the LLC, the initial managers and/or members, the organizers, the state of formation, the LLC's purpose, the duration of the company, and other important information.

beneficiary (noun): The future recipient of all or part of an estate, trust, or insurance policy.

blue sky laws (noun): Securities laws that protect the public from fraudulent companies that don't offer investments of substance.

board of directors (noun): Elected by the entity's shareholders or members, the directors set company policy and choose the corporation's officers.

buy-sell agreement (noun): An agreement that outlines the terms of the purchase of a shareholder's interest in an entity.

bylaws (noun): The document created and ratified by the shareholders and/or board of directors of a corporation that outlines basic corporate policy.

C corporation (noun): An entity, unlike a partnership, which is completely separate from its owners. Corporations have their own level of taxation, which varies greatly from personal income tax.

capital (noun): The total amount of assets that an individual or entity owns, which includes liquid cash, real estate, equipment, stocks and bonds, and so on.

capital assets (noun): All assets, including real estate, equipment, and cash, that are owned by an entity.

capital gains (noun): In real property, the sale price minus the purchase price, plus improvements.

case law (noun): Interpretations of the law by the courts that can be used as precedents in future cases.

cell (noun): A unit in a series LLC that acts like a separate LLC but is still under the same common umbrella.

charging order (noun): A type of court order that restricts the claim of certain assets, such as property or securities, to their fiscal income only. Under charging order protections, assets can't be liquidated or sold.

common law (noun): The laws brought over from England that are still generally accepted.

company kit (noun): A binder that contains the items essential for the running and maintaining of a limited liability company. Items can include sample minutes and operating agreement, membership certificates, a company seal, and membership transfer ledger.

consolidation (noun): The act of two companies coming together to form a new entity that they both operate under.

corporation (noun): A separate entity that has been accepted by the government and does business or other activities, can offer ownership shares to raise capital (except in the case of a nonprofit), and can sue and be sued in a court of law.

deed: 1. (noun) In the case of real property, the document that transfers the ownership from one party to another. 2. (verb) The act of transferring ownership of real property by use of a deed.

dissolution (noun): The winding up of affairs and termination of an entity either voluntarily by the entity's owners or by a government action.

distribution (noun): An actual distribution of the profit in the form of cash, usually proportionate to the number of shares in the corporation.

doing business (verb): Normally a term that connotes whether an entity is carrying out normal and regular business activities within a jurisdiction. If an entity is "doing business" in a foreign state, it may be subject to state taxes and required to register with the Secretary of State in that jurisdiction.

domicile (noun): The state in which an entity is registered and headquartered — its home state.

double taxation (noun): When a corporation pays taxes on the profits, then distributes those profits to shareholders in the form of dividends, which are taxed again on a personal level.

Employer identification number (EIN) (noun): Used to differentiate entities, such as corporations or LLCs, from others; the company equivalent of a Social Security number.

entity (noun): A general legal term for any company, corporation, LLC, partnership, institution, government agency, educational body, or any other form of organization that has a completely separate identity from that of the individuals behind it.

face value (noun): The number of shares of stock, as shown on the certificate, multiplied by the stock's par value, also shown on the certificate.

foreign corporation or LLC (noun): An entity that is formed in a different state or nation than the one it is doing business in. Foreign entities must register with all states that they are conducting regular business in.

franchise tax (noun): A common state-level tax that is imposed on businesses.

fraudulent conveyance (noun): The act of transferring assets to another party for the sole purpose of making them inaccessible to a creditor or the party of a lawsuit or divorce. If the assets are transferred before the knowledge of any such lawsuit exists, then the assets are not being fraudulently conveyed.

general partner (noun): One of the managers of a limited partnership. The business's liability is shared by all general partners in a limited partnership.

general partnership (noun): A business partnership that has two or more partners wherein each partner is equally liable for any of the business's debts.

gross estate (noun): The total value of an individual's estate before taxes, attorney's fees, administration fees, and even funeral expenses are deducted.

heir (noun): One who has acquired the assets of a deceased person, normally by familial lineage — normally a child or close relative of the deceased.

holding company (noun): A company whose sole purpose is to own the stock or membership shares of other entities to simultaneously oversee the management and policies of all entities.

impute (verb): The act of holding one person responsible for the acts of another. If someone in business has knowledge of another's actions, such as an employee, then they are imputed to that person and held responsible for their acts.

incorporate (verb): To obtain the Secretary of State's approval of the articles of incorporation. When you incorporate, your company is now officially a corporation. When forming an LLC, this act is loosely termed *organizing*.

joint liability (noun): When two or more parties (or entities) are held equally responsible for a debt or judgment.

joint venture (noun): When two or more people (or entities) create an entity for a limited time and for a specific project, such as raising funds or a shorter-term real estate transaction. After the business has been completed and the affairs have been wound up, the joint venture is terminated, and the entity is dissolved.

judgment creditor (noun): When a person or organization sues you and wins (the court decides that you owe that party money), that party becomes a "judgment creditor" until you pay them what you owe.

judgment debt (noun): When a lawsuit is lost, the "judgment debt" is the money owed to the winning party by the losing party.

liability (noun): A legal term for responsibility and one of the most common words used in corporate and partnership law. When you have liability for yourself, your business, or even your partners, you are held personally responsible for the acts of those parties, meaning you can be subject to a lawsuit or criminal charges.

lien (noun): A legal claim against an asset that is used to secure a loan or debt.

limited liability protection (noun): The protection of an owner, manager, or employee of a business against being responsible for the debts and/or obligations of the business.

limited partner (noun): One of the two kinds of partners in a limited partnership; a limited partner has no say in the day-to-day management of the company and isn't personally responsible for the liabilities and debts of the company.

limited partnership (noun): A type of partnership that consists of one or more limited partners, who are silent in the day-to-day management and aren't personally liable for the LLC's debts, and one or more general partners, who manage the business but *are* personally responsible for the company's debts.

living trust (noun): A trust that is created by the trustor during that person's lifetime, where the trustor is distributed profits from his assets in the trust until his death, when the trust continues on and instead gives those distributions to the new beneficiaries — normally the trustor's children. (*Note:* This is not to be confused with a *living will,* which comes into effect only during a person's lifetime if he becomes incapacitated in any way.)

member (noun): An individual or entity that has an ownership interest in the LLC with or without voting rights.

membership certificate (noun): An official document, issued by the LLC to a member that states the LLC's name and state of formation. When issued, it is signed by the managers and/or members and lists the number of shares and the member's name.

membership interest (noun): A member's percentage of ownership in the company.

membership or shareholder register (noun): The record of members (in an LLC) or shareholders (in a corporation) that lists current and past issuances and transfers.

merger (noun): The instance in which two businesses decide to become one and transfer all assets into one of the entities (the surviving entity) and then dissolve the other.

minutes (noun): The official record of the events that took place at a company meeting.

nominee (noun): 1. The successor to one person's rights and obligations on a contract; 2. The person or entity that acts on another's behalf, either to protect the privacy of that individual or entity or to handle the affairs during an absence.

nonprofit corporation (noun): Also called a *not-for-profit corporation,* an organization incorporated and ratified by the state that operates for purposes of charity or public benefit. A nonprofit corporation has no shareholders and can apply for federal and state tax-exempt status.

off-shore corporation or LLC (noun): Any corporation or LLC that is created and domiciled in any country other than the United States.

operating agreement (noun): A contract among the members of the LLC that governs the operation, management, membership, and distribution of the company's profits.

organize (verb): See *incorporate.*

pass-through tax status (noun): A type of taxation, inherent in LLCs, that passes the income or loss generated by the business to the partners to be reflected on their personal income tax returns.

phantom income (noun): Income that is allocated to a partner that he must pay tax on but doesn't actually receive in the form of cash.

piercing the veil (noun): When a judge allows the plaintiff to hold the members of the LLC, otherwise immune, personally responsible for the damages caused by the LLC under their control.

provision (noun): A clause or stipulation in a document or agreement.

quorum (noun): During a corporation or LLC's annual or special meetings, the number of people required to be present so voting can take place. Unless otherwise stated in the bylaws or operating agreement, a quorum is usually just a majority.

registered agent (noun): A person or company that is designated in the articles of organization as authorized to receive service of process and other important documents from the state on behalf of the company. In most states, an LLC is required to have a registered agent.

regulatory law (noun): Rules and regulations created by government agencies that are based on statutes.

resolution (noun): An agreement of policy, rules, and guidelines that have been voted on by the corporation's board of directors or the LLC's managers and/or members.

S corporation (noun): A designation made by a corporation that elects a pass-through tax status, thereby eliminating the double taxation that corporations are normally subject to.

series LLC (noun): A unique type of LLC, only available in certain states, under which you can create numerous cells that act as separate entities and can own separate assets.

service of process (noun): When sued, the initial delivery of a legal summons, or the delivery of other legal documents such as a subpoena, complaint, and so on.

several liability (noun): When multiple people are responsible for a debt, however, they fail to pay and the burden falls on only one person, that person is severally liable (as in "joint and several").

silent partner (noun): An investor who puts in money but doesn't deal with the business's day-to-day operations nor makes any operational decisions. In a limited partnership, this person is called a *limited partner.*

single-member LLC (noun): An LLC that is wholly owned by one person or institution — typically also the manager. Not all states allow single-member LLCs.

sole proprietorship (noun): An unincorporated business that is owned and managed by a single person (or husband and wife).

statutory law (noun): Laws and statutes that have been enacted by the legislative branches of state or federal governments.

stock certificate (noun): An official document, issued by the corporation, that states the name of the corporation, the state of incorporation, the type of stock the certificate represents, as well as the number of shares of stock in the corporation and the par value of that stock. When issued, it's normally signed by the president and secretary and lists the number of shares and the shareholder's name.

taxable estate (noun): The total value of a deceased person's assets that are taxable, deducted by their debts and liabilities and any allowable tax deductions.

trademark: 1. (noun) A name, tag line, slogan, or symbol that identifies a product that is officially registered and legally restricted by use of the registrant only. 2. (verb) To register a name, tag line, slogan, or symbol as a trademark.

trust (noun): A legal arrangement where an individual or enterprise, the trustor, gives economic control of assets to an individual or institution, the trustee, for the benefit of the beneficiaries.

trustor (noun): An individual who creates a trust; also called a grantor.

unlimited marital deduction (noun): A provision in the tax code that allows one spouse, upon his or her death, to transfer — tax-free — an unlimited amount of property to his or her surviving spouse.

winding up the affairs (verb): Prior to dissolving, liquidating the entity's assets, paying the final bills, distributing remaining assets to the members/shareholders, and then filing a formal dissolution with the Secretary of State.

Index

• E •

Wiley Publishing, Inc.
End-User License Agreement

READ THIS. You should carefully read these terms and conditions before opening the software packet(s) included with this book "Book". This is a license agreement "Agreement" between you and Wiley Publishing, Inc. "WPI". By opening the accompanying software packet(s), you acknowledge that you have read and accept the following terms and conditions. If you do not agree and do not want to be bound by such terms and conditions, promptly return the Book and the unopened software packet(s) to the place you obtained them for a full refund.

1. **License Grant.** WPI grants to you (either an individual or entity) a nonexclusive license to use one copy of the enclosed software program(s) (collectively, the "Software") solely for your own personal or business purposes on a single computer (whether a standard computer or a workstation component of a multi-user network). The Software is in use on a computer when it is loaded into temporary memory (RAM) or installed into permanent memory (hard disk, CD-ROM, or other storage device). WPI reserves all rights not expressly granted herein.

2. **Ownership.** WPI is the owner of all right, title, and interest, including copyright, in and to the compilation of the Software recorded on the physical packet included with this Book "Software Media". Copyright to the individual programs recorded on the Software Media is owned by the author or other authorized copyright owner of each program. Ownership of the Software and all proprietary rights relating thereto remain with WPI and its licensers.

3. **Restrictions on Use and Transfer.**

    (a) You may only (i) make one copy of the Software for backup or archival purposes, or (ii) transfer the Software to a single hard disk, provided that you keep the original for backup or archival purposes. You may not (i) rent or lease the Software, (ii) copy or reproduce the Software through a LAN or other network system or through any computer subscriber system or bulletin-board system, or (iii) modify, adapt, or create derivative works based on the Software.

    (b) You may not reverse engineer, decompile, or disassemble the Software. You may transfer the Software and user documentation on a permanent basis, provided that the transferee agrees to accept the terms and conditions of this Agreement and you retain no copies. If the Software is an update or has been updated, any transfer must include the most recent update and all prior versions.

4. **Restrictions on Use of Individual Programs.** You must follow the individual requirements and restrictions detailed for each individual program in the "About the CD" appendix of this Book or on the Software Media. These limitations are also contained in the individual license agreements recorded on the Software Media. These limitations may include a requirement that after using the program for a specified period of time, the user must pay a registration fee or discontinue use. By opening the Software packet(s), you agree to abide by the licenses and restrictions for these individual programs that are detailed in the "About the CD" appendix and/or on the Software Media. None of the material on this Software Media or listed in this Book may ever be redistributed, in original or modified form, for commercial purposes.

5. **Limited Warranty.**

   (a) WPI warrants that the Software and Software Media are free from defects in materials and workmanship under normal use for a period of sixty (60) days from the date of purchase of this Book. If WPI receives notification within the warranty period of defects in materials or workmanship, WPI will replace the defective Software Media.

   (b) WPI AND THE AUTHOR(S) OF THE BOOK DISCLAIM ALL OTHER WARRANTIES, EXPRESS OR IMPLIED, INCLUDING WITHOUT LIMITATION IMPLIED WARRANTIES OF MER-CHANTABILITY AND FITNESS FOR A PARTICULAR PURPOSE, WITH RESPECT TO THE SOFTWARE, THE PROGRAMS, THE SOURCE CODE CONTAINED THEREIN, AND/OR THE TECHNIQUES DESCRIBED IN THIS BOOK. WPI DOES NOT WARRANT THAT THE FUNC-TIONS CONTAINED IN THE SOFTWARE WILL MEET YOUR REQUIREMENTS OR THAT THE OPERATION OF THE SOFTWARE WILL BE ERROR FREE.

   (c) This limited warranty gives you specific legal rights, and you may have other rights that vary from jurisdiction to jurisdiction.

6. **Remedies.**

   (a) WPI's entire liability and your exclusive remedy for defects in materials and workman-ship shall be limited to replacement of the Software Media, which may be returned to WPI with a copy of your receipt at the following address: Software Media Fulfillment Department, Attn.: *Limited Liability Companies For Dummies*, Wiley Publishing, Inc., 10475 Crosspoint Blvd., Indianapolis, IN 46256, or call 1-800-762-2974. Please allow four to six weeks for delivery. This Limited Warranty is void if failure of the Software Media has resulted from accident, abuse, or misapplication. Any replacement Software Media will be warranted for the remainder of the original warranty period or thirty (30) days, whichever is longer.

   (b) In no event shall WPI or the author be liable for any damages whatsoever (including without limitation damages for loss of business profits, business interruption, loss of business information, or any other pecuniary loss) arising from the use of or inability to use the Book or the Software, even if WPI has been advised of the possibility of such damages.

   (c) Because some jurisdictions do not allow the exclusion or limitation of liability for conse-quential or incidental damages, the above limitation or exclusion may not apply to you.

7. **U.S. Government Restricted Rights.** Use, duplication, or disclosure of the Software for or on behalf of the United States of America, its agencies and/or instrumentalities "U.S. Government" is subject to restrictions as stated in paragraph (c)(1)(ii) of the Rights in Technical Data and Computer Software clause of DFARS 252.227-7013, or subparagraphs (c) (1) and (2) of the Commercial Computer Software - Restricted Rights clause at FAR 52.227-19, and in similar clauses in the NASA FAR supplement, as applicable.

8. **General.** This Agreement constitutes the entire understanding of the parties and revokes and supersedes all prior agreements, oral or written, between them and may not be modified or amended except in a writing signed by both parties hereto that specifically refers to this Agreement. This Agreement shall take precedence over any other documents that may be in conflict herewith. If any one or more provisions contained in this Agreement are held by any court or tribunal to be invalid, illegal, or otherwise unenforceable, each and every other pro-vision shall remain in full force and effect.

BUSINESS, CAREERS & PERSONAL FINANCE

0-7645-9847-3   0-7645-2431-3

Also available:
- Business Plans Kit For Dummies
  0-7645-9794-9
- Economics For Dummies
  0-7645-5726-2
- Grant Writing For Dummies
  0-7645-8416-2
- Home Buying For Dummies
  0-7645-5331-3
- Managing For Dummies
  0-7645-1771-6
- Marketing For Dummies
  0-7645-5600-2

- Personal Finance For Dummies
  0-7645-2590-5*
- Resumes For Dummies
  0-7645-5471-9
- Selling For Dummies
  0-7645-5363-1
- Six Sigma For Dummies
  0-7645-6798-5
- Small Business Kit For Dummies
  0-7645-5984-2
- Starting an eBay Business For Dummies
  0-7645-6924-4
- Your Dream Career For Dummies
  0-7645-9795-7

HOME & BUSINESS COMPUTER BASICS

0-470-05432-8   0-471-75421-8

Also available:
- Cleaning Windows Vista For Dummies
  0-471-78293-9
- Excel 2007 For Dummies
  0-470-03737-7
- Mac OS X Tiger For Dummies
  0-7645-7675-5
- MacBook For Dummies
  0-470-04859-X
- Macs For Dummies
  0-470-04849-2
- Office 2007 For Dummies
  0-470-00923-3

- Outlook 2007 For Dummies
  0-470-03830-6
- PCs For Dummies
  0-7645-8958-X
- Salesforce.com For Dummies
  0-470-04893-X
- Upgrading & Fixing Laptops For Dummies
  0-7645-8959-8
- Word 2007 For Dummies
  0-470-03658-3
- Quicken 2007 For Dummies
  0-470-04600-7

FOOD, HOME, GARDEN, HOBBIES, MUSIC & PETS

0-7645-8404-9   0-7645-9904-6

Also available:
- Candy Making For Dummies
  0-7645-9734-5
- Card Games For Dummies
  0-7645-9910-0
- Crocheting For Dummies
  0-7645-4151-X
- Dog Training For Dummies
  0-7645-8418-9
- Healthy Carb Cookbook For Dummies
  0-7645-8476-6
- Home Maintenance For Dummies
  0-7645-5215-5

- Horses For Dummies
  0-7645-9797-3
- Jewelry Making & Beading For Dummies
  0-7645-2571-9
- Orchids For Dummies
  0-7645-6759-4
- Puppies For Dummies
  0-7645-5255-4
- Rock Guitar For Dummies
  0-7645-5356-9
- Sewing For Dummies
  0-7645-6847-7
- Singing For Dummies
  0-7645-2475-5

INTERNET & DIGITAL MEDIA

0-470-04529-9   0-470-04894-8

Also available:
- Blogging For Dummies
  0-471-77084-1
- Digital Photography For Dummies
  0-7645-9802-3
- Digital Photography All-in-One Desk Reference For Dummies
  0-470-03743-1
- Digital SLR Cameras and Photography For Dummies
  0-7645-9803-1
- eBay Business All-in-One Desk Reference For Dummies
  0-7645-8438-3
- HDTV For Dummies
  0-470-09673-X

- Home Entertainment PCs For Dummies
  0-470-05523-5
- MySpace For Dummies
  0-470-09529-6
- Search Engine Optimization For Dummies
  0-471-97998-8
- Skype For Dummies
  0-470-04891-3
- The Internet For Dummies
  0-7645-8996-2
- Wiring Your Digital Home For Dummies
  0-471-91830-X

* Separate Canadian edition also available
† Separate U.K. edition also available

Available wherever books are sold. For more information or to order direct: U.S. customers visit www.dummies.com or call 1-877-762-2974.
U.K. customers visit www.wileyeurope.com or call 0800 243407. Canadian customers visit www.wiley.ca or call 1-800-567-4797.

SPORTS, FITNESS, PARENTING, RELIGION & SPIRITUALITY

0-471-76871-5

0-7645-7841-3

Also available:
- Catholicism For Dummies
  0-7645-5391-7
- Exercise Balls For Dummies
  0-7645-5623-1
- Fitness For Dummies
  0-7645-7851-0
- Football For Dummies
  0-7645-3936-1
- Judaism For Dummies
  0-7645-5299-6
- Potty Training For Dummies
  0-7645-5417-4
- Buddhism For Dummies
  0-7645-5359-3

- Pregnancy For Dummies
  0-7645-4483-7 †
- Ten Minute Tone-Ups For Dummies
  0-7645-7207-5
- NASCAR For Dummies
  0-7645-7681-X
- Religion For Dummies
  0-7645-5264-3
- Soccer For Dummies
  0-7645-5229-5
- Women in the Bible For Dummies
  0-7645-8475-8

TRAVEL

0-7645-7749-2

0-7645-6945-7

Also available:
- Alaska For Dummies
  0-7645-7746-8
- Cruise Vacations For Dummies
  0-7645-6941-4
- England For Dummies
  0-7645-4276-1
- Europe For Dummies
  0-7645-7529-5
- Germany For Dummies
  0-7645-7823-5
- Hawaii For Dummies
  0-7645-7402-7

- Italy For Dummies
  0-7645-7386-1
- Las Vegas For Dummies
  0-7645-7382-9
- London For Dummies
  0-7645-4277-X
- Paris For Dummies
  0-7645-7630-5
- RV Vacations For Dummies
  0-7645-4442-X
- Walt Disney World & Orlando
  For Dummies
  0-7645-9660-8

GRAPHICS, DESIGN & WEB DEVELOPMENT

0-7645-8815-X

0-7645-9571-7

Also available:
- 3D Game Animation For Dummies
  0-7645-8789-7
- AutoCAD 2006 For Dummies
  0-7645-8925-3
- Building a Web Site For Dummies
  0-7645-7144-3
- Creating Web Pages For Dummies
  0-470-08030-2
- Creating Web Pages All-in-One Desk
  Reference For Dummies
  0-7645-4345-8
- Dreamweaver 8 For Dummies
  0-7645-9649-7

- InDesign CS2 For Dummies
  0-7645-9572-5
- Macromedia Flash 8 For Dummies
  0-7645-9691-8
- Photoshop CS2 and Digital
  Photography For Dummies
  0-7645-9580-6
- Photoshop Elements 4 For Dummies
  0-471-77483-9
- Syndicating Web Sites with RSS Feeds
  For Dummies
  0-7645-8848-6
- Yahoo! SiteBuilder For Dummies
  0-7645-9800-7

NETWORKING, SECURITY, PROGRAMMING & DATABASES

0-7645-7728-X

0-471-74940-0

Also available:
- Access 2007 For Dummies
  0-470-04612-0
- ASP.NET 2 For Dummies
  0-7645-7907-X
- C# 2005 For Dummies
  0-7645-9704-3
- Hacking For Dummies
  0-470-05235-X
- Hacking Wireless Networks
  For Dummies
  0-7645-9730-2
- Java For Dummies
  0-470-08716-1

- Microsoft SQL Server 2005 For Dummies
  0-7645-7755-7
- Networking All-in-One Desk Reference
  For Dummies
  0-7645-9939-9
- Preventing Identity Theft For Dummies
  0-7645-7336-5
- Telecom For Dummies
  0-471-77085-X
- Visual Studio 2005 All-in-One Desk
  Reference For Dummies
  0-7645-9775-2
- XML For Dummies
  0-7645-8845-1

HEALTH & SELF-HELP

0-7645-8450-2

0-7645-4149-8

Also available:

Bipolar Disorder For Dummies
0-7645-8451-0

Chemotherapy and Radiation
For Dummies
0-7645-7832-4

Controlling Cholesterol For Dummies
0-7645-5440-9

Diabetes For Dummies
0-7645-6820-5* †

Divorce For Dummies
0-7645-8417-0 †

Fibromyalgia For Dummies
0-7645-5441-7

Low-Calorie Dieting For Dummies
0-7645-9905-4

Meditation For Dummies
0-471-77774-9

Osteoporosis For Dummies
0-7645-7621-6

Overcoming Anxiety For Dummies
0-7645-5447-6

Reiki For Dummies
0-7645-9907-0

Stress Management For Dummies
0-7645-5144-2

EDUCATION, HISTORY, REFERENCE & TEST PREPARATION

0-7645-8381-6

0-7645-9554-7

Also available:

The ACT For Dummies
0-7645-9652-7

Algebra For Dummies
0-7645-5325-9

Algebra Workbook For Dummies
0-7645-8467-7

Astronomy For Dummies
0-7645-8465-0

Calculus For Dummies
0-7645-2498-4

Chemistry For Dummies
0-7645-5430-1

Forensics For Dummies
0-7645-5580-4

Freemasons For Dummies
0-7645-9796-5

French For Dummies
0-7645-5193-0

Geometry For Dummies
0-7645-5324-0

Organic Chemistry I For Dummies
0-7645-6902-3

The SAT I For Dummies
0-7645-7193-1

Spanish For Dummies
0-7645-5194-9

Statistics For Dummies
0-7645-5423-9

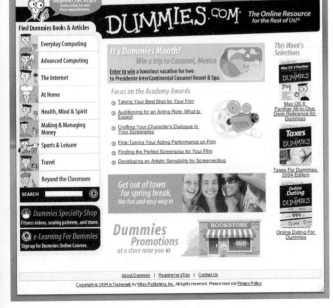

Get smart @ dummies.com®

- **Find a full list of Dummies titles**
- **Look into loads of FREE on-site articles**
- **Sign up for FREE eTips e-mailed to you weekly**
- **See what other products carry the Dummies name**
- **Shop directly from the Dummies bookstore**
- **Enter to win new prizes every month!**

* Separate Canadian edition also available
† Separate U.K. edition also available

Available wherever books are sold. For more information or to order direct: U.S. customers visit www.dummies.com or call 1-877-762-2974.
U.K. customers visit www.wileyeurope.com or call 0800 243407. Canadian customers visit www.wiley.ca or call 1-800-567-4797.